HOW *to* USE

Macromedia® Flash™ 5

SAMS

Sams Publishing
201 West 103rd Street, Indianapolis, Indiana 46290

Denise Tyler
Gary Rebholz

Visually in Full Color

How to Use Macromedia Flash 5

International Standard Book Number: 0-672-32004-5

Library of Congress Catalog Card Number: 00-105609

Printed in the United States of America

First Printing: November 2000

03   02   01   00   4   3   2   1

Trademarks

All terms mentioned in this book that are known to be trademarks or service marks have been appropriately capitalized. Sams Publishing cannot attest to the accuracy of this information. Use of a term in this book should not be regarded as affecting the validity of any trademark or service mark.

Macromedia and Flash are trademarks or registered trademarks of Macromedia, Inc.

Warning and Disclaimer

Executive Editor
Jeff Schultz

Development Editor
Kate Small

Managing Editor
Charlotte Clapp

Project Editor
Elizabeth Finney

Copy Editor
Michael Henry

Indexer
Chris Barrick

Proofreader
Tony Reitz

Technical Editor
Lynn Baus

Team Coordinator
Amy Patton

Interior Designers
Nathan Clement and
Ruth Lewis

Cover Designers
Nathan Clement and
Aren Howell

Layout Technicians
Ayanna Lacey
Heather Hiatt Miller
Stacey Richwine-DeRome
Mark Walchle

Contents at a Glance

Contents

About the Authors

Denise Tyler is no stranger to graphics, animation, and multimedia-related software. Currently a Consulting and Training Specialist for Sonic Foundry in Madison, Wisconsin, she combines her passion for multimedia with an equal passion for teaching others how to create it. During many years of working as a freelance graphics artist and animator, she attained wide and varied experience with many computer graphics, animation, and Web-related software programs, including Flash.

An author for Sams Publishing since 1994, Denise has authored, co-authored, or revised a dozen books. Her most recent projects include the fourth edition and professional reference edition updates for Laura Lemay's international best-selling book, *Sams Teach Yourself Web Publishing with HTML 4 in 21 Days.*

As a Training and Development Specialist for Sonic Foundry in Madison, Wisconsin, **Gary Rebholz** spends most of his time developing in-depth training materials aimed at teaching people how to express themselves through mastery of creative software. He has been involved with training and creative services for over 15 years. Gary worked for several years as a freelance graphic designer, copywriter, and trainer. He has developed instructional materials for, and taught various training classes ranging from QuarkXPress to HTML.

Gary has developed and delivered training via every delivery vehicle from the World Wide Web to CD-ROM to flip chart to chalk board to bar napkin. This is Gary's first book.

Dedication

To Michael, Gary, Mary, Peter, and Nathan.
You're the best. —Denise Tyler

For Rebecca, Jake, Leah, and baby Kyri.
I love you all. —Gary Rebholz

Acknowledgments

Each time I sit down to write words of thanks to the many people who work so hard behind the scenes at Macmillan USA, the first thing that comes to mind is how great the editorial staff at Sams Publishing is to work with. I can't say enough about the dedication and professionalism that every one of them demonstrates. I'm also thrilled that I finally had the opportunity to meet all my longtime friends...yes, *friends*...at Sams face-to-face during the development of this book!

To Jeff Schultz, thanks for getting me back into the swing of things again with a project that more than satisfied my creative urges. Most especially, thanks for your cheery wit and great sense of humor—it went a long way toward keeping the energy level high! Thanks, as always, to Mark Taber, for continued support, excellent advice, and all those atta-girls. To Kate Small, I love your very humorous email reminders and notes. You truly are a Super-DE, and I'm looking forward to working with you on those other projects we've got in the works! To Amy Patton, thanks so much for your sharp attention to detail and for keeping the project running smoothly. Your hearty "Hey Denise, how's it going?" also served as additional motivation whenever I called with questions. To the rest of the editors, indexers, proofreaders, designers, and layout technicians, *Thank you, team!*

Last but not least, one more very special thank you goes to Gary Rebholz, my ever-friendly and very talented co-author. It was a great pleasure working on this project with you. Your hard work and dedication to this project has been appreciated throughout!

—Denise Tyler

Denise has already done a great job of thanking all the folks behind the scenes at Macmillan USA. I'd like to add simply that I don't know how you all do it. It can't be easy keeping people like me on task! Thank you to Jeff Schultz and Mark Taber for giving me this chance. I look forward hopefully to a long relationship with my new colleagues at Macmillan USA.

I owe a huge thank you to my co-author and friend, Denise Tyler. Not many people are given the opportunity to collaborate with one of the industry's absolute best. Your long record of success as a best-selling author earns you the right to choose who you work with. I'm honored that you chose me. I could always cram a few words together to make a sentence, but you made me an author.

Next, I want to thank my good friend and ardent supporter, Michael Bryant, who makes work a fun place to be. Barb Rau, who has never given up on me. Kevin Rau, who constantly challenges and inspires me. And Jack and Rose Rebholz, who have guided me.

Finally, how could I even begin to thank my truest loves, and greatest inspirations, for their incredible support and patience through it all? Kyrianna, Leah, and Jake, everything I do, I do for you. Becky, everything I am, I am with you.

—Gary Rebholz

Tell Us What You Think!

As the reader of this book, *you* are our most important critic and commentator. We value your opinion and want to know what we're doing right, what we could do better, what areas you'd like to see us publish in, and any other words of wisdom you're willing to pass our way.

You can email or write me directly to let me know what you did or didn't like about this book—as well as what we can do to make our books stronger.

Please note that I cannot help you with technical problems related to the topic of this book, and that due to the high volume of mail I receive, I might not be able to reply to every message.

When you write, please be sure to include this book's title and author as well as your name and phone or fax number. I will carefully review your comments and share them with the author and editors who worked on the book.

Email: graphics_sams@mcp.com

Mail: Mark Taber
Associate Publisher
Sams Publishing
201 West 103rd Street
Indianapolis, IN 46290 USA

How To Use This Book

The Complete Visual Reference

Each part of this book consists of a series of short instructional tasks designed to help you understand all the information you need to get the most out of Flash 5.

Click: Click the left mouse button once.

Double-click: Click the left mouse button twice in rapid succession.

Right-click: Click the right mouse button once.

Pointer Arrow: Highlights an item on the screen you need to point to or focus on in the step or task.

Selection: Highlights the area onscreen discussed in the step or task.

Click and Type: Click once where indicated and begin typing to enter your text or data.

Click & Drag

Release

How to Drag: Point to the starting place or object. Hold down the mouse button (right or left per instructions), move the mouse to the new location, and then release the button.

Key icons: Clearly indicate which key combinations to use.

Each task includes a series of easy-to-understand steps designed to guide you through the procedure.

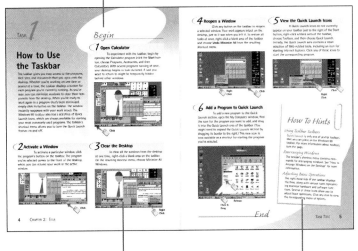

Each step is fully illustrated to show you how it looks onscreen.

Extra hints that tell you how to accomplish a goal are provided in most tasks.

Menus and items you click are shown in **bold**. Words in *italic* are defined in more detail in the glossary.

Continues

If you see this symbol, it means the task you're in continues on the next page.

Introduction

*I*n case you haven't noticed, the Internet is coming alive. Web pages aren't static any more—many are vibrant with movement, color, and sound. To keep that media moving at a reasonable clip while it pushes its way through low-bandwidth connections, you need an application that helps you create lean-and-mean multimedia.

Enter Macromedia Flash, an ingenious software tool that helps you create engaging, colorful, and *compact* animations for the Internet. Its clever drawing and animation tools are easy (and fun) to learn and use. And this book shows you exactly how to use them.

In This Book

If you want to learn Flash quickly, you don't want a lot of explanation or wordy introductions, and you don't want to bog yourself down with a lot of technical features and jargon. If you just want to dig right in and learn the basics, have we got a book for you!

We wrote this book with a specific goal in mind. We wanted to teach you the basics of Flash in a systematic way that would be easy to follow. You will learn how to create animations, but we won't tie you down with having to draw each frame by hand. Instead, we'll show you how to make Flash do all the animating for you.

In addition, we won't bog you down with a lot of technical details and features. Although a lot of Flash's power lies in using advanced scripting features, the steps to explain how to use them would fill another book *at least* this size. Remember, we want to get you started quickly. Therefore, we'll show you some very basic scripting techniques that will perform basic navigation functions.

In these pages, you'll find a visual guide that will get you started (if you'll pardon the pun) in a flash. A picture that shows the process or the result accompanies each step. By the time you complete this book, you'll know how to use Flash to accomplish the following tasks, plus a whole lot more:

- ✓ Paint and draw shapes using all the tools in the Flash toolbox
- ✓ Create your own custom colors and palettes
- ✓ Import artwork that you create in other software applications
- ✓ Use layers in your Flash movies
- ✓ Create buttons that navigate to Web pages, other Flash movies, and other scenes in the same Flash movie
- ✓ Use keyframes and tweens to create animations
- ✓ Add sounds to your Flash movies
- ✓ Optimize and publish your Flash projects

Pull up your favorite chair to your monitor and keyboard, fire up the CPU, and turn the pages in this book to learn what Flash is about. We promise that you'll be up and running in no time!

Task

Introducing Flash

*I*f you're reading this book, you're probably already familiar with Flash. Flash is used on innumerable Web sites to enhance content with rich, clean, sharp multimedia that downloads and streams quickly. When you selected Flash as the way to integrate multimedia into your Web sites, you made a wise choice. In spite of all its features, Flash is easy to use! You'll also enjoy hearing that you'll be up and running in no time with the help of the examples that we provide in this book.

As with any well-designed software program, Flash is easy to learn. After you're familiar with the lay of the land, you'll find the interface to be very intuitive—things make sense. In addition, Flash contains a depth that just keeps unfolding before you as you work with the program.

Every project begins with a first step. The tasks in this part of the book begin with a general overview of the Flash interface and continue by explaining where you can find the commands and features that you need.

Welcome to Flash

This task will walk you through opening and exiting Flash, and familiarize you with its basic interface—which features standard Windows commands, toolbars, and shortcuts. We'll also open one of the sample files that ships with Flash. Let's get started!

Begin

1 Open Flash

To open Flash from the Windows start menu, choose **Start, Programs, Macromedia Flash 5, Flash 5.** To open Flash on your Macintosh, locate the folder that contains the Flash 5 shortcut. Double-click the shortcut to open the program.

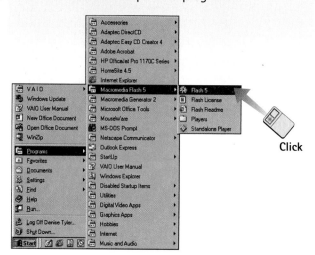

Click

2 General Interface Layout

The toolbars located at the left side of the screen provide quick access to drawing tools and commands. The Timeline gives you a bird's eye view of the layers and actions that take place in your movie. Use the Stage to develop and view the objects and symbols in your movie.

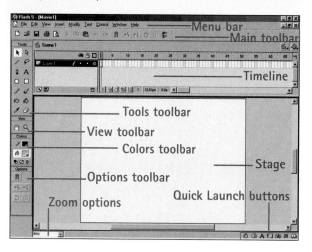

- Menu bar
- Main toolbar
- Timeline
- Tools toolbar
- View toolbar
- Colors toolbar
- Options toolbar
- Stage
- Zoom options
- Quick Launch buttons

3 Open the Spotlight Mask.fla File

To follow along with the remaining tasks in this part, choose **File, Open.** The **Open** dialog appears. Use the **Look In** field to navigate to the Flash 5\Samples folder installed with your Flash program. Click on Spotlight Mask.fla to select it, and then click on **Open.**

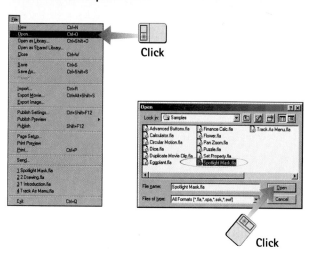

Click

Click

4 Exit the Program

After you complete your Flash projects, it's a very simple process to exit the program. In Windows, choose **File, Exit**, or use the keyboard shortcut **Ctrl+Q**. Mac users can choose **File, Quit**, or use the keyboard shortcut **Cmmd+Q**. Flash prompts you to save any unsaved changes to your projects before you exit the program.

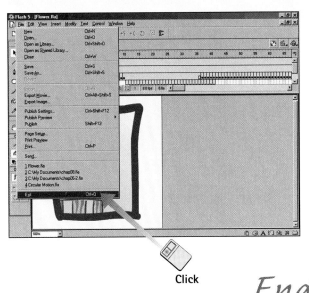

Click

End

How-To Hints

Opening Multiple Projects

Flash enables you to work on more than one project at a time. Simply choose **File, Open**, and select additional Flash projects. A list of the currently opened projects appears at the bottom of the Window menu. Use this project list to switch between projects as you work on them.

How to Use the Flash Interface

The first step in learning Flash is to become familiar with the Flash interface. Obviously, we'll talk about each of these pieces in more detail later in the book. For now, get to know the very basic layout of the application window. This essential knowledge takes you a long way; without it, you'll go nowhere.

Begin

1 The Flash Menu Bar

The Flash menu bar looks very familiar to anyone with even a small amount of experience with other Windows programs. It includes familiar menu items such as **File**, **Edit**, **View**, and **Help.** It also includes menus that are specific to Flash. All these menus work in a similar manner to menus in other applications with which you are familiar.

Menu bar

2 The Main Toolbar

In Windows, Flash contains a **Main** toolbar that is similar to those found in other Windows programs. To view the Main toolbar, choose **Window, Toolbar, Main.** This toolbar provides shortcut buttons for some of the most common Flash operations. Each button has an associated ToolTip that tells you instantly what the button's function is. Hover the mouse pointer over the **New** button to see its ToolTip. Use the **New** button as a shortcut alternative to choosing **File, New** when creating a new project.

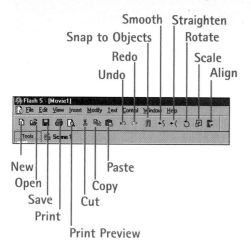

3 The Vertical Toolbar

The vertical toolbar in the Flash interface contains four sections. The **Tools** toolbar provides a number of useful drawing tools that help you create original vector-based artwork. When you click on a tool to select it, Flash presents a different set of tool options in the **Options** toolbar, located at the bottom of the vertical toolbar. The **View** toolbar enables you to pan and zoom your view of the Stage. You can select fill and stroke colors from the **Colors** toolbar.

4 The Timeline

The Timeline defines and controls the frames, keyframes, and layers that appear in your Flash movie. When you move the play head forward or backward through the Timeline, you see a visual reference of where you are in the animation, and exactly how the Stage appears at that point. For example, drag the play head back and forth along the Timeline. As you do so, watch as the blue circle moves toward the left or right of the Stage.

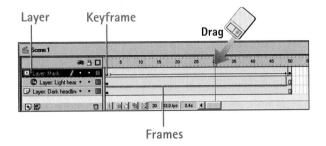

Layer   Keyframe

Drag

Frames

5 The Stage and Work Area

The Stage appears as a white rectangle in the drawing area. Symbols and objects that appear on the Stage also appear in your movie when it plays. The gray space around the Stage is the work area. Choose **View, Work Area** to toggle the work area on and off. You can develop and store objects in the work area, and move them onto the Stage when it is time for them to appear in your movie. In the first frame of the Spotlight Mask.fla movie, the blue mask is completely off stage, and therefore will not appear onscreen.

End

How-To Hints

Dockable/Floatable Windows

The **Main** toolbar (in Windows), **Drawing** toolbar, and Timeline are all dockable/floatable windows. When you first open Flash, all windows appear in their default "docked" positions. Click and drag them to a new position on the screen so that they either float independently, or dock to a new area. This functionality enables you to arrange your workspace to best suit your working style.

TASK 3

How to Use the Flash Menus

Just as does any Windows-based program, Flash makes extensive use of menus for the operation of basic and advanced program features. As with any other Windows program, you choose a command by first clicking on the appropriate menu item (such as **File, Edit,** or **View**) to expand the list of command options. Then, you select a command from the available options. If a keyboard shortcut exists for a command, it is listed next to the command.

1 The File and Edit Menus

The **File** menu contains commands that provide basic functions such as opening, closing, and saving files. It also contains import and export, publish, and print functions. The **Edit** menu includes commands that enable you to apply basic changes to the objects in your movie. Among the basic features of the **Edit** menu are the common **Undo, Redo, Cut, Copy,** and **Paste** commands.

2 The View and Window Menus

The **View** menu commands control the magnification of the Stage, the grid and rulers, and the smoothness of image quality (antialiasing). The **Window** menu opens or closes the various toolbars and panels and enables you to switch quickly between several open projects.

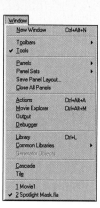

3 The Insert Menu

Use the **Insert** menu commands to create the basic building blocks of your movies. Commands in this menu enable you to create symbols, layers, frames, keyframes, tweens, and scenes. You'll learn about each of these building blocks as you work through the examples in this book.

10 PART 1: INTRODUCING FLASH

4 The Modify Menu

The commands in the **Modify** menu enable you to make changes to specific pieces of your animation. Use these commands to change properties of symbols, instances, frames, layers, scenes, and movies. Other commands enable you to adjust, rotate, and align shapes, to group or ungroup objects, and to convert between frames and keyframes.

5 The Text Menu

The **Text** menu, new to Flash 5, provides quick access to the fonts on your system and enables you to format the size, style, alignment, and tracking of the text you add to your movies. Additional commands enable you to adjust spacing and kerning for text and paragraphs.

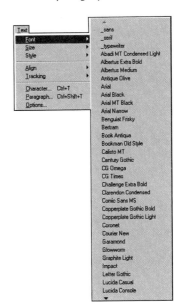

6 The Control Menu

The **Control** menu provides commands that relate to playing and testing your movies. You can play, rewind, and step forward or backward through your animation one frame at a time. You can test a scene or the entire movie to get an accurate sense of the performance of the animation. You also enable buttons and actions, and mute all sounds by using commands from this menu.

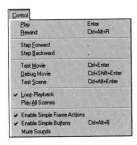

How-To Hints

Floating Panels

Most of the commands available under the **Modify** and **Text** menus can also be accessed through various tabbed panels that you open under the **Window** menu. To see a list of these panels, choose **Window, Panels**. Expand the flyout menu for a list of all the tabbed panels that are available. We'll talk in much more detail about these panels—new to Flash 5—throughout this book.

End

Task

Getting Started with Flash

*T*he main purpose for Flash is to create lean and mean animations for the Web. Flash keeps your movies lean by using *vector graphics*, which store the elements in your project as mathematical formulas that make up color or gradient-filled shapes rather than as a screen filled with differently colored pixels. Vector graphics consume fewer bytes than do pixel-based graphics. As a result, they download much faster.

As you create movies, Flash offers several features that help you draw lines and objects more easily. You can zoom in and out of your drawing to levels up to 2000%, enabling you to design objects with extreme precision. You can use the Timeline to control when and where changes take place, and to place objects on layers. Flash also provides the capability to copy items to the clipboard for pasting into other applications such as Fireworks or Photoshop.

Additionally, Flash has a unique capability to "fix" lines and shapes as you draw them, and you can control the amount of tolerance and correction. This feature is of great benefit to those who have little experience with computer graphics and animation, but also helps advanced users keep their objects and symbols neat and trim in size.

How to Create and Configure a New Movie

Every Flash project you create is called a *movie*. When you create a movie, you specify the dimensions of the movie and the speed of the movie in frames per second. If you use Flash's **Publish** feature to create the HTML page that will house the movie, the background color of the movie determines the color of the Web page on which it is placed. You can also specify the spacing and color of the grid that lines and objects snap to.

Begin

1 Creating a New Movie

Flash starts a new movie every time you open the application. You can also start new movies at any time while Flash is running. To create a movie, choose **File, New,** or click on the **New** button on the **Standard** toolbar. Alternatively, you can use the keyboard shortcut **Ctrl+N** (Windows) or **Cmmd+N** (Macintosh).

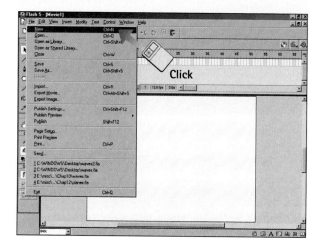

2 Set the Movie Frame Rate

To set the frame rate (or playback speed) of the movie, choose **Modify, Movie** to open the **Movie Properties** dialog. Enter the number of frames per second (fps) in the **Frame Rate** field. Lower numbers can be more economical in file size, but setting the fps too low can cause the movie to appear choppy. Higher fps values play more smoothly, but can increase file size. Web animations typically use frame rates of 8–12 fps, with 12 fps as the default setting.

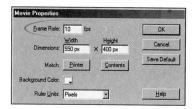

3 Set the Movie Size

When you create a new movie, the default size is 550 pixels wide and 400 pixels high. To specify a different size, enter numbers between **18** and **2880** in the **Width** and **Height** fields of the **Movie Properties** dialog. You can also set the size using one of two **Match** options. Click the **Printer** button to set the Stage size according to the maximum printable area. Click the **Contents** button to set the Stage size so that equal space exists around the Stage contents on all sides.

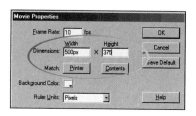

4 Set Background and Ruler Units

To modify the color of the movie background, click on the **Background** color square in the **Movie Properties** dialog. Select a color from your current color palette. Choose the desired ruler units from the **Ruler Units** drop-down. Pixels are chosen by default.

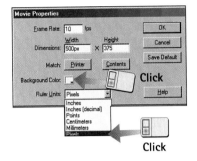

Click

Click

5 Save New Default Movie Settings

If you frequently use the same settings for your movies, you can save your settings as the new default startup values. After you enter your movie properties as outlined previously in this task, click on the **Save Default** button in the **Movie Properties** dialog. The next time you create a new movie, your custom movie properties will be used.

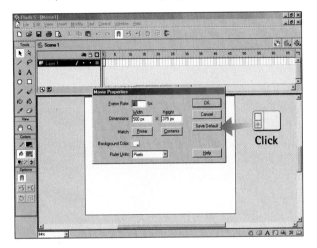

Click

6 Set the Grid and Guides

Flash provides a Grid and Guides as aids in placing and drawing objects. Choose **View, Grid, Show Grid** to turn the Grid on. Choose **View, Grid, Snap to Grid** to toggle the Snap to Grid feature off and on. Choose **View, Grid, Edit Grid** to change grid spacing, color, and snap-to accuracy. Under the **View** menu, the **Guides** options are **Show Guides, Lock Guides, Snap to Guides,** and **Edit Guides.** Use **Edit Guides** to change guide color and snap accuracy.

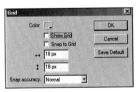

Choose View, Grid,
Edit Grid

Choose View, Guides,
Edit Guides

End

How-To Hints

Customizing Movie Background Colors

When you click the color squares in the **Grid, Guides,** or **Movie Properties** dialogs, Flash opens your current palette. By default, Flash loads a palette that consists of 216 Web-safe colors. If you want to customize your movie colors, create a custom palette as outlined in Part 3, Task 2.

Setting Ruler Units

The default unit of measurement for the ruler is pixels. Use the **Ruler Units** drop-down in the **Movie Properties** dialog to select another unit of measurement: **Inches, Inches (decimal), Points, Centimeters,** or **Millimeters.** To toggle the rulers on and off, choose **View, Rulers,** or type **Ctrl+Alt+Shift+R** (Windows) or **Cmmd+Opt+Shift+R** (Macintosh).

How to Zoom

As you develop your Flash projects, you might need to zoom in closer to specific elements to draw fine details, or zoom out to see all the elements on your Stage. Flash provides several different ways to zoom in and out of the Stage. The Zoom tool, which appears in the toolbox as a small magnifying glass, provides a quick way to zoom in or out of your projects. The Zoom **Percentage** field, located near the lower-left corner of the screen, enables you to enter specific zoom percentages, or to choose a percentage from the drop-down list.

Begin

1 Zoom In to an Element

To zoom in to an element in your movie, select the Zoom tool from the toolbox, and click the **Enlarge** modifier. With the Zoom tool, click the element that you want to zoom into. Flash doubles the zoom percentage each time you click up to 2000%. Flash also automatically moves the center point to where you clicked.

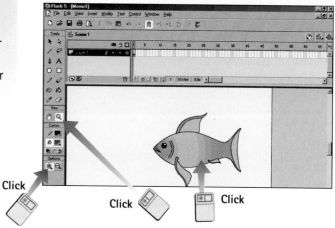

Click   Click   Click

2 Zoom Out from an Element

To zoom out from an element in your movie, select the Zoom tool from the toolbox and click the **Reduce** modifier. With the Zoom tool, click the element that you want to zoom out from. With each click, Flash cuts the zoom level in half.

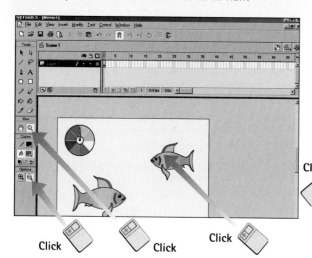

Click   Click   Click

3 Zoom to a Specific Area

To zoom into a specific area in your movie, select the Zoom tool from the toolbox. Click and drag the mouse from one corner of a rectangle to its diagonally opposite corner. The Stage zooms into a rectangular area. This method works the same no matter which modifier you have chosen.

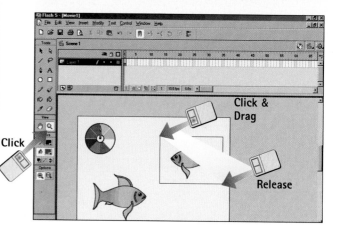

Click

Click & Drag

Release

4 Use the Zoom Control Menu

Use the **Zoom Percentage** text field to enter a zoom percentage. Double-click in the field and then type in the new value, or click the field's drop-down arrow to select a value from the preset list. The percentages available as presets are **25%, 50%, 100%, 200%, 400%,** and **800%.** Choose **Show Frame** to zoom out to view the entire movie frame. Choose **Show All** to zoom in to show just the elements in the current frame.

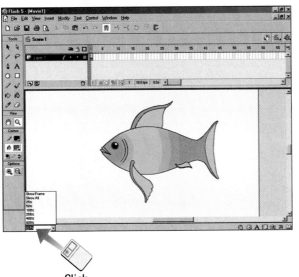

Click

5 Pan Your Movie

Use the Hand tool to pan your movie when you cannot see the entire Stage. Select the Hand tool. Then click and drag the Stage to view a different area. If you have any other tool selected, hold down the **Spacebar** to temporarily switch to the Hand tool.

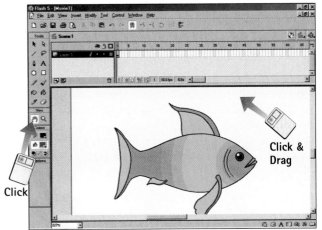

Click

Click & Drag

End

How-To Hints

Toggling Between Zoom In and Zoom Out

Hold down **Alt** (Windows) or **Option** (Macintosh) when using the Zoom tool to toggle between the **Enlarge** and **Reduce** modifiers.

How to Use the Timeline

The Timeline is one of the central components that you use while you create Flash animations. Use the Timeline to add layers, frames, and keyframes. As we discuss in detail later in this book, frames and keyframes represent specific points in time where elements, transitions, and sounds that make up your movie appear on the stage (or, in the case of sounds, start playing). You can dock and undock the Timeline to position it in any convenient place. In addition, you can customize how the Timeline displays the frames.

Begin

1 Undock the Timeline

To undock the Timeline, click in the blank area right above the layers list, and drag the Timeline to tear it away from the main application window. Release the mouse button to position the Timeline in its own floating window.

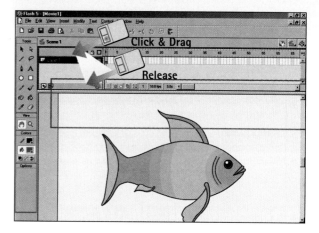

2 Redock the Timeline

To redock the Timeline, drag it back to any edge of the application window. The Timeline can be docked to the left, right, top, or bottom of the application window. Release the mouse button to dock the Timeline.

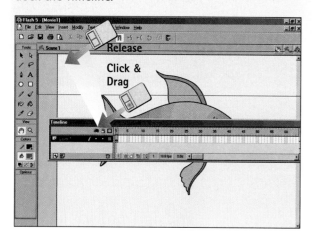

3 View Layers in the Timeline

As discussed in detail in Part 6 of this book, you can add as many layers to your movie as you like. If you have more layers than can be displayed at one time in the Timeline, use the right Timeline scrollbar to move up and down through the layers list. Click the up and down arrows to move in small increments, or drag the slider up or down to move in larger increments.

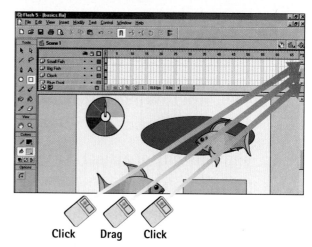

Click   Drag   Click

4 Resize the Timeline

You can also resize the Timeline to display more layers. To resize the Timeline, position the cursor over the bottom edge of the Timeline. When you see a double-arrow cursor, click and drag the bottom edge up or down.

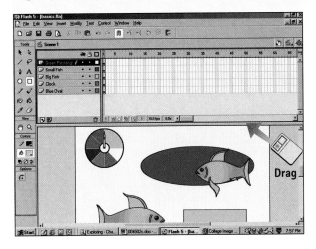

5 Scroll Through the Timeline

If your animation has more frames than you can see in the Timeline, you can drag the bottom scrollbar left to move backward through your animation, or right to move forward. Click the back and forward arrows to move in increments of five frames at a time.

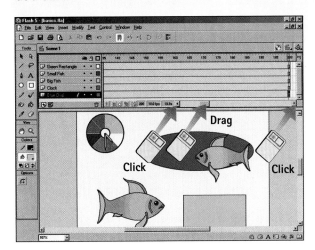

6 Change the Timeline Frame View

To change the width of the frames in the Timeline, click the **Frame View** button at the right side of the Timeline to open the **Frame View** drop-down list. Select a frame size. Choose **Preview** to view thumbnail versions of each frame in the Timeline. Choose **Preview in Context** to view exact thumbnails of the Stage at each frame (including blank areas of the Stage).

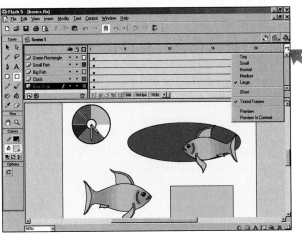

How-To Hints

How to Prevent the Timeline from Redocking

You can move the Timeline over the top of the Stage without redocking it. Simply press the **Ctrl** key while you move the Timeline. To permanently prevent redocking, choose **Edit, Preferences,** and check the **Disable Timeline Docking** option in the **Preferences** dialog box.

End

How to Use the Library

Each Flash project has its own library that stores all the symbols that appear in the movie. The Library helps you organize, sort, and manage the symbols that appear in your Flash projects. It also keeps track of the number of times that each symbol is used in the current project. The Library is especially useful when a project contains many symbols because you can organize these symbols in folders, assign useful names to them, and sort them in various ways.

Begin

1 Open the Library

To open the Library for your current Flash project, choose **Window, Library**. Alternatively, use the keyboard shortcut **Ctrl+L** (or **Cmmd+L** on the Macintosh).

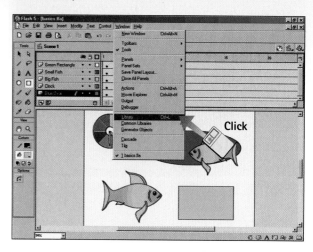

2 Resize the Library Window

To resize the Library window, position the cursor over any edge or corner of the window. When you see a double-arrow cursor, click and drag to resize the window. Alternatively, click the **Wide State** button to display all the columns in the library, or click the **Narrow State** button to display only the Name column.

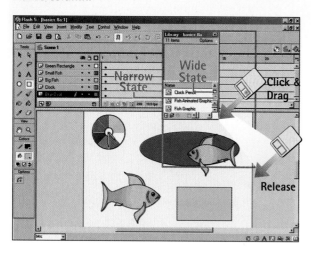

3 Resize the Column Widths

To resize Library column widths, position the cursor between column headers. Click and drag to resize the columns.

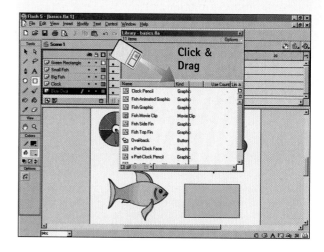

4 Create Folders

Use folders to organize your symbols into logical groups. To create a folder, click on the **New Folder** button at the bottom of the Library window. Alternatively, choose **New Folder** from the **Library Options** menu. After you create a new folder, Flash selects the folder name so that you can assign a name to it.

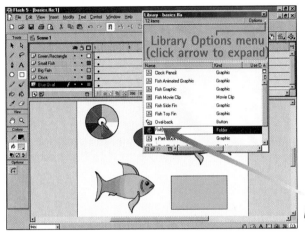

Library Options menu (click arrow to expand)

5 Move Objects Between Folders

To move objects from one folder to another, highlight one or more objects. Then, drag them to the new folder and release the mouse button.

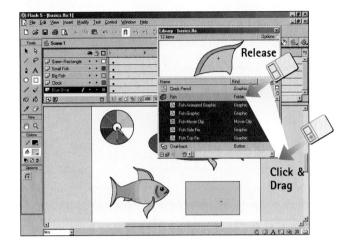

Release

Click & Drag

6 Sort Objects in Folders

With the Library in **Wide** state, click a column header to sort your Library items by the category you select (**Name, Kind, Use Count, Linkage,** or **Date Modified**). To toggle between listing the items in ascending or descending order, click the **Triangle** button at the right edge of the column headers.

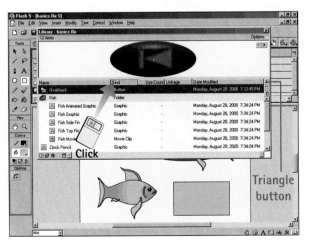

Click

Triangle button

How-To Hints

Renaming Library Items

To quickly rename a Library item, double-click on the item name, enter the new name, and press **Enter.** Alternatively, choose **Rename** from the Library's **Option** menu; or click the **Information** icon at the bottom of the Library window to rename the item in the **Symbol Properties** dialog; or right-click (Windows) or Ctrl+click (Macintosh) and choose **Rename** from the menu that appears.

Deleting Library Items

To help keep your project organized, delete unused items from your library. Use the **Select Unused Items** command in the **Library Options** menu to highlight the unused Library items. To delete selected items, click the **Delete** button at the bottom of the Library window.

End

How to Set General and Clipboard Preferences

Flash provides a number of user-definable preferences to help you customize certain aspects of the program according to your preferred work style. In this task, we talk about two sets of preferences, General and Clipboard. Although we won't talk about every preference, we will touch on many of the important settings. In the next task, we'll talk about Flash's third category of preferences, Editing. To access the **Preferences** dialog, choose **Edit, Preferences**.

Begin

1 Increase or Decrease Undo Levels

Click the **General** tab of the **Preferences** dialog. Here the **Undo Levels** field enables you to enter the number of undo levels that Flash retains in memory. You might improve system performance when you reduce the number of undo levels in your Flash projects from its default number of **100**.

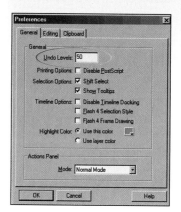

2 Control the Selection of Objects

The **Shift Select** setting in the **General** tab of the **Preferences** dialog controls how you select multiple objects in Flash. When this setting is on (the default), you must hold down the **Shift** key to select additional elements after you select the first item. When the **Shift Select** option is not checked, clicking additional items automatically adds them to the previous selection.

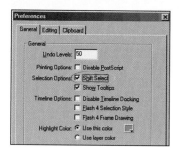

3 Set the Blank Keyframe Behavior

By default, Flash provides no visual clue that a keyframe exists in the Timeline if there are no objects on the Stage at that keyframe. Flash refers to this as a *blank keyframe*. Check the **Flash 4 Frame Drawing** option if you want Flash to identify blank keyframes with a hollow circle in the Timeline. Part 8 discusses keyframes in detail.

4 Set Color Depths for Copied Items

Flash enables you to select a bitrate and color depth for items that you copy into the clipboard. Select the **Clipboard** tab. In Windows, select the bit depth from the **Color Depth** drop-down menu, and choose the dots per inch (DPI) resolution from the **Resolution** drop-down. The **Size Limit** field enables you to specify a maximum kilobyte (KB) limit for the clipboard. For Macintosh, choose **bit depth** from the **Type** drop-down, and enter the DPI in the **Resolution** field.

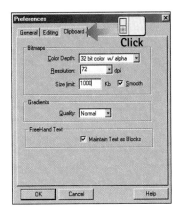

5 Set Gradient Preferences

It can sometimes take a while to copy gradients onto the clipboard because of limitations in the Windows Metafile and PICT (Macintosh) file formats that store clipboard information. The **Gradients** setting enables you to control the quality of the gradients that you copy onto the clipboard. The default setting, **Normal,** is adequate for most purposes. To reduce the time it takes to copy to the clipboard, choose **Fast.** The **Best** setting results in the highest quality, but takes the longest amount of time to copy. If you are copying a gradient to reuse elsewhere in your Flash project, choose **None.**

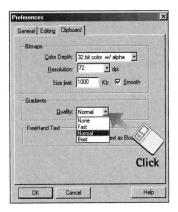

End

How-To Hints

Resolving Windows PostScript Printing Problems

If you are having difficulty printing to a PostScript printer in Windows, check the **Disable PostScript** check box in the **General** tab of the **Preferences** dialog. Unchecking this option disables the PostScript output from Flash, but it might also result in slower printing.

Disabling ToolTips

If you don't want to display ToolTips when your mouse pointer hovers over a window emblem, uncheck the **Show Tooltips** option in the **General** tab of the **Preferences** dialog. This option is checked by default.

How to Set Editing Preferences

Even the most skillful artists have a difficult time getting great results from a mouse. If you aren't able to use a graphics tablet, Flash's **Editing Preferences** tab will come to your rescue. You can specify how close lines have to be before they snap together and connect, control the smoothness of your curves or the straightness of your lines, and determine how Flash recognizes the shapes you draw. To follow the steps in this task, choose **Edit, Preferences,** and click the **Editing** tab.

1 Define Pen Tool Behavior

With the **Show Pen Preview** box checked, a line segment appears as soon as you place the first end point and move the mouse. The **Show Solid Points** option determines whether a selected point on a line will appear as a solid or hollow circle. The **Show Precise Cursors** option toggles the Pen tool cursor between the default pen icon, and a crosshair for precise drawing.

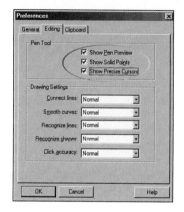

2 Connect Endpoints of Lines

The **Connect lines** setting controls how close the endpoint you draw must be to an existing line segment before it snaps to the existing line. The default setting is **Normal** (2–3 pixels). Other settings are **Must be close** (1–2 pixels), and **Can be distant** (3–4 pixels). If you have **Snap to Objects** engaged, this setting determines how close one object needs to be to a second object before they snap together.

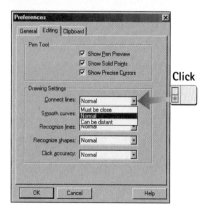

Click

3 Smooth Curves

The **Smooth curves** setting controls the amount of smoothing applied to the curved lines you draw with the Pencil tool when it is set to the **Straighten** or **Smooth** line type. The default setting is **Normal**. Other choices, from least amount of smoothing to greatest, are **Off, Rough,** and **Smooth.**

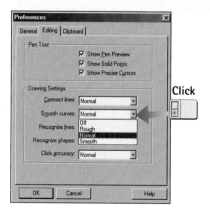

Click

4 Adjust Straight Line Recognition

The **Recognize lines** setting controls how nearly straight a line must be for Flash to realize that it should be perfectly straight. The **Off** setting leaves lines exactly as you draw them. The **Strict** setting dictates that the line must be almost straight before Flash will make it perfectly straight. The **Tolerant** setting straightens lines that are actually quite far from straight as drawn. The default setting of **Normal** falls between **Strict** and **Tolerant**.

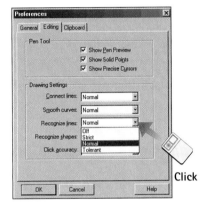

Click

5 Control Shape Recognition

Similar to the **Recognize lines** setting, the **Recognize shapes** setting controls how precisely you must draw basic shapes such as circles, ovals, squares, rectangles, and 90 degree or 180 degree arcs. Based on the tolerance you select, Flash redraws these shapes more accurately for you. The same options exist for shape recognition as those discussed for straight-line recognition in step 4, and they work exactly the same way.

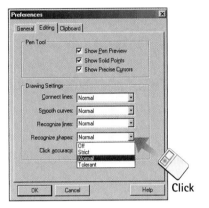

Click

6 Control Click Accuracy

The **Click accuracy** setting controls how close to an item you must click with the mouse before Flash recognizes the item and selects it. The **Strict** setting requires that you click very nearly on the item before Flash recognizes it. With the **Tolerant** setting, you can actually click quite far from an object, and Flash still selects it. The default is **Normal**, and falls between **Strict** and **Tolerant**.

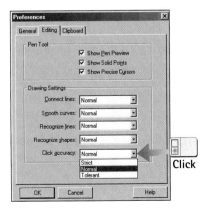

Click

How-To Hints

More About Smoothing Curves

Smooth curves are much easier to reshape. To soften curves and reduce the number of steps and bumps in them, select the curves you want to fix. Choose **Modify, Smooth.** Repeat the command to smooth the curve further if necessary.

Correcting Lines and Shapes After You Draw Them

It is also easy to straighten lines and shapes after you draw them. Simply select the lines or shapes you want to correct and choose **Modify, Straighten.**

End

Task

Drawing and Choosing Colors

Flash provides a variety of tools and panels that make it easy to draw and color objects for your Flash movies. You gain quick access to the drawing and painting tools from the toolbox, located at the left side of the interface screen by default.

Flash's Oval and Rectangle tools enable you to create basic shapes. For more complicated artwork, use the Pencil tool, the Brush tool, and the Pen tool. The Pencil tool is used to create strokes, and the Brush tool paints with fills. The Pen tool, new to Flash 5, enables you to create shapes with vector-based Bézier curves.

Flash also makes it easy to work with colors and gradients. The Swatches and Mixer panels help you quickly select Web-safe colors, but also enable you to create and save your own custom color palettes and gradients.

In this part, we explain how to create your own colors and palettes, and how to draw and modify shapes with the many tools available in the Flash toolbox. ●

How to Use the Color Picker

The Color Picker is located in the toolbox. It enables you to quickly choose outline and fill colors for use in your Flash artwork. You can also create fills without outlines, and outlines without fills.

1 Choose the Stroke Color

To select a stroke color, click on the small arrow in the stroke color square in the toolbox. This expands the color palette. Keep the left mouse button pressed as you drag to choose a new color and release the mouse.

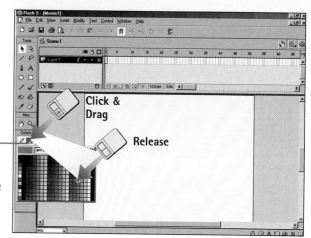

Stroke color square

2 Choose the Fill Color

The steps to choose a fill color are similar to those in choosing a stroke color. To select a fill color, click on the small arrow in the fill color square in the toolbox. This expands the color palette. Keep the left mouse button pressed as you drag to choose a new color and release the mouse.

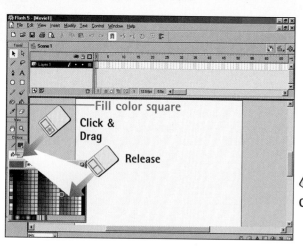

3 Choose Default Colors

To quickly select black for your outline color and white for your fill color, click on the **Default Colors** button, located at the bottom of the Color Picker.

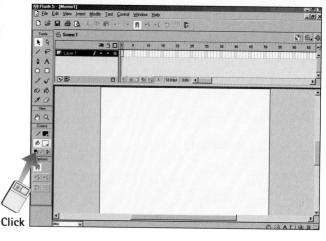

4 Turn Off the Stroke Color

If you want to create an oval or rectangle without an outline, first select the Oval tool (keyboard shortcut O) or the Rectangle tool (keyboard shortcut R). Then click on the **Pencil** icon in the Color Picker (do not confuse this icon with the Pencil tool in the toolbox!). Finally, click on the **No Color** button located at the bottom of the Color Picker.

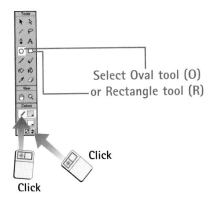

Select Oval tool (O)
or Rectangle tool (R)

Click

Click

5 Turn Off the Fill Color

To create an oval or rectangle that does not have a fill, first select the Oval tool (O) or the Rectangle tool (R). Then click on the **Paint Bucket** in the Color Picker (do not confuse this with the Paint Bucket tool in the toolbox!). Finally, click on the **No Color** button located at the bottom of the Color Picker.

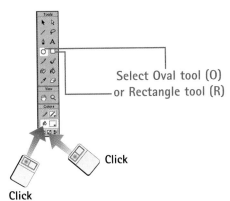

Select Oval tool (O)
or Rectangle tool (R)

Click

Click

6 Swap Outline and Fill Colors

The Color Picker provides a quick way to swap the stroke and fill colors. This changes the stroke color to the fill color, and the fill color to the stroke color at the same time. To swap stroke and fill colors, click on the **Swap Colors** button located at the bottom of the Color Picker.

Click

End

How-To Hints

When to Use the Outline Color

Use the outline color with the Line tool, the Pen tool, the Pencil, and the Ink Bottle tool. The Oval tool and Rectangle tool also use the outline color to outline the shapes.

When to Use the Fill Color

Use the fill color with the Brush tool and the Paint Bucket. The Oval tool and Rectangle tool also use the fill color to fill the shapes. You can also fill with linear or radial gradients.

TASK 2

How to Use the Color Mixer

When you first install Flash, you use a palette of Web-safe colors to create your artwork. On occasion, you might need to create and use colors that are not Web-safe. For example, one of your clients might want you to reproduce a logo that uses specific colors. Or you might want to use a color scheme that requires more subtle color transitions than the default Web-safe palette provides. In this task, you'll learn how to use the Color Mixer to choose and create custom colors that you can add to your own palettes.

1 Open the Color Mixer

To open the Color Mixer, choose **Window, Panels, Mixer**. The **Mixer** panel appears. The left portion of the **Mixer** panel includes the same controls found in the Color Picker, discussed in Task 1. Click on the Pencil icon to create a stroke color, or click on the **Paint Bucket** icon to create a fill color.

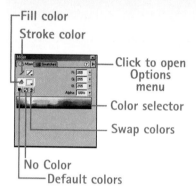

Fill color
Stroke color

Click to open Options menu
Color selector
Swap colors

No Color
Default colors

2 Use the Color Selector

The Color Selector enables you to visually select a stroke color or an outline color. To choose a color from the Color Selector, left-click and drag until you find a color to use. Release the mouse to select the color.

Click & Drag
Release

3 Specify a Color by Decimal Values

If you know the RGB (Red, Green, Blue) color formula for a specific color, you can reproduce it in the **Mixer** panel. Enter a number from 0 to 255 in each of the Red (R), Green (G), and Blue (B) fields. Alternatively, click on the arrow that appears at the right of each color field to use a color slider. Zero (0) represents the darkest value of each color, and a value of **255** represents the brightest.

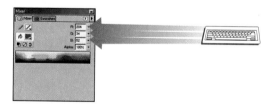

4 Specify a Hexadecimal Color

Hexadecimal numbers are used to specify colors in HTML code. The color formula is composed of three alphanumeric strings, one each for red, green, and blue. The lowest value is 00 and the highest value is FF. To specify a hexadecimal color formula, click on the arrow at the upper-right corner of the **Mixer** panel to expand the **Options** menu. Choose **Hex** from the menu that appears. Then enter hexadecimal values in the **R, G,** and **B** fields.

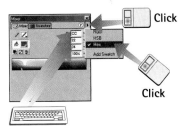

Click

Click

5 Specify a Color by HSB Values

The **Mixer** panel enables you to specify a color by HSB (Hue, Saturation, and Brightness) values. Enter a hue setting between and including **0** and **360**. A hue of **0** or **360** is red, **120** is green, and **240** is blue. Values between generate intermediate colors. Saturation settings range from **0** to **100%**. Lower values create colors that are muted, and higher values create purer colors. Brightness settings range from **0** to **100%**, with **0%** being black and **100%** representing full brightness.

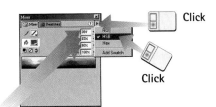

Click

Click

6 Create Transparent Colors

The **Alpha** setting controls the amount of transparency in the color. Enter a number between **0** and **100** in the **Alpha** field, or click on the arrow at the right of the **Alpha** field to move the **Alpha** slider up or down. An **Alpha** value of **0%** is fully transparent, and an **Alpha** value of **100%** is fully opaque.

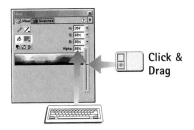

Click & Drag

End

How-To Hints

Web-Safe Color Tip

It's actually very easy to determine a Web-safe color by its RGB or hexadecimal color formula. When mixing custom RGB colors, you use values ranging from 0 to 255 for each color. Web-safe colors only use combinations of the decimal numbers 0, 51, 102, 153, 204, and 255. The equivalent Web-safe hexadecimal values are 00, 33, 66, 99, CC, and FF, respectively. For example, using standard RGB values pure red is 255, 0, 0; using hexadecimal Web-safe values it is FF0000.

How to Customize Color Palettes

Every Flash file that you create stores its own color palette in the Flash project. You can save your custom colors into palettes to use later. You can also use one of your custom palettes as your default palette when you begin a new project. Use the Color Swatches panel to add, append, and change palette colors.

Begin

1 Open the Swatches Panel

To open the **Swatches** panel, choose **Window, Panels, Swatches.** Alternatively, you can click on the **Swatches** tab if you already have the **Mixer** panel open. All commands that add, replace, or delete colors from your current palette appear in the **Swatches** options menu. To open the menu, click on the arrow that appears at the upper-right corner of the **Swatches** panel.

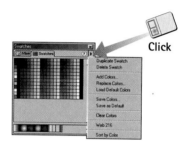

Click

2 Remove Colors from the Palette

If you want to begin your own custom palette from scratch, you can delete all colors except black, white, and a black-to-white gradient from the current color palette. To remove all other color, choose **Clear Colors** from the **Swatches** options menu.

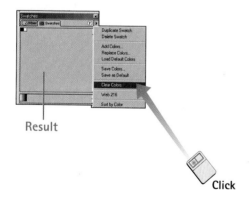

Result

Click

3 Add a New Color to the Palette

After you create a color as outlined in Task 2, you can add it to your current palette. To add a new color to your palette, first click on the **Mixer** tab to open the **Mixer** panel. Then, choose **Add Swatch** from the **Mixer** panel options menu. Finally, click on the **Swatches** tab to open the **Swatches** panel. Your new color now appears in the **Swatches** panel.

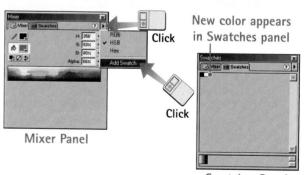

Click

New color appears in Swatches panel

Mixer Panel

Click

Swatches Panel

4 Append Colors to the Palette

Flash enables you to import colors from Flash color files (CLR extension), color table files (ACT extension), and GIF images (GIF extension). To append colors to the current palette, choose **Add Colors** from the **Swatches** options menu. Use the **Import Color Swatch** dialog to navigate to the folder that contains the palette you want to add. Select the CLR, ACT, or GIF palette file that you want to import, and choose **Open.**

Click to choose Add Colors

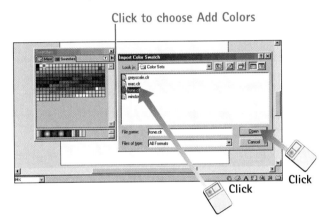

Click

Click

5 Replace Colors in a Palette

To replace the colors in your current palette with colors from a palette that you previously saved, choose **Replace Colors** from the **Swatches** options menu. Use the **Import Color Swatch** dialog to navigate to the folder that contains the palette you want to import. Select the CLR, ACT, or GIF palette that you want to import, and choose **Open.** The new colors replace the old colors.

Click to choose Replace Colors

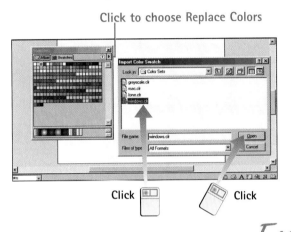

Click

Click

End

How-To Hints

Removing One Color from the Palette

Use the **Swatches** panel to remove one or more colors from the current palette. Select the color you want to remove, and then choose **Delete Swatch** from the **Swatches** options menu.

Sorting Palette Colors

By default, colors appear in the order in which you add them to a palette. To sort colors based on luminosity (brightness) values, choose **Sort by Color** from the **Swatches** options menu.

Duplicating Palette Colors

To duplicate a color in your current palette, click on the color in the **Swatches** panel that you want to dupli-cate. Next, click on the arrow that appears in the upper-right corner of the **Swatches** panel, and choose **Duplicate Swatch** from the menu that appears.

How to Save and Reuse Palettes

After you add your own colors to an existing palette or create an entirely new palette, you can specify your custom palette as the default. Flash uses the default palette whenever you create a new project. This task tells you how to save and load palettes that are compatible with Flash and other applications. You can find all the commands discussed in this task in the **Swatches** options menu. Click on the arrow that appears in the upper-right corner of the **Swatches** panel to open this menu.

Begin

1 Save a Flash Color Set

Flash color sets save RGB colors and gradients that you can reuse in another Flash project. To save the current palette as a Flash color set, choose **Save Colors** from the **Swatches** options menu. The **Export Color Swatch** dialog appears. From the **Save as type** field, choose **Flash Color Set (*.clr)**. Enter a filename for the palette in the **File name** field, and click on the **Save** button to save the palette into the selected folder.

Click to choose Save Colors

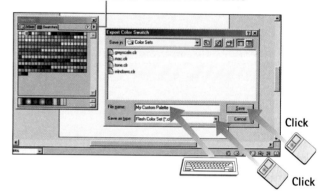

Click

Click

2 Save a Color Table File

Color table files save RGB colors, but not gradient information. To save the current palette as a color table file for use in other applications, choose **Save Colors** from the **Swatches** options menu. The **Export Color Swatch** dialog appears. From the **Save as type** field, choose **Color Table (*.act)**. Enter a filename for the palette in the **File name** field, and click on the **Save** button to save it into your selected folder.

Click to choose Save Colors

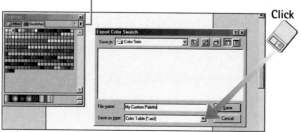

Click

3 Save a Default Palette

If you find that you use one of your custom palettes more frequently than the default Web-safe palette, you can save your custom palette as the default. Any new files that you create afterward will use your custom palette. To save your current palette as the default palette, choose **Save as Default** from the **Swatches** options menu.

Click

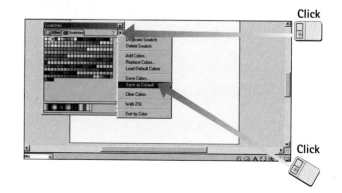

Click

4 Reload Your Default Palette

You can reload your default palette at any time. To replace the current palette with the default palette, choose **Load Default Colors** from the **Swatches** options menu.

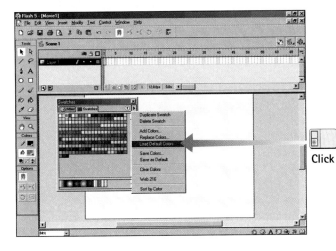

Click

5 Load the Web-Safe Palette

If you replace the default Web-safe palette with your own default custom palette, you can restore and use the Web-safe palette at any time. Simply choose **Web 216** from the **Swatches** options menu.

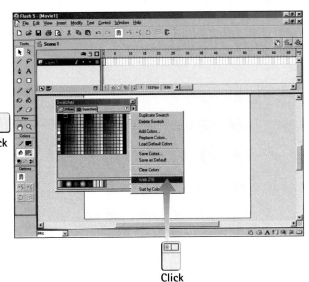

Click

End

How-To Hints

Use the Web-Safe Palette Whenever Possible

Flash provides you with a Web-safe color palette for good reason. When you use Web-safe colors in your Flash animations, it ensures that your Flash movies look their best in browsers that are written for Windows, Macintosh, OS/2, UNIX, Linux, and other operating systems. When you deviate from Web-safe colors, you might see unpredictable results when you view your movies in browsers that were written for other platforms.

Don't Forget to Save Palettes

It's always a good idea to save any custom palettes you create. Flash retains all changes that you make to your palettes until you exit the program. The next time you start Flash, it will start with your default palette. Therefore, if you think you'll use your custom colors again, don't forget to save the palette before you exit the program.

TASK

How to Create Gradients

A *gradient* is two or more colors that blend as they transition from one color to another. *Linear gradients* blend the colors from one end of the gradient to the other. *Radial gradients* blend the colors from the center of a circle or oval outward toward the outer edges. Objects that you fill with gradients appear more rich and realistic. Use the **Fill** panel to select or create gradients that contain up to sixteen colors. Gradient fills do increase the size of your Flash movies, however, so it is best to use them sparingly.

Begin

1 Open the Fill Panel

Use the **Fill** panel to create and edit gradients. To open the **Fill** panel, choose **Window, Panels, Fill**.

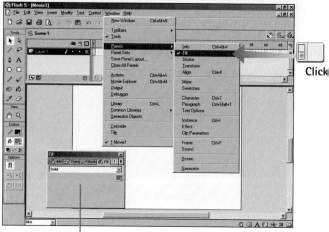

Click

Fill panel

2 Choose a Gradient Type

Click on the arrow beside the **Fill** drop-down menu to choose the type of gradient you want to create. Choose **Linear Gradient** to create a gradient that blends colors linearly from one end to the other. Choose **Radial Gradient** to create a gradient that blends colors from the center point to the outer edges of the shape. Either option displays a preview of the gradient as you create or modify the colors.

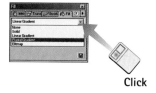

Click

3 Choose an Existing Gradient

Alternatively, you can begin with a gradient that already exists in your current palette. To open the current palette, click on the arrow that appears in the lower-right corner of the fill color square in the toolbox. Then, click to select a gradient from the bottom portion of the palette.

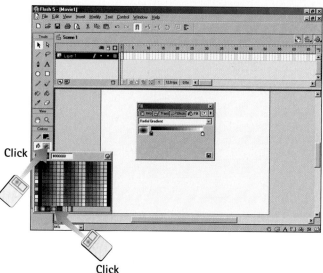

Click

Click

Click

4 Select a Color Pointer

Color pointers, which define the colors and their locations in the gradient, appear beneath the gradient definition bar. Click to select the color pointer that you want to change. A color square appears at the right side of the gradient definition bar.

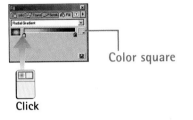

Color square

Click

5 Change the Color of the Pointer

To change the color of the selected pointer, click on the color square to open the current palette. Click and drag through the palette and move the cursor over the color you want to select. Then release the mouse button to assign the color to the color pointer. Repeat this step for additional color pointers as necessary.

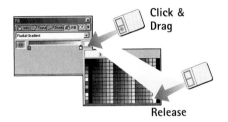

Click & Drag

Release

6 Save the Gradient

To add a gradient to the **Swatches** panel, click on the arrow in the upper-right section of the **Fill** panel, and choose **Add Gradient** from the menu that appears. The gradient now appears in the **Swatches** panel.

Click

End

How-To Hints

Filling with Radial Gradients

When you fill an object with a radial gradient using the **Paint Bucket**, the point at which you click determines the center of the gradient.

Adding, Moving, and Removing Color Pointers from Gradients

To add a color pointer to a gradient, click below the gradient definition bar. Choose a color for the new color pointer as outlined in step 5. To change the location at which the color appears, click and drag a color pointer left or right. To remove a color pointer, drag it down and away from the gradient definition bar.

How to Change Gradients

After you fill an object with a gradient, you can modify the width of the gradient, adjust its center point, and rotate the gradient at a different angle. The **Transform Fill** modifier enables you to accomplish these tasks. This task shows how to change a radial gradient, but the steps to change a linear gradient are similar.

Begin

1 Use the Transform Fill Modifier

With a gradient fill selected, use the Oval tool to draw a circle. Select the Paint Bucket tool from the toolbox, or use the keyboard shortcut **U**. Then, click on the **Transform Fill** modifier in the toolbox to enable it. Click to select the gradient fill of the object you want to edit. For a radial gradient, a large circle representing the gradient fill appears. For a linear grid, a rectangle appears.

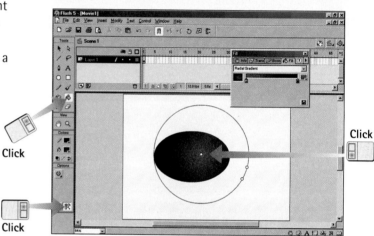

Click

Click

Click

2 Move the Center of the Gradient

To move the center point of the gradient, click and drag the small circle that appears at the center of the gradient. Release the mouse when the circle is at the desired location.

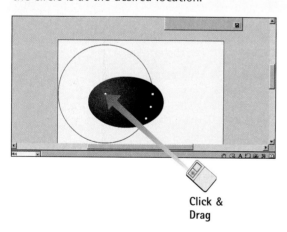

Click & Drag

3 Adjust the Shape of a Gradient

To adjust the width or height of the gradient, drag the square control point that appears on the circle or box that defines the gradient.

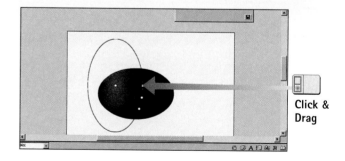

Click & Drag

4 Rotate the Gradient

You can rotate a gradient to any angle you desire. To rotate the gradient, hover the mouse over the circular control point that appears on the gradient's bounding shape until it turns into a rotation pointer. Drag the mouse clockwise or counterclockwise, and release the mouse at the desired angle.

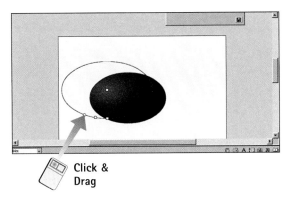

Click & Drag

5 Change the Radius of a Gradient

To increase or decrease the radius of a radial gradient, click and drag the middle circular control point that appears on the bounding circle. Drag inward or outward to resize the radius, and release the mouse.

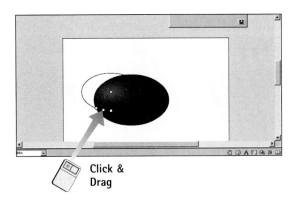

Click & Drag

6 Disable the Transform Fill

After you have altered your gradient, click on the **Transform Fill** modifier in the toolbar to disable the option.

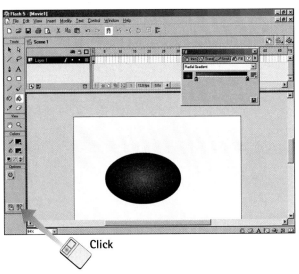

Click

How-To Hints

Filling Lines with Gradients

Flash enables you to fill only shapes with gradients. If you want to fill a line with a gradient, you must first convert the line to fills. To do this, select the line or lines that you want to convert, and choose **Modify, Shape, Convert Lines to Fills.**

End

How to Draw with the Pencil

Use the Pencil tool to draw lines and shapes in your Flash movies. The Pencil tool uses the stroke color to draw its lines and shapes. The **Options** section of the toolbox displays three drawing modes. The Straighten mode converts any lines you draw into straight lines and basic geometric shapes such as circles, ovals, squares, rectangles, and triangles. The Smooth mode reduces the jaggedness in the lines you draw and creates very smooth curves. The Ink mode renders your lines as you draw them.

Begin

1 Select a Pencil Mode

Click to select the Pencil tool from the toolbox. From the **Options** section of the toolbox, click on the **Pencil Mode** button. From the drop-down, choose **Straighten, Smooth,** or **Ink.**

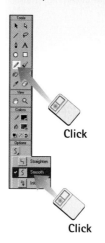

Click

Click

2 Choose a Color from the Toolbox

To quickly select a color for your pencil lines, click on the stroke color box in the toolbox to open your current palette. Drag the mouse to the color that you want to choose, and release the mouse button to select the color. Alternatively, you can choose your color in the **Stroke** panel, described next.

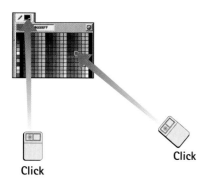

Click

Click

3 Use the Stroke Panel

You can also choose a color from the **Stroke** panel. Choose **Window, Panels, Stroke** to open the **Stroke** panel. Click on the color square to choose a color from the current palette. Alternatively, you can enter a hexadecimal value in the text box.

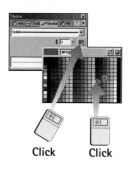

Click   Click

4 Choose a Line Style

The **Stroke** panel also enables you to select a line style. Click on the arrow that appears at the right of the **Line Style** drop-down menu, and click to choose one of several line styles shown here.

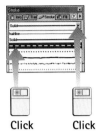

Click   Click

5 Choose a Stroke Height

Use the **Stroke height** field to enter the number of pixels in width for your pencil line. Double-click to highlight the number that appears in the field. Enter a new value and press **Enter** to assign the width. Alternatively, click on the triangle to open the **Stroke height** slider, and adjust the slider up or down to increase or decrease the stroke height. As you adjust the height, a preview appears in the **Stroke** panel.

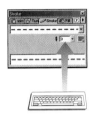

6 Draw on the Stage

After you choose your Pencil tool options, use it to draw on the Stage. Examples of each pencil-drawing mode are shown here.

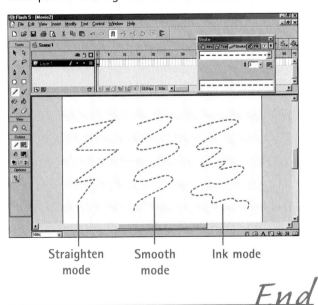

Straighten   Smooth   Ink mode
mode   mode

End

How-To Hints

Rescaling Pencil Lines

Lines that you draw with the Pencil tool remain the same width when you rescale an object. Therefore, don't use wide pencil lines when you create objects that you will eventually scale down. If you scale them down too small, the lines will cover the fills.

Watch That File Size!

Be careful when choosing a line style. Anything other than a solid line generally creates a larger file size. Dashed or dotted lines might also be more of a burden on your computer's processor.

TASK

How to Paint with the Brush Tool

Because the Brush tool creates fills instead of strokes, you can paint or draw with gradients or bitmap fills. You can adjust the width and the angle of the brush to create lines that appear like those from calligraphy pens. The Brush tool also supports pressure-sensitive tablets and styli. Finally, it provides a number of different painting options that enable you to fine-tune what you want to paint, and how you want to paint it.

Begin

1 Select the Brush Tool

Click to choose the Brush tool from the toolbox. The Brush tool options appear in the **Options** section of the toolbox.

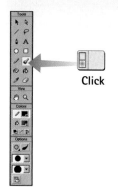

Click

2 Choose a Fill

Click the fill color square to select a color from your current palette. Alternatively, choose **Window, Panels, Fill** to select the **Fill** panel. Choose **Solid** from the fill options to select a solid fill color. Choose **Linear Gradient** or **Radial Gradient** to choose a gradient fill. Choose **Bitmap** to fill your paint strokes with any bitmap that you have imported into your Flash movie.

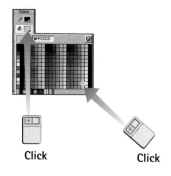

Click   Click

3 Choose a Painting Mode

Click on the **Brush Mode** modifier in the **Options** section of the toolbox to select a painting mode. **Paint Normal** covers everything that you paint over. **Paint Fills** paints over the Stage and fills in your artwork, but leaves strokes untouched. **Paint Behind** covers the Stage, but paints behind any previously existing strokes or fills. **Paint Selection** paints inside a selected fill. **Paint Inside** paints over the fill you begin painting on, but will not affect or cross over lines. It acts like a coloring book that won't allow you to go out of the lines.

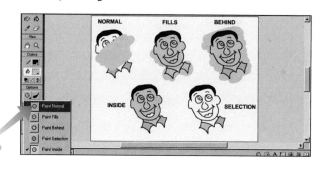

Click

42   PART 3: DRAWING AND CHOOSING COLORS

4 Select Your Brush Size and Shape

Click on the **Brush Size** modifier in the Options section of the toolbox to choose one of ten brush sizes. Click on the **Brush Shape** modifier in the Options section to select a brush shape.

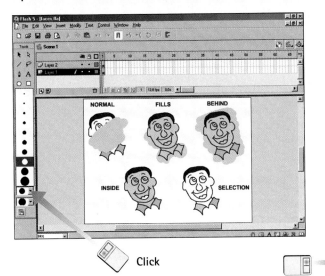

Click

5 Enable the Pressure Modifier

When you have a pressure-sensitive stylus and tablet installed on your system, you can configure the Brush tool to draw with pressure sensitivity. The **Use Pressure** option appears at the right of the **Brush Mode** modifier in the toolbox. If you are drawing with a pressure-sensitive stylus and tablet and want to vary the width of your paint strokes, click on the **Use Pressure** modifier in the **Options** section of the toolbox to turn on this option.

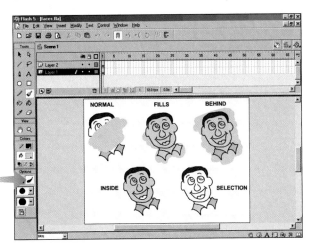

Click

6 Paint on the Stage

Paint on the Stage with the Brush tool. Strokes appear in the color, gradient, or bitmap that you selected for a fill.

Paint

How-To Hints

Painting with Bitmaps

Many interesting effects can be achieved when you choose a bitmap for a fill, and then paint with the Brush tool. You'll learn how to paint with bitmaps in Part 4, "Importing Artwork."

End

How to Draw Straight Lines with the Pen Tool

The Pen tool, new to Flash 5, enables you to draw shapes with Bézier lines and curves. When you draw with the Bézier Pen tool, you click to place control points along a path. You can adjust the shape of the curve by moving handles that are linked to each control point. This task explains how to use the Bézier Pen tool to create straight lines.

Begin

1 Choose the Pen Tool

Choose the Pen tool from the toolbox, or press **P** on the keyboard.

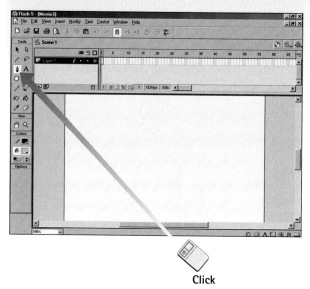

Click

2 Set the Stroke Attributes

To set the stroke attributes, choose **Window, Panels, Stroke** to open the **Stroke** panel. Select a line type from the drop-down menu. Choose or enter a line width (in pixels) from the **Width** field. Then click on the color square to select a stroke color from the current palette.

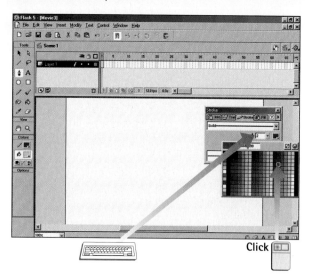

Click

3 Set the Fill Attributes

Click on the **Fill** tab to switch to the **Fill** panel (or choose **Window, Panels, Fill**). Select the fill type (**Solid, Linear Gradient, Radial Gradient,** or **Bitmap**).

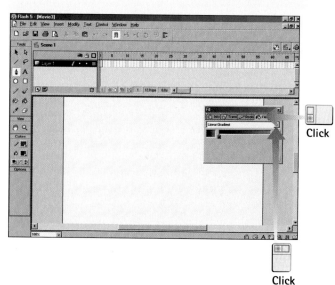

Click

Click

4 Create the First Segment

Click on the Stage to place the first anchor point for a line segment. Release the mouse, and move the cursor to the location where you want the line to end. Click again to place the next anchor point.

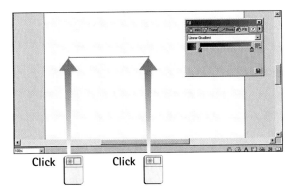

Click   Click

5 Add Additional Segments

Click to add additional anchor points for more line segments. To constrain the lines to snap to 45- or 90-degree angles, hold down the **Shift** key.

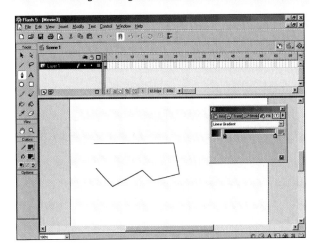

6 Complete the Path

Use one of the following methods to complete an open path: Double-click at the location where you want to place the last anchor point; or click on the Pen tool in the toolbox; or **Ctrl+click** (Windows) or **Cmmd+click** (Macintosh) away from the path. To complete a closed path, position the Pen tool over the first anchor point. When the cursor turns into a small loop, click or drag the Pen tool to close the path.

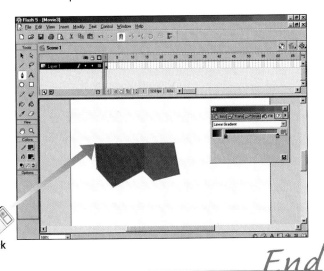

Click

End

How-To Hints

Use Snap to Grid

When you use the **Snap to Grid** option, the lines you draw can snap to the grid lines in your movie. **Snap to Grid** works whether or not the grid is visible on the Stage. To use **Snap to Grid**, choose **View, Grid, Snap to Grid**, or use the keyboard shortcut **Ctrl+Shift+'**. The **View, Grid, Show Grid** command toggles the display of the grid on or off. Use the **View, Grid, Edit Grid** command to alter grid spacing.

About Straight or Corner Anchor Points

When you draw a straight-line segment with the **Pen** tool, or a straight line that connects with a curved segment, you create *corner points*. Corner points are anchor points that are placed on a straight path, or at the junction of a straight and curved path. Selected corner points appear as hollow squares by default.

TASK 10

How to Draw Curved Lines with the Pen Tool

The steps to create curves with the Bézier Pen tool might seem confusing in comparison to drawing with the Pencil tool. Whenever you click with the Pen tool, you place a control point that defines the start or end point of a curve. Tangent handles appear at each side of the control point. The length and angle of the tangent handles determines the shape of the curve. The following task shows you how to create curved lines with the Pen tool.

1 Choose the Pen Tool

Choose the Pen tool from the toolbox, or enter **P** on the keyboard. Select the **Stroke** and **Fill** attributes as described in the previous task.

Click

2 Place the First Anchor Point

Position the cursor on the Stage at the location where you want the curve to begin. Click to position the first anchor point, and continue to hold down the mouse button. The cursor changes to an arrowhead.

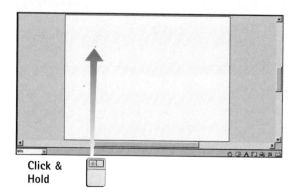

Click & Hold

3 Drag to Shape the Curve

While still holding down the mouse button, drag in the direction you want to draw the curve segment. Tangent handles for the curve appear as you drag the mouse. Adjust the length and slope of the tangent handles to shape the curve segment. **Shift**+drag the tangent handles to constrain the tangent handles to multiples of 45 degrees. Then release the mouse button.

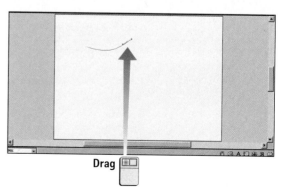

Drag

4 End the Curve

Position the cursor where you want the curve segment to end. Click and drag the mouse in the opposite direction of the curve to complete the curve segment. **Shift**+drag to constrain the tangent handles to multiples of 45 degrees.

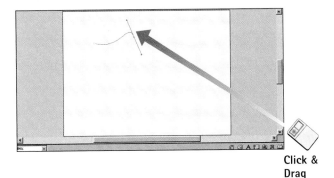

Click &
Drag

5 Add Additional Curves

To draw additional curve segments, click at the location where you want the next segment to end, and drag away from the curve.

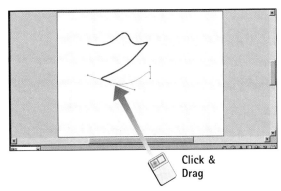

Click &
Drag

6 Complete the Shape

Use one of the following methods to complete an open path: Double-click at the location where you want to place the last anchor point; or click on the Pen tool in the toolbox; or **Ctrl**+click (Windows) or **Cmmd**+click (Macintosh) away from the path. To complete a closed path, position the Pen tool over the first anchor point. When the cursor turns into a small loop, click or click and drag to close the path.

Click

How-To Hints

Experiment to Learn

If you have never worked with Bézier curves before, they can be a little awkward at first and you might need to experiment for a while to get a feel for them. If your curves don't come out as you expect, you can always begin again, or adjust the curves with the Arrow tool later on. Don't be afraid to dive in!

About Curve Anchor Points

When you draw a curved segment with the Pen tool, you create curve points. Curve points are anchor points that are placed on a curved path. Selected curve points appear as hollow circles by default.

End

How to Set Pen Tool Options

To assist in the way you draw lines and curves, Flash enables you to configure some options for the Pen tool. You can turn the display of line segments on and off while you draw, control how selected anchor points are displayed, and change the appearance of the cursor when you use the Pen tool. All these options are available in the **Preferences** dialog, as described in this task.

Begin

1 Choose Edit, Preferences

To set Pen tool options, choose **Edit, Preferences**. Click on the **Editing** tab in the **Preferences** dialog.

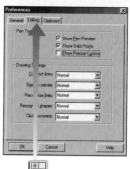

Click

2 Preview Line Segments

The **Show Pen Preview** option controls how line segments are displayed while you draw them. Check this option to preview line segments while you draw them (before you click to create the end point of the segment). If this option is not checked, the line will not display until after you click to create the end point.

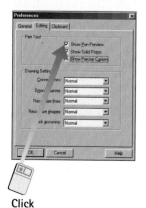

Click

3 Display Selected Anchor Points

The **Show Solid Points** option controls anchor points that appear on the Stage. When this option is checked (the default choice), unselected anchor points appear as solid, and selected anchor points appear as hollow. Uncheck this option to display unselected anchor points as hollow, and selected anchor points as solid.

Click

4 Choose Cursor Display Options

The **Show Precise Cursor** option controls the appearance of the cursor when you draw anchor points. Check this option to display the cursor as a crosshair pointer. This enables you to place lines more precisely. Uncheck this option to display the cursor as the default **Pen Tool** icon.

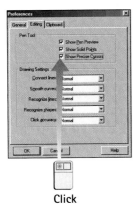

Click

5 Click on OK

After you select your Pen tool options, click on **OK** to close the **Preferences** dialog.

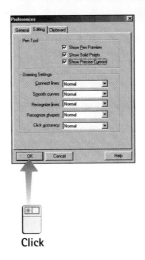

Click

End

How-To Hints

How-To Hints

Toggling Between Cursor Types

In step 4 of the previous task, you learned how to set cursor display options. You can use the **Caps Lock** key to toggle between the standard Pen tool cursor and the crosshair cursor. For example, if you normally work with the standard Pen tool cursor, you can press the **Caps Lock** key once to switch to the crosshair cursor. Press the **Caps Lock** key again to switch back to the standard Pen tool cursor. Note that even though you press the **Caps Lock** key, the cursor does not change until you move the mouse.

How to Edit Shapes Drawn with the Pen

After you draw shapes with the Pen tool, you can select one or more anchor points and change the shape to improve its appearance. After you select anchor points, you can move or delete them. You can also add additional points to the curves and segments in your shape. This task explains how to modify shapes that you create with the Pen tool.

Begin

1 Select Anchor Points

To select one or more anchor points on a shape that you created with the Pen tool, click on the Subselect tool in the toolbox. Click on an anchor point to select it. Then, **Shift**+click to select additional anchor points. To select several anchor points at once, use the Subselect tool to marquee around the points you want to select.

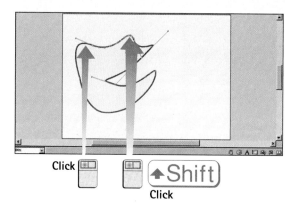

Click   Click ⬆Shift
              Click

2 Move Anchor Points

To move an anchor point, move the Subselect tool near the point you want to move, until a hollow square or circle appears beside the cursor. This indicates that you can move the point that you are near. Click and drag the anchor point to a new location.

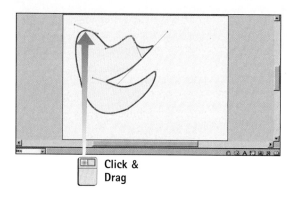

Click & Drag

3 Add Anchor Points

If the line is not already selected, click it with the Pen tool to select it. Once the line is selected, position the Pen tool over the location on the line segment where you want to add a point. A small plus sign (+) appears beside the cursor. Click on the line segment with the Pen tool to add a point.

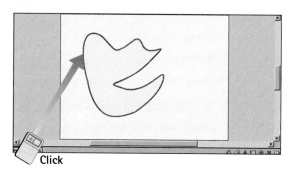

Click

4 Delete Anchor Points

If the line is not already selected, click it with the Pen tool to select it. Once the line is selected, position the Pen tool over the point you want to delete. A small minus sign appears by the cursor. Click on the point with the Pen tool to delete it.

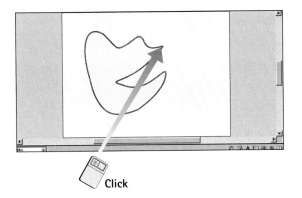

Click

5 Convert Corner or Curve Points

When you draw two straight lines at an angle using the Pen tool, you create a corner point at the intersection of the two line segments that make up the angle. When you select a corner point, it does not have tangent handles. **Alt+drag** (Windows) or **Option+drag** (Macintosh) a corner point with the Subselect tool to convert it to a curve point. A curve point has tangent handles. To convert a curve point to a corner point, hold down the **Alt** (Windows) or **Option** (Macintosh) key and click once on the point with the Subselect tool.

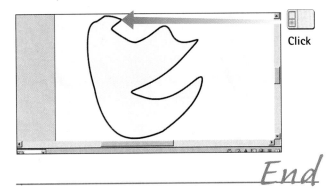

Click

End

How-To Hints

Nudging Anchor Points

You can use the arrow keys on your keyboard to nudge anchor points to a new location. With the Subselect tool, select the point or points you want to move, and then use the Up-arrow, Down-arrow, Left-arrow, and Right-arrow keys to nudge the anchor points one pixel at a time.

Reshaping Lines and Curves with the Arrow Tool

You can also use the Arrow tool to reshape lines, curves, and shapes. Choose the Arrow tool from the toolbox, or use the keyboard shortcut **A.** Hover the Arrow tool over a line segment or shape until you see a small curve beside the Arrow tool cursor. This indicates that you can reshape the line or shape over which you are hovering. Click and drag to reshape the line or curve, and then release the mouse.

How to Draw Ovals and Rectangles

The Oval tool and the Rectangle tool use stroke and fill colors to create the shapes. The steps to create ovals and rectangles are basically the same, with one exception. The Rectangle tool provides an option to round the corners of the rectangle. To create a rectangle or oval, follow the steps outlined here.

Begin

1 Choose the Appropriate Tool

Choose the Oval tool (O) or the Rectangle tool (R) from the toolbox.

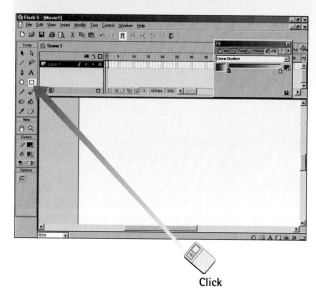

Click

2 Set the Stroke Attributes

Choose **Window, Panels, Stroke** to open the **Stroke** panel. Select the stroke attributes with which you want to outline the oval or rectangle.

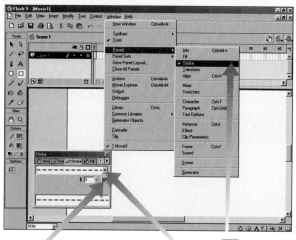

Click

Click Click

3 Set the Fill Attributes

Choose **Window, Panels, Fill** to open the **Fill** panel. Select the fill attributes with which you want to fill the oval or rectangle.

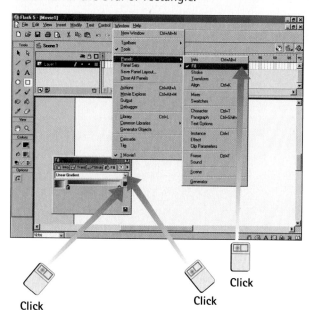

Click

Click Click

4 Draw on the Stage

Click on the Stage, and drag to a new location. As you drag, an outline of the rectangle or oval appears so that you can evaluate the shape you are creating. When you have the shape you want, release the mouse button. An oval or rectangle appears on the Stage with the stroke and fill attributes you chose in steps 2 and 3.

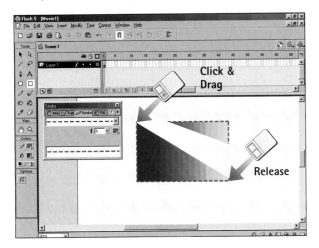

5 Draw a Perfect Circle or Square

To create a perfect circle with the Oval tool or a square with the Rectangle tool, press the **Shift** key while you drag the oval or rectangle. The dimensions of the oval or rectangle will be constrained to equal measurements.

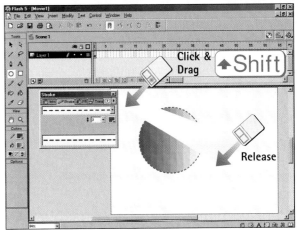

End

How-To Hints

Creating Rectangles with Rounded Corners

To create a rectangle that has rounded corners, choose the Rectangle tool from the toolbox. Click on the **Rounded Rectangle Radius** modifier in the **Options** section of the toolbox to open the **Rectangle Settings** dialog. Enter the radius (in points) for the rounded corners, and then click on **OK** to apply the settings. All rectangles will use this setting until you change it. To create rectangle with perpendicular corners, enter 0 in the **Radius** field.

TASK 14

How to Use the Eraser

The Eraser tool offers several different erasing modes that enable you to control how much information to erase from the Stage. The following task describes the various erasing methods.

Begin

1 Select the Eraser Tool

To erase lines, fills, and objects from the Stage, choose the Eraser tool (E) from the toolbox.

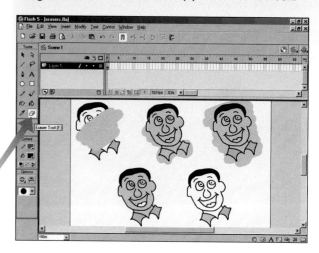

Click

2 Choose an Erasing Mode

Click on the **Eraser Mode** modifier in the **Options** section of the toolbox to expand the list of eraser modes. Choose a mode with which to erase. The figure displays the results of each eraser mode.

Click

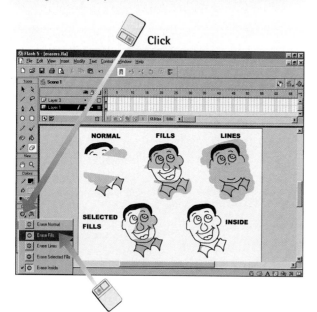

Click

3 Select an Eraser Shape and Size

Click on the **Eraser Shape** modifier in the **Options** section of the toolbox to select an eraser shape and size. Choose from several sizes of round or square erasers.

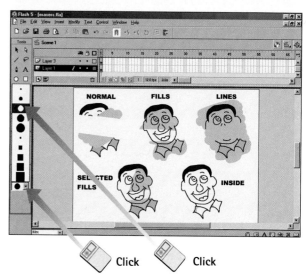

Click   Click

54 PART 3: DRAWING AND CHOOSING COLORS

4 Drag on the Stage

Drag on the Stage to erase lines, fills, or objects with the Eraser tool.

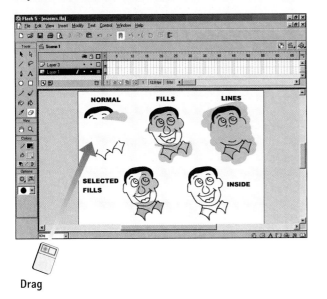

Drag

5 Use the Faucet Modifier

The **Faucet** modifier is a quick way to erase individual strokes and fills by clicking on them. Click on the **Faucet** modifier in the **Options** section of the toolbox to turn on the **Faucet** modifier. Then, click on a stroke or fill to erase it from the Stage.

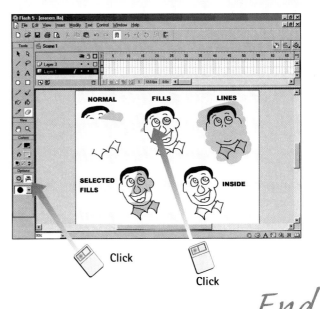

Click

Click

End

How-To Hints

Erasing Everything on the Stage

To quickly erase everything on the Stage, double-click on the **Eraser Tool** icon in the toolbox. This erases everything from the Stage, and affects all layers.

How to Fill Shapes with the Paint Bucket

Use the Paint Bucket tool to fill or change the fill of shapes in your Flash projects. You can also use the Paint Bucket tool to fill an unfilled area. The Paint Bucket tool enables you to fill an object with a solid color, a radial gradient, a linear gradient, or a bitmap. This task shows you how to use the Paint Bucket tool to fill an object.

Begin

1 Choose the Paint Bucket Tool

Select the Paint Bucket tool from the toolbox, or use the keyboard shortcut **K**.

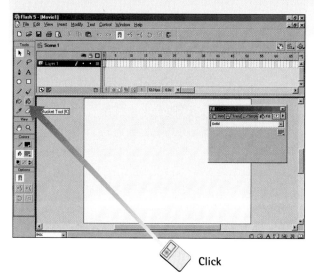

Click

2 Select a Solid Fill Color

Use the **Fill** Panel to select a fill color for the Paint Bucket tool. Choose **Window, Panels, Fill** to open the **Fill** panel. To fill the object with a solid color, choose **Solid** from the options drop-down list. Then, click on the solid color square to select a color from your current palette.

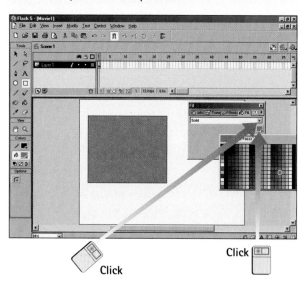

Click
Click
Click

3 Select a Gradient Fill

To fill an object with a gradient, choose either **Linear Gradient** or **Radial Gradient** from the options drop-down list. Create the gradients as outlined in Task 5.

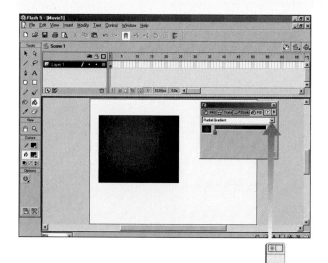

Click

4 Select a Bitmap Fill

To fill an object with a bitmap, choose **Bitmap** from the options drop-down list. You learn more about filling objects with bitmaps in Part 4.

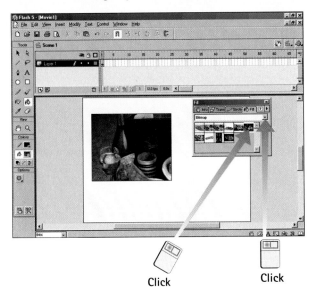

Click   Click

5 Choose a Gap Size

The Paint Bucket tool does not fill open shapes. Sometimes, the areas that you fill appear to be closed, but in actuality gaps exist between the line segments. You can control how much of a gap the Paint Bucket tool ignores before it considers a shape to be open, and thus does not fill it. Click on the **Gap Size** modifier in the **Options** section of the toolbox to specify the amount of gap that the Paint Bucket tool will ignore.

Click

Click

6 Click to Fill

To change the fill of an object that already has a fill, click on the current fill to apply the new properties. To fill an enclosed area that is empty (as shown in this example), click inside the enclosed area.

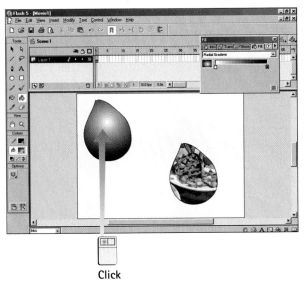

Click

How-To Hints

Changing the Background Color

With Flash, you cannot use the Paint Bucket tool to change the color of the entire Stage. Instead, choose **Modify, Movie** to open the **Movie Properties** dialog. Then click on the **Background Color** square, and choose a new color from the color palette. This changes the Stage color for the entire movie, not just the chosen frame or scene.

Using Rectangles for Backgrounds

If you want to change the background color for a limited number of frames, choose the Rectangle tool. Select the desired fill color, but do not use a stroke color. Create a rectangle that is the same size as the Stage. Place that rectangle on the bottom-most layer of your movie. You can remove it as necessary in later frames.

End

How to Stroke Shapes with the Ink Bottle Tool

The Ink Bottle tool serves a similar function to the Paint Bucket tool, except that you use it to apply or change the stroke around an object. You can use the Ink Bottle tool to apply a stroke around an object that does not have one. You can also use the Ink Bottle tool to change the width, color, or line style of an existing stroke. Follow the steps outlined in this task to learn how to use the Ink Bottle tool in this manner.

Begin

1 Choose the Ink Bottle Tool

Select the Ink Bottle tool from the toolbox, or use the keyboard shortcut **S**.

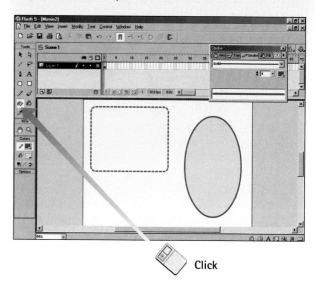

Click

2 Select a Stroke Color

Use the **Stroke** panel to select a stroke color for the Ink Bottle tool. Choose **Window, Panels, Stroke** to open the **Stroke** panel. To select a stroke color, click on the solid color square to select a color from your current palette.

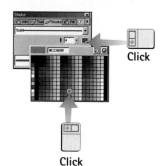

Click

Click

3 Select a Line Style

To select a line style, click on the line options drop-down to display the line style choices. Click on the line style you want to apply. Your new choice appears in the dialog after the drop-down collapses.

Click

Click

4 Select a Line Width

To select a line width, double-click on the width entry that appears in the **Width** field, and enter a new value in pixels. Alternatively, click on the arrow at the lower-right corner of the **Width** field, and drag the slider up or down to increase or decrease the width.

5 Click on the Object

To apply a stroke to an area that does not have one, click on the fill to which you want to apply a stroke. To change an existing stroke, click on the fill or the stroke to change the stroke properties.

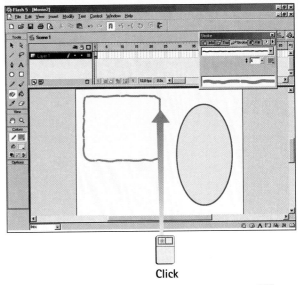

Click

End

How-To Hints

Making Strokes Narrower

You can use the Ink Bottle to reduce the height of the strokes in a shape. Choose **Window, Panels, Stroke** to open the **Stroke** panel. Enter a new stroke height in the Height field, or move the slider down to reduce the stroke height. Then, choose the Ink Bottle from the toolbox, and click to assign the new stroke height to any of the strokes on the stage.

How to Copy Fill and Line Colors

You can use the Dropper tool to copy fill and line colors from one object to another.

Begin

1 Choose the Dropper Tool

Choose the Dropper tool from the toolbox, or use the keyboard shortcut I.

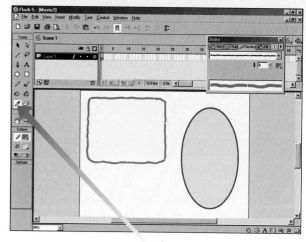

Click

2 Copy the Properties of a Fill

To copy the properties of a fill, hover the cursor over the fill until you see a small brush icon appear beside the Dropper. Then click on the fill to copy its properties.

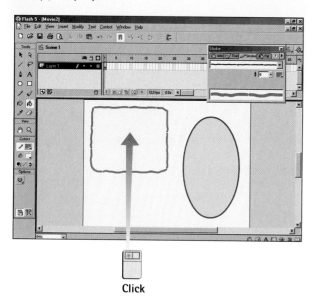

Click

3 Click the Fill that Will Change

The Paint Bucket tool is automatically selected. Move over the fill that you want to change, and click on the fill with the Paint Bucket. The fill from the first object is applied to the second object.

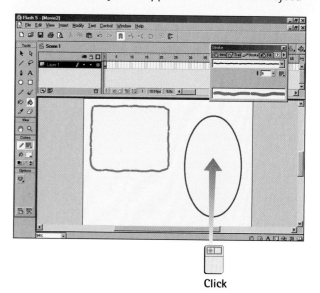

Click

4 Copy the Properties of a Stroke

To copy the properties of a stroke, choose the Dropper tool from the toolbox again. Hover the cursor over an existing stroke until you see a small Pencil icon appear beside the Dropper. Then click on the stroke to copy its properties.

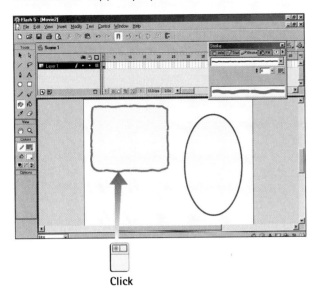

Click

5 Click the Stroke that Will Change

The Ink Bottle tool is automatically selected. Move over the stroke that you want to change, and click on the stroke with the Ink Bottle. The stroke from the first object is applied to the second object.

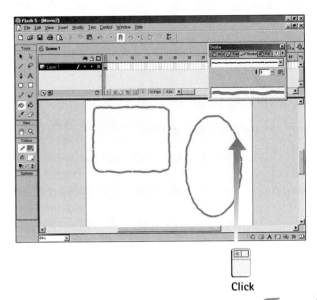

Click

End

How-To Hints

Copying Strokes and Fills to Multiple Objects

You can repeat step 5 from this task to change the fills or strokes of more than one object. As long as the Ink Bottle tool or Paint Bucket tool remains selected, you can apply the new stroke or fill to as many objects as you like.

How to Lock a Gradient Fill

The Brush tool and the Paint Bucket tool include a **Lock Fill** modifier that enables you to spread a fill across a group of selected objects. This is especially useful when you want to apply a gradient fill across a number of boxes that you will later use as buttons. Instead of sizing the gradient to the individual object, the **Lock Fill** modifier sizes the gradient as if it fills the entire Stage. The following task helps clarify this technique.

Begin

1 Select the Appropriate Tool

Choose either the Brush tool (**B**) or the Paint Bucket tool (**K**) from the toolbox. In this example, we selected the Paint Bucket tool. The **Options** section of the toolbox shows the Paint Bucket options.

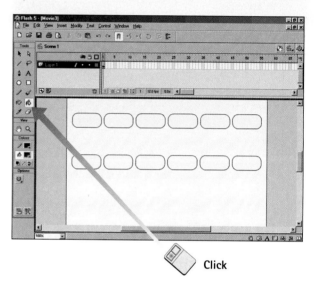

Click

2 Select a Gradient or Bitmap Fill

Choose the **Window, Panels, Fill** command to open the **Fill** panel. To fill objects with a gradient, choose **Linear Gradient** or **Radial Gradient** from the fill options drop-down list.

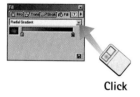

Click

3 Turn On the Lock Fill Modifier

Click on the **Lock Fill** modifier in the **Options** panel to toggle this option on.

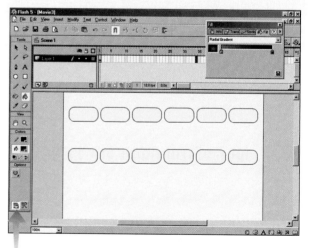

Click

4 Paint the Areas You Want to Fill

Paint with the Brush tool or click over one of the selected objects with the Paint Bucket tool. The object you clicked on becomes filled with the selected gradient. The top row in the example shows the result when each button is clicked on with the **Lock Fill** modifier turned off. The bottom row in the example shows the result when each button is clicked on with the **Lock Fill** modifier turned on.

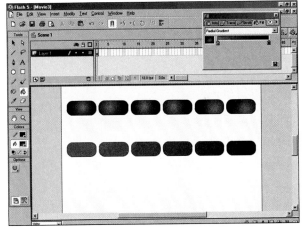

End

How-To Hints

Experiment with Locked Fills

You can use locked gradients to fill many types of objects. You can also create interesting text effects with this feature. Remember, however, that you will need to use the **Modify, Break Apart** command to break text apart before you fill it with a gradient or bitmap fill.

Task

Importing Artwork

Flash is best suited for creating lean-and-mean animations for the Internet, and it is a wonderful tool for that purpose. There are a host of other graphics tools that have their strengths in helping you create bitmap and vector graphics, and you might already make frequent use of some of the more popular graphics tools.

Flash enables you to create artwork in your favorite paint or vector graphic program, and then use that artwork in your latest Flash projects. In this part, we show you how to import graphics and video clips that you created in other programs for use in your Flash movies.

How to Import Bitmap Files into Flash

Flash enables you to import a wide variety of bitmap file types (BMP, GIF, JPEG, and PNG images). If you install QuickTime 4 on your computer, a few additional bitmap file formats become available to Flash's import function. These formats include MacPaint (.pntg), Photoshop 2.5 and 3.0 (.psd), PICT (.pct, .pic), QuickTime Image (.qtif), Silicon Graphics (.sgi), TGA (.tga), and TIFF (.tif).

Begin

1 Choose the Import Command

To begin the import process, choose **File, Import**. Alternatively, press the keyboard shortcut **Ctrl+R** (Windows) or **Cmmd+R** (Macintosh). This brings up the **Import** dialog box.

 Click

2 Choose a File Format

Click on the **Files of type** drop-down list (the **Show** drop-down on Macintosh). This list displays all the file types that you can import into Flash. If you know the file format of the file you want to import, choose it from the list. This makes it much easier to find the file or files you want.

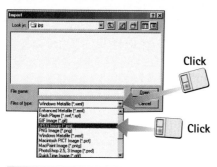

Click

Click

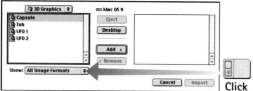

Click

3 Select the File (PC)

On the PC, click on the **Look in** drop-down, and navigate through the folders on your computer until you locate the file or files you want to import. To import a range of files, click on the name of the first file, hold down the **Shift** key, and click on the last file. To import nonadjacent files, hold down **Ctrl** while clicking on each individual filename.

4 Select the File (Macintosh)

On the Macintosh, navigate to the correct folder, click on the name of each file you want to import, and click on the **Add** button to add it to the list on the right. Remove files from the list by clicking on **Remove**.

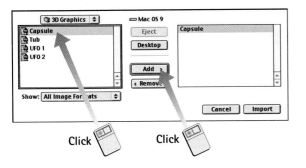

Click   Click

5 Open the Selected File

On the PC, after you select the desired file, click on the **Open** button to import the file. On the Macintosh, click on the **Import** button. The file appears in the center of the Flash Stage.

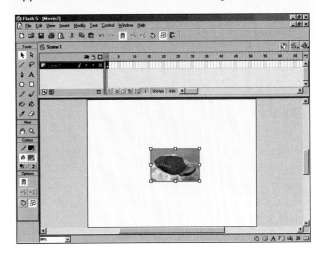

6 Import Sequentially Numbered Files

If you choose to import an image called popart1.png, and another image in the same folder has the name popart2.png, Flash views these images as a sequence. Flash asks you if you want to import all the images in the sequence. Click on **Yes** to add the entire sequence. Flash imports the images in numerical order, and places them on consecutive keyframes on the same layer in the Timeline. In effect, you create a frame-by-frame animation with this technique.

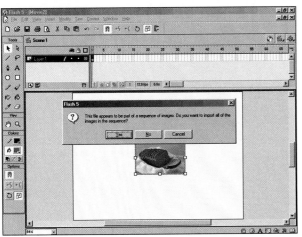

How-To Hints

Copy and Paste

You can also use the **Copy** and **Paste** commands to import graphics. Open or create a bitmap in your favorite paint program, and then use the **Edit, Copy** command to copy it into the clipboard. Next, switch to Flash. Click on the Timeline at the frame and layer in which you want to place the bitmap, and choose **Edit, Paste** to place the artwork on the Stage.

Watch Those File Sizes!

Using a lot of bitmaps increases the size of your Flash project and of your Flash movie, which can slow download. If you use bitmaps in your Flash movies, try to reduce file sizes *before* you import them. Crop or size the images no larger than you intend to display them in your Flash movie. (Scaling the image down in your Flash movie will not reduce the byte size of the bitmap.)

End

How to Import Vector Files into Flash

Flash also enables you to import vector-based graphics, including Macromedia FreeHand versions 7 through 9, Adobe Illustrator (AI and EPS), AutoCAD (DXF), Enhanced Metafile (EMF), and Windows Metafile (WMF). Even though Flash works directly with vector graphics, many flash artists use draw programs to provide advanced text and graphic effects that are beyond the capabilities of Flash. Later, they import it into Flash to add the animation and interactivity. This task shows you how to import vector images into Flash.

Begin

1 The Import Command

Choose **File, Import,** or use the keyboard shortcut **Ctrl+R** (Windows) or **Cmmd+R** (Macintosh). The **Import** dialog appears.

Click

2 Choose a File Format

From the **Files of type** drop-down list (the **Show** drop-down on Macintosh), select the file format that you want to import.

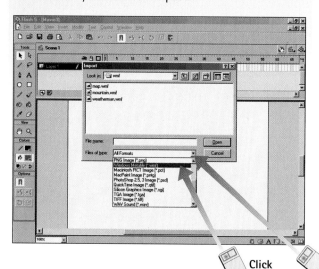

Click

Click

3 Select the File and Import It

On the PC, navigate to the file you want to open, and click on **Open** to import the file. On the Macintosh, select the file you want to open and click on **Add** them, click on **Import**. The file appears in the center of the Stage. Selection boxes surround all individual objects in the file.

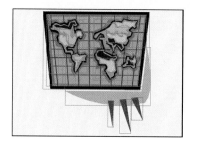

4 Move Objects to a Different Layer

When you import vector graphics, Flash places all objects on a single layer. To relocate objects to different layers, click on the **Insert Layer** button at the lower-left corner of the Timeline to create a new layer. Rename the new layer. Select one or more objects to move to the new layer.

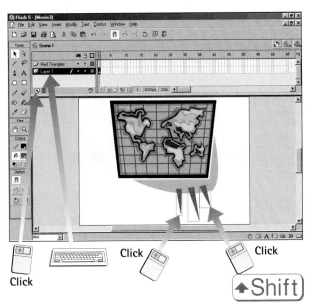

Click   Click   Click
Click
⬆Shift

5 Cut and Paste to the New Layer

To cut the objects from the current layer and place them into the clipboard, use the **Edit, Cut** command or click on the **Cut** button on the toolbar. Then, click to select the new layer on the Timeline to make it the current layer. Choose **Edit, Paste in Place** to paste the objects from the clipboard to the same location on the new layer.

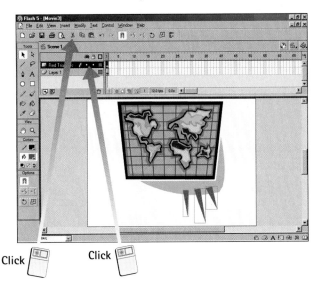

Click   Click

6 Add Layers and Convert to Symbols

Repeat step 5 as necessary to place objects on different layers. Choose **Insert, Convert to Symbol** to convert the objects to Flash symbols that you can animate. Several layers and symbols are created from the original vector file shown here.

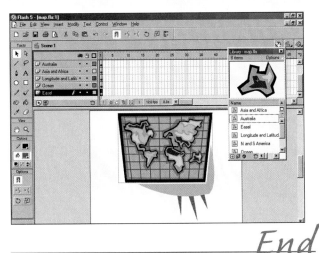

How-To Hints

Editing Vector Art

You might need to perform some editing on the vector artwork that you import. You can edit imported vector art by using the same methods that you use to edit artwork that you draw directly into Flash. Reshape lines, change stroke and fill colors, and break apart objects as necessary to change the artwork to fit your animation.

A Note About Illustrator

Ungroup all objects on each layer of your Adobe Illustrator file before you import a file into Flash. This is necessary to manipulate the objects like any other Flash object.

End

How to Import PNG and FreeHand Files

Flash utilizes additional features when you import files built in other Macromedia programs. This task discusses some of the choices available to you when importing PNG files created in Fireworks, and images that you create in FreeHand.

Begin

1 Import a Fireworks PNG File

Follow steps 1 through 4 in Task 1 to navigate to and open a Fireworks PNG file. When you click on **Open**, the **Fireworks PNG Import Settings** dialog box appears. This dialog enables you to import the PNG file as an editable object. You can also choose to preserve placed bitmaps, text blocks, and guides from Fireworks. If you instead choose **Flatten Image**, Flash *rasterizes* the file, or converts it to a bitmap image. After you've made your choices, click on **OK** to import the file.

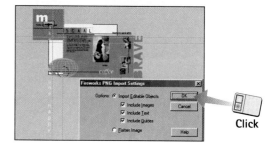

Click

2 Import Other PNG Files

If you import a PNG file that you created in a paint program other than Fireworks, Flash treats the file like any other bitmap graphic. The image appears as one object and Flash places it on one layer.

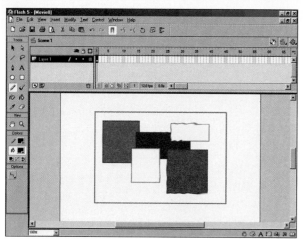

3 Import a FreeHand File

Follow steps 1 through 4 in Task 1 to navigate to and open a FreeHand 7-9 file. After you click **Open** the **FreeHand Import** settings dialog pops up. The **Pages** options in the **Mapping** section control how Flash imports individual pages in the FreeHand document. Choose **Scenes** to place each page in the FreeHand document into a separate scene in Flash. Choose **Key Frames** to place each FreeHand page into a separate keyframe within the same scene in Flash.

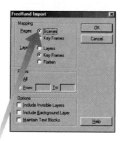

 Click

4 Select a Layer Treatment

The **Layers** section provides options that control how Flash converts the layers in your FreeHand file. Choose **Layers** to convert each layer in the FreeHand document to a layer in Flash. Choose **Key Frames** to convert each layer in FreeHand to a keyframe in Flash. Finally, choose **Flatten** to combine all of FreeHand's layers into one Flash layer.

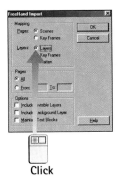

Click

5 Select a Page Treatment

The options in the **Pages** section control the number of pages from the original FreeHand document that import into a Flash movie. To import all pages in the FreeHand document, click on the **All** option. To import a range of pages in the original FreeHand document, click on the **From** option. Then, enter a starting and ending number for the pages you want to import in the **From** and **To** fields.

Click

6 Select Additional Options

The **Options** section enables you to define the import operation further. Choose **Include Invisible Layers** to include hidden layers when you import the FreeHand document. Choose **Include Background Layer** to import the background layer from FreeHand. Finally, choose **Maintain Text Blocks** to preserve the FreeHand document's text boxes so that they appear as editable text boxes in Flash.

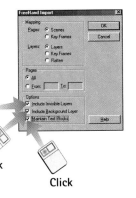

Click

How-To Hints

Controlling File Size

When you create files in FreeHand for import into Flash, use fewer than eight colors in your gradient fills, and as few steps in your blends as possible. This helps keep your Flash file size down. Also, be aware that when you import a file that contains placed grayscale images, Flash converts the grayscale images to RGB format. This increases file size.

Using FreeHand Objects That Overlap

FreeHand maintains the integrity of two objects that overlap on the same layer, whereas Flash cannot. If you need to keep the objects separated, place them on different layers in FreeHand. When you import the file into Flash, choose **Layers** in Flash's **FreeHand Import** dialog box.

End

How to Convert Bitmaps to Vector Graphics Files

Converting a bitmap image to a vector image enables you to manipulate a graphic as you would any graphic created in Flash. Generally, it does not save space when you convert a bitmap to vector image. In fact, the file size might actually become larger when you convert a photographic image or a complex bitmap to a vector image. Line art drawings, cartoon art, and images with mostly solid areas of color are suitable for conversion to vector art, but you will need to experiment with various settings to keep file sizes down. This task explains the steps for converting a bitmap image to a vector graphic.

Begin

1 Import a Bitmap Image

Choose **File, Import** to access the **Import** dialog. Navigate to the desired bitmap file on you computer, and click on **Open** to import that image. The import operation adds the bitmap image to the Stage at the currently selected frame and layer. The operation also automatically selects the image on the Stage. If the image already exists in your Flash movie, click on it to select it, and move on to step 2.

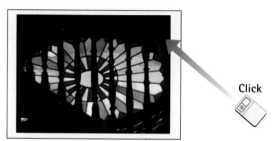

Click

2 Trace the Bitmap Image

Choose **Modify, Trace Bitmap.** The **Trace Bitmap** dialog appears. In the next few steps, you make choices to fine-tune the conversion to suit your needs.

3 Enter a Color Threshold Value

In the **Color Threshold** field, enter a value between **1** and **500.** You will need to adjust threshold values to suit the image you are tracing. Find a compromise between image quality and file size. A larger number in this field (such as **350** in this example) results in a vector graphic that contains fewer colors than the original bitmap image. This reduces image quality, but it also reduces the file size.

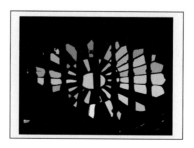

4 Set a Minimum Area Value

Enter a value between **1** and **1000** in the **Minimum Area** field. Higher numbers result in lower image quality in comparison to the original bitmap, but they also reduce file size. In the example shown here, the **Color Threshold** value is set at the default of **100**. The **Minimum Area** field is set to **250**. Now you have more colors in the traced version, but the colors do not blend as much.

5 Set a Curve Fit

Choose an option from the **Curve Fit** drop-down list. Choose **Pixels, Very Tight, Tight, Normal, Smooth,** or **Very Smooth** to determine how closely curves match the shapes in the original bitmap. Tighter curves result in bigger file sizes, but remain more true to the original bitmap. Smoother curves result in smaller file sizes, but reduce the quality of the traced image. Experiment with the options until you find the one that gives you the results you are looking for.

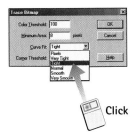

Click

6 Set a Corner Threshold

In the **Corner Threshold** drop-down list, choose from among **Many corners, Normal,** and **Few Corners.** This setting determines how the conversion process treats sharp corners. **Many corners** preserves sharp edges, whereas **Few corners** smoothes out some of the edges. Again, experiment with these options to determine which one gives you the results you like best.

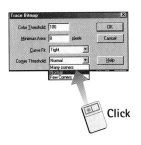

Click

End

How-To Hints

When to Trace Bitmaps

Generally, you want to use the **Trace Bitmap** feature when it saves time and when there is no other alternative available. For example, if your client has only a bitmap version of a logo or symbol available, it *might* save some time to use the **Trace Bitmap** feature instead of trying to reproduce it yourself in Flash. Make sure that you begin with an image that is free of compression artifacts, and sufficiently large enough to trace smoothly. This ensures the best results.

How to Break Apart a Bitmap

When you break apart an imported bitmap, you can fill ovals, rectangles, and brush strokes with a bitmap fill. You can also use the Lasso and Magic Wand tools to select and modify portions of a bitmap image. The following task shows you how to break apart a bitmap so that you can use it as a fill.

Begin

1 Open the Import Dialog

In order to paint with a bitmap, you have to import it into your Flash movie. To import a bitmap, choose **File, Import** to access the **Import** dialog.

Click

2 Select a Bitmap to Import

Navigate to the drive and folder that contains the bitmap you want to import. On the PC, click to highlight the bitmap file you want to import, and click **Open** to import that image. On the Macintosh, **Add** the image to the list on the right, and then click on **Import**.

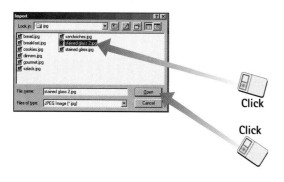

Click

Click

3 Break Apart the Bitmap

With the bitmap selected, choose **Modify, Break Apart,** or use the keyboard shortcut **Ctrl+B** (Windows) or **Cmmd+B** (Macintosh) to break apart the bitmap.

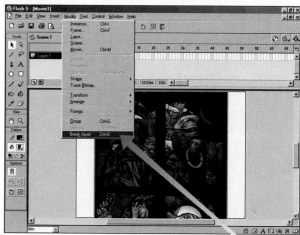

Click

4 Use the Bitmap for a Fill

After you break apart a bitmap, small white dots fill the image as a visual indicator that the bitmap is broken apart. A small thumbnail of the bitmap appears beside the **Paint Bucket** in the **Colors** section of the toolbox to indicate that the bitmap is selected as the current fill. Choose the Oval tool or the Rectangle tool to draw an object on the Stage. Notice that the bitmap fills the object.

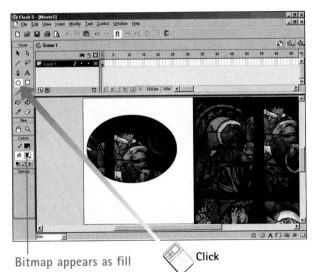

Bitmap appears as fill

Click

5 Modify the Broken-Apart Bitmap

Use the Arrow tool to adjust the shape of the filled oval or rectangle to create some interesting effects for your filled shape. The bitmap fill expands as necessary to fill the shape as you adjust it.

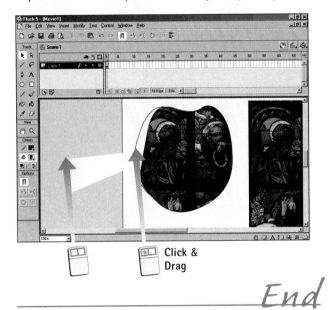

Click

Click & Drag

End

How-To Hints

Breaking Apart and Tracing Bitmaps

Note the differences between breaking apart bitmaps and tracing them. When you trace a bitmap, you convert it into smaller vector graphics object. When you break apart a bitmap, it is still one object. However, you can edit smaller portions of the bitmap as discussed in Task 7.

Deleting the Bitmap from the Stage

If you use a bitmap as a fill, as shown in the previous task, you can delete the broken-apart bitmap from the Stage. Click to select the broken-apart bitmap, and press the **Delete** key. The objects that you filled with the bitmap remain on the Stage, and remain filled with the bitmap. Do not delete the original bitmap from the library, however. If you do, the objects that you filled with the bitmap have no fill at all.

How to Paint with a Bitmap

You can fill rectangles, ovals, and other shapes with any bitmap that you have imported into your Flash movie. One of the nicest features of Flash enables you to paint with a bitmap. This adds artistic flair to bitmap images. The following task demonstrates another way that you can select a bitmap as a fill, and shows you how to paint with a bitmap.

Begin

1 Open the Fill Panel

To open the Fill panel, choose **Window, Panels, Fill.**

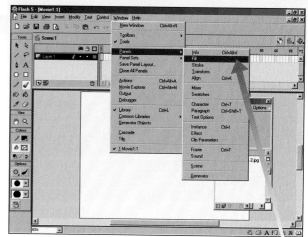

Click

2 Select the Bitmap Fill

Click on the drop-down arrow, and choose **Bitmap** from the list of fill options. Flash shows thumbnails of all the bitmaps in your movie (in this case, there is only one).

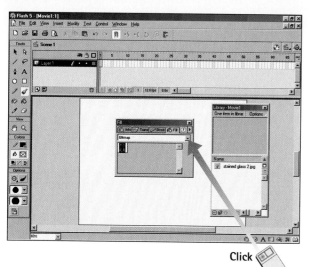

Click

3 Choose the Bitmap with Which to Fill

Click on the thumbnail of the image you want to use as your fill. The bitmap fill appears as a small icon in the **Colors** section of the toolbox.

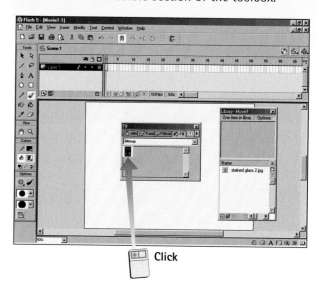

Click

4 Select and Set Brush Tool Options

For this example, select the Brush tool from the toolbox, or use the keyboard shortcut **B** to use the Brush tool. Use the controls in the **Options** section of the toolbox to select the shape, pressure, and size of the brush. These options are described in Part 3, "Drawing and Choosing Colors."

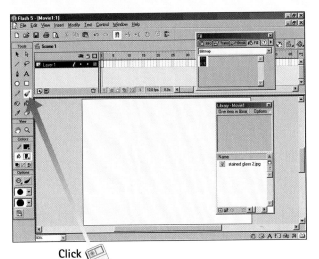

Click

5 Paint on the Stage

Paint on the Stage with the brush. Initially, your paint strokes appear red as you drag the mouse. Release the mouse, and watch the bitmap fill the stroke!

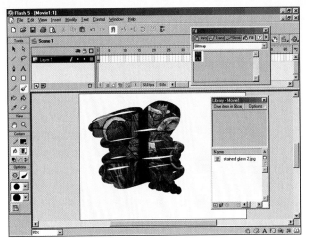

End

How-To Hints

Using Solid Colors and Bitmap Fills Together

You can combine bitmap fills with solid color fills to create some interesting effects and patterns in your Flash movies. Use the Brush tool to paint with the bitmap to place an interesting shape on the stage. Then select a solid color or gradient to paint over other areas in the bitmap. If you create the solid colored strokes before you group the bitmap fill, you can also use solid colored strokes or the Eraser tool to "cut out" areas of the bitmap fill.

How to Change Fills in Bitmaps

You can use the Lasso tool and the Magic Wand to change colors in selected areas of a bitmap that has been broken apart. Some experimentation will be necessary to achieve the settings that are appropriate for each bitmap you choose to edit in this manner. The following steps show you how to edit colors in a bitmap.

Begin

1 Break Apart a Bitmap

Drag a bitmap from the library onto the Stage. Choose the **Modify, Break Apart** command to break apart the bitmap.

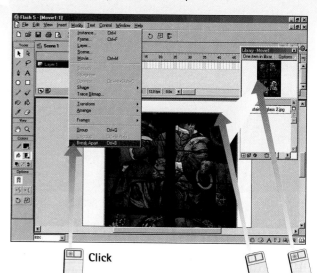

Click

Drag

2 Choose the Lasso Tool

Click outside the broken-apart image to deselect it. Next, click on the Lasso tool in the toolbox, or use the keyboard shortcut **L** to select it.

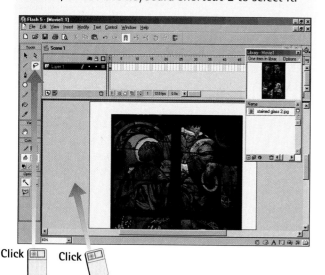

Click   Click

3 Choose the Magic Wand Modifier

Click on the **Magic Wand** button in the **Options** section of the toolbox to activate the **Magic Wand** modifier.

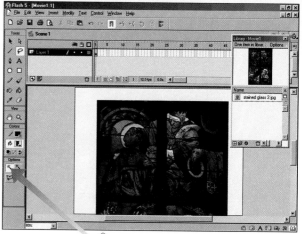

Click

4 Set Magic Wand Properties

Click on the **Magic Wand Properties** button to open the **Magic Wand Settings** dialog. In the **Threshold** field enter value between **0** and **200**. The higher the **Threshold** value, the less similar the colors must be before the wand tool includes them in the selection. Then, choose a **Smoothing** option from the drop-down list. The options (from least to greatest) are **Pixels, Rough, Normal,** and **Smooth.** Click **OK.**

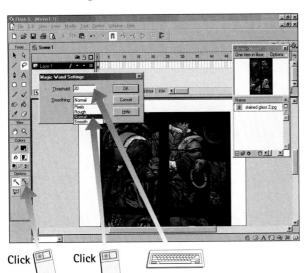

Click   Click

5 Modify a Color with the Magic Wand

With the wand, click on the bitmap to select the color you want to modify. Flash selects areas based on the parameters you defined in the **Magic Wand Settings** dialog. The selected areas become highlighted with small white dots.

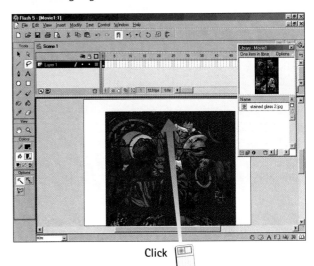

Click

6 Choose a New Fill Color

Click on the **Fill** color square in the **Colors** section of the toolbox. Drag through the current palette, and then click to select a new fill color.

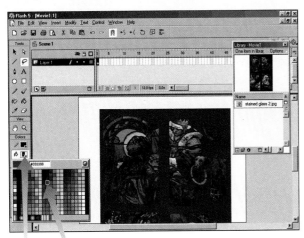

Click   Click

End

How-To Hints

Editing Bitmaps in an Image-Editing Program

If you want to use your favorite image-editing program to edit your bitmap, you can launch that program directly from Flash, edit the image, and then have Flash update the image in your project. To do so, right-click on the bitmap icon in the **Library** window. Choose **Edit with** or **Edit with Fireworks** if you have Fireworks on your computer. Navigate to the image editor of your choice (unless you chose **Edit with Fireworks**), edit the image, and save it. If the image doesn't automatically update in Flash, right-click on its icon in the **Library** window and choose **Update.**

How to Modify Bitmap Fills with the Paint Bucket

When you use the **Paint Bucket** to fill your artwork with a bitmap image, you can modify the look of the bitmap within the object it fills. This task explains how to do so.

Begin

1 Choose a Bitmap Fill

Import a bitmap into your movie as outlined in Task 1. Select the bitmap you want to use as a fill as outlined in Task 6. Any new objects that you create with the Oval tool, Rectangle tool, Brush tool, or Paint Bucket tool will use this bitmap as a fill. For this step, use the Rectangle tool to create a bitmap-filled box.

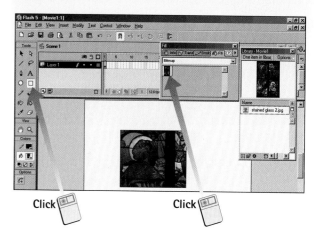

Click

Click

2 Select the Paint Bucket Tool

Click with the Arrow tool to select the rectangle you created in the previous step. Then click to select the Paint Bucket tool from the toolbox.

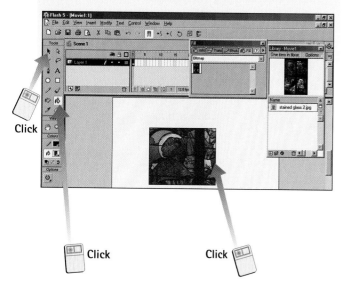

Click

Click

Click

3 Reposition the Fill

Click on the **Transform Fill** modifier button for the **Paint Bucket** to toggle the modifier on. When you click on the rectangle with the **Paint Bucket** tool, a rectangular resizing box appears around it. The resizing box is the same size as the entire bitmap (rather than the object it's filling), and provides six resize handles on the outside and one in the center. Zoom out as necessary to see the entire resizing box. Click and drag the center handle to reposition the fill inside the rectangle.

Click & Drag

4 Resize the Fill

Click and drag the lower-left handle to proportionately resize the bitmap fill. Notice that if you make the fill smaller than the object, Flash "tiles" the fill so that more than one copy of the bitmap image appears in the object. Click and drag the bottom handle to resize the bitmap's height only, and the left handle to resize the bitmap's width only. Notice that the three handles used to resize the bitmap are square.

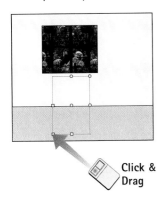

Click &
Drag

5 Rotate the Fill

Notice that the three handles on the upper-right side of the box are circular. Click and drag the upper-right handle to rotate the bitmap fill image inside the rectangle. The position box rotates around an anchor at the very center of the box.

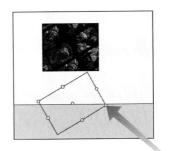

Click &
Drag

6 Skew the Fill

The top handle enables you to skew, or slant, the box left and right. As you slide the handle to the left, the top of the box follows it as the bottom moves to the right. Drag to the right, and the top goes right, and the bottom goes left. The right handle behaves similarly.

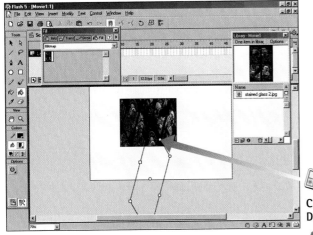

Click &
Drag

End

How to Set Bitmap Properties

The **Bitmap Properties** dialog provides detailed information about the bitmap, and enables you to make choices regarding file compression and anti-aliasing. This task explores the **Bitmap Properties** dialog in detail.

Begin

1 Import a Bitmap to the Library

Choose **File, Import** to access the **Import** dialog. Navigate to the desired bitmap file on you computer. On the PC, click on **Open** to import that image. On the Macintosh, **Add** the image to the list on the right, and then click on **Import**. The import operation adds the bitmap image to the Stage at the currently selected frame and layer. It also adds the bitmap to the library. Choose **Window, Library** to open the library.

Click

2 Open the Bitmap Properties

In the Library window, click on the name of the bitmap whose properties you want to set. In this case, there is only one bitmap in the list. Click on the **Properties** button to open the **Bitmap Properties** dialog. Alternatively, right-click (Windows) or double-click (Macintosh) on the image's name in the library list, and choose **Properties** from the menu, or choose **Properties** from the **Options** drop-down list at the top of the Library window.

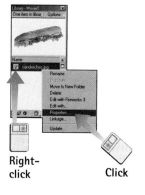

Right-click   Click

3 Set Anti-Aliasing

Anti-aliasing helps make an image appear smoother by softening hard edges. For example, if a red pixel sits directly next to a blue pixel, the edge where the two meet is very noticeable, and can make the image look hard or blocky. Anti-aliasing creates transition pixels of varying shades of the two colors so that the line is smoothed and less noticeable. Check the **Allow smoothing** box to engage anti-aliasing. Keep in mind that anti-aliased images have a larger file size than images that are not anti-aliased because of all the transitional colors that are created.

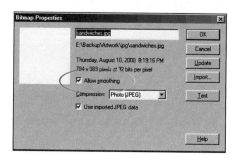

4 Choose a Compression Setting

Click on the **Compression** drop-down to choose between **Photo (JPEG)** or **Lossless (PNG/GIF)**. In general, use **Photo (JPEG)** for images with many colors and color transition areas, such as full-color photographs. Use **Lossless (PNG/GIF)** for simple images that contain large blocks of solid colors. For the **Photo (JPEG)** option, click on the **Use imported JPEG data** box to use the default quality. To set it manually, uncheck the box, and enter a value between **1** and **100**. Higher quality settings result in superior image quality, but quality comes with a price in larger file size. Experiment with various settings to find a suitable trade-off.

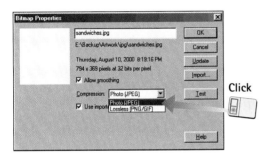

Click

5 Test the File Compression Setting

Click on the **Test** button to update the summary file information and the preview window when you make anti-aliasing and compression choices. Summary information appears at the bottom of the **Bitmap Properties** dialog. The preview window at the top left of the dialog enables you to see how the changes you make affect the image quality. If the image is larger than the window, click and drag the preview to view different parts of the image.

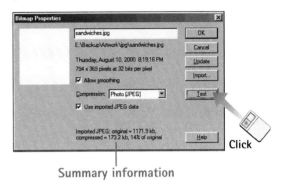

Click

Summary information

6 Update a Bitmap Image

Sometimes you have a need to edit a bitmap image with another graphics program outside of Flash. If this is the case, you don't have to import the revised image into Flash again. Save the revised image over the previous version, using the same file location and filename. Then click on the **Update** button if you have edited the bitmap in an outside image-editing program. This updates Flash to reflect the changes made in the image editor.

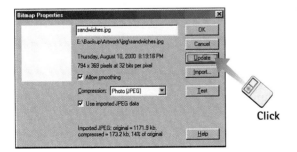

Click

7 Import a New Bitmap Image

Click on the **Import** button to import a new bitmap image to replace the old image in the **Library** and on the Stage. For example, you can place a temporary image into your movie as a placeholder and use the **Import** button to replace it later with the final version. When you click on the **Import** button, a dialog enables you to navigate to the drive and folder that contains your image. When you locate the image, click on **OK** to choose it.

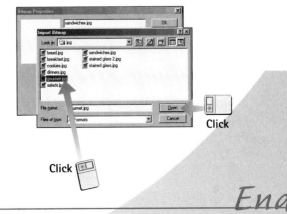

Click

Click

End

Task

PART

5

Using Type

*I*n Flash, type can do much more than sit on a page. Text takes on a new dimension in Flash...you can animate the size, position, skewing, rotation, transparency, and color of type to bring life to an otherwise dull text-only page.

There was a time when you had to use fonts with great care. If you used fonts that were not resident on other users' systems, your movies looked entirely different to them. Now, Flash embeds most TrueType and Adobe Type 1 PostScript fonts into your Flash movies, so your movies look the same from one computer to another. When Flash cannot embed a font, it's easy to tell: embedded fonts appear smooth and anti-aliased. When a font appears rough and "pixelly," that means Flash can't embed it. So, you have to find an alternative font.

If you have to use a font that Flash can't export, there is another solution. You can break the text apart and convert it to shapes. Be aware that converting text to shapes slightly increases the size of your movies. In addition, after you convert your text to shapes, you won't be able to edit it. You can, however, create some interesting effects with text that has been converted to shapes. ●

How to Add Type and Set Attributes

Before you enter text on the Stage, you need to select a font and specify the size, color, and alignment properties. Any new text block that you create afterward will use the same settings, until you select new properties. When you edit a text block, the settings used in the text block you are editing will become the new default for adding new text. These points will be illustrated in the following tasks.

Begin

1 Select the Text Tool

To add type, select the Text tool from the toolbox.

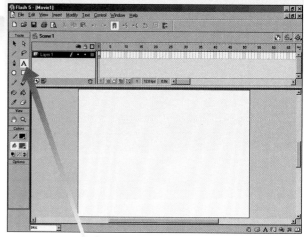

Click

2 Choose Your Font

The **Character** panel provides a means for you to choose font, font size, and other text attributes quickly. To open the **Character** panel, choose **Window, Panels, Character**. To select a font, expand the **Font** drop-down, and highlight the name of a font in the font list. A preview of the selected font appears in a flyout box. Click to select the font you want to use.

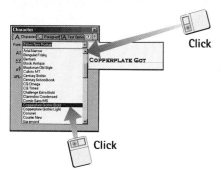

Click

Click

3 Choose the Font Size

To choose the font size, enter a new point size in the **Size** field directly beneath the **Font** drop-down. Alternatively, click-and-drag the slider up or down to increase or decrease the font size.

Click & Drag

4 Select the Text Color

To select a color for your text, click on the **Font Color** swatch in the **Character** panel. Then, click to select a color from your current Flash palette. You can also use the Fill color swatch in the **Colors** panel of the toolbox to select a text color from your current palette.

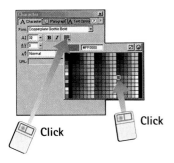

Click

Click

5 Choose the Text Style

Click on the **Bold, Italic,** or both buttons in the **Character** panel to format the text as the button indicates. Click on a button again to turn off bold or italic. Note that bold or italic styles might not be available for all fonts that you have installed on your system.

6 Align the Paragraphs

Use options in the **Paragraph** panel to align your text. To open the **Paragraph** panel, choose **Window, Panels, Paragraph.** You can also switch between the **Character** panel and the **Paragraph** panel by clicking the appropriate tabs in the dialog as indicated in this figure. To align your text, click to choose from **Left, Center, Right,** or **Justify** alignment.

Click to use   Click to use
Character panel   Paragraph panel

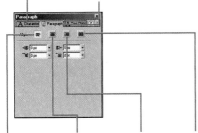

Align Left   Align Center   Justify   Align Right

End

How-To Hints

Smoothing the Appearance of Text

When you enter your text on the stage, verify that it appears smoothed (or anti-aliased) after you type it. This indicates that Flash will embed the font so that other viewers will see the font properly when they play your movie. Your text appears rough or jagged when Flash cannot embed the font in your movie. In that case, you can either select a different font or break the text apart into lines and fills.

How to Create Static Text Fields

Text content that does not change, either dynamically or by user input, is referred to as *static text*. You can animate and apply effects to static text blocks just as you can with any other graphic element in your Flash movies. Flash enables you to add type in single-line or multiple-line text fields. Single-line text fields expand horizontally as you type. For longer paragraphs, you can use fixed-width blocks that expand vertically as you enter your type. The following steps show you how to create single-line and multiple-line static text blocks.

1 Create Short Text Phrases

To create a text field that consists of short words or phrases, select the Text tool from the toolbox and choose your font properties as outlined in Task 1. Click on Stage where you want the text to appear and type. The text field expands horizontally to fit the text on one line. To begin a new line, press **Enter** (Windows) or **Return** (Macintosh). Click outside the text box to complete the operation.

 Click

2 Create Fixed-Width Paragraphs

To create a fixed-width text field, select the Text tool and choose your font properties as outlined in Task 1. Click where you want the type to start, and drag to the desired width of the text block. Release the mouse to define the width of your text field. Enter the text for your paragraph. The text wraps when it reaches the end of the field. Click outside the text box to complete the operation.

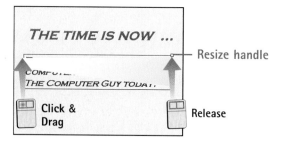

Resize handle

Click & Drag

Release

3 Change the Width of a Text Field

To change the width of a text field, click inside the text field with the Text tool to display the resize handle. Click and drag the resize handle and release at the desired width.

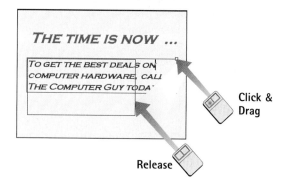

Click & Drag

Release

4 Reset to a Text Field

To remove the width setting from a text field, select the Text tool, and click once inside the text field to display the resize handle. Then double-click the resize handle with the Text tool. The text field expands to fit the contents of the text field on one line.

Double-click

5 View All Text in Wide Text Fields

If you create a text block that extends horizontally, it might continue beyond the boundaries of the Stage. To view the portion of the text field that extends beyond the Stage, choose **View, Work Area**. Then, choose **Show All** from the **Zoom** drop-down at the bottom-left corner of the stage. After you zoom out, you can add line breaks or move the resize handle to resize the text field.

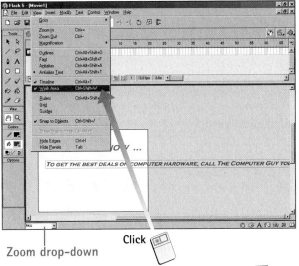

Zoom drop-down

Click

End

How-To Hints

The Text Options Panel

The **Text Options** panel enables you to choose how you want Flash to use the text in your movies. In addition to creating static text fields, which are used in the examples in this chapter, Flash enables you to create two other types of text fields also. Dynamic text and input text are advanced text options that display text retrieved from databases, or text that users input into forms. They require advanced scripting techniques that are beyond the scope of this book. Refer to *Sams Teach Yourself Macromedia Flash in 24 Hours* for further information on how to use dynamic text and input text.

Using Device Fonts

The **Text Options** panel also includes a **Use Device Fonts** option, which can decrease the file size of your movie and increase readability for small type sizes. When you enable this option, Flash does not embed the font for that text. Instead, Flash substitutes the closest device font that most resembles the font you select. Device fonts come in three types: _sans, which most closely resembles fonts such as Arial or Helvetica; _serif, which most closely resembles fonts such as Times New Roman; and _typewriter, which resembles fixed-width fonts such as Courier or Courier New.

How to Select and Edit Text

You can edit any text field in Flash as long as it has not been converted to shapes. To edit text, you must first select the text that you want to change. Select a text block with the Arrow tool or text itself with the Text tool. After you select text for editing, you can change the font properties or edit the contents of the text field.

Begin

1 Select All Text in a Text Field

To select all text in a text field, choose the Text tool and click inside the text field to place the cursor. Then use the keyboard shortcut **Ctrl+A** (Windows) or **Cmmd+A** (Macintosh) to select all text in the text field.

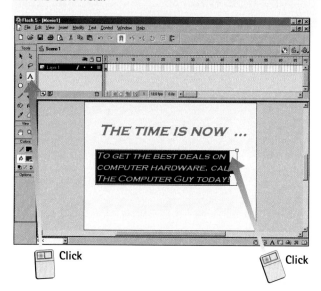

Click   Click

2 Select Part of a Text Field

To select specific characters or words within a text field, choose the Text tool and click inside the text field to place the cursor. Select text by dragging to select characters, double-clicking to select a word, or by clicking at the beginning of the selection and **Shift**+clicking to end the selection.

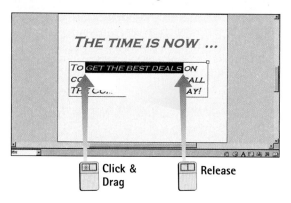

Click & Drag   Release

3 Select One or More Text Fields

To select one or more text fields for editing, choose the Arrow tool from the toolbox. Then, click on a type block to select it. **Shift**+click to add additional text blocks to the selection.

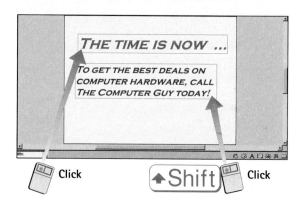

Click   Shift   Click

4 Edit Selected Text

After you select text for editing, you can change the font, font size, color, style, and alignment using the same techniques that you learned in Task 1 in this part.

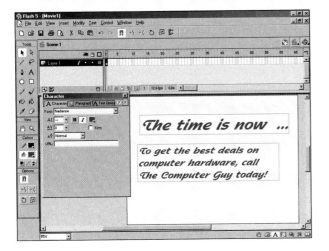

5 Use the Clipboard to Move Text

You can also use the **Cut, Copy,** and **Paste** commands to remove text or to copy text elsewhere into your Flash projects. For example, you can cut some text from one text block, and place it into another as shown here. You can also use the clipboard to copy text from Flash into other applications, or to copy text from other applications into Flash.

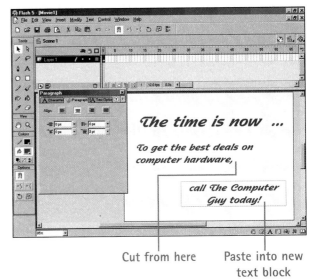

Cut from here   Paste into new
                            text block

End

How-To Hints

Creating Text with Drop Shadows

Flash does not create text with drop shadows automatically. An easy way to create drop-shadowed text is to select a text block with the Arrow tool. Choose **Edit, Duplicate** to create a copy of the text. Offset the duplicated text and change the color to the desired shadow color. Then choose **Modify, Arrange, Move Behind** to move the shadow behind the foreground text. Finally, group the foreground text and shadow with the **Modify, Group** command.

TASK 4

How to Adjust Margins, Kerning, and Spacing

Other options in the **Character** panel enable you to increase the amount of space between characters, either automatically or manually. This is most commonly known as *kerning*. Additionally, the **Paragraph** panel enables you to adjust the amount of spacing used for right and left margins, indentation of the first line, and the amount of space between multiple lines of text.

Begin

1 Adjust Text Margins

To open the **Paragraph** panel, choose **Window, Panels, Paragraph.** To adjust text margins, enter the values, in pixels, inside the **Left margin** and **Right margin** fields.

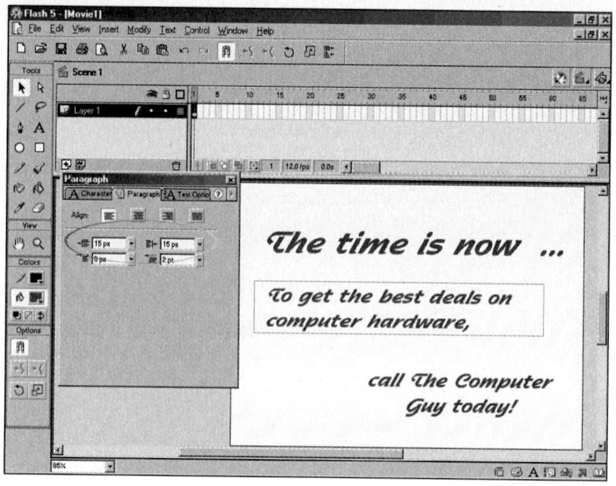

2 Indent Paragraphs

The **Indentation** setting in the **Paragraph** panel controls how far the first line of each paragraph in a text field is indented. You specify the amount of indentation in pixels. The default is 0 pixels, or no indentation. If you want to indent the first line of each paragraph, enter a value in pixels in the **Indentation** field.

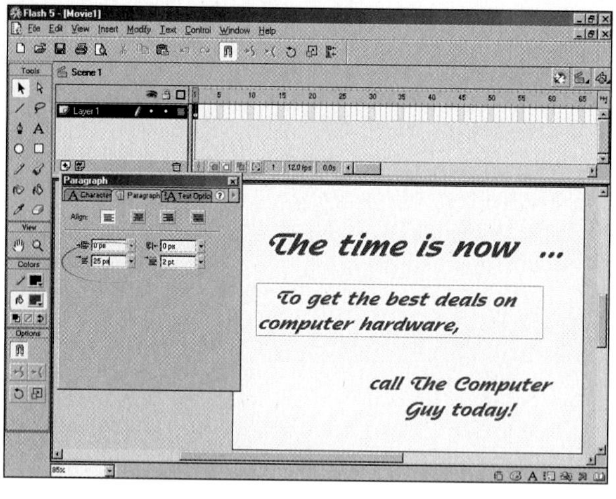

3 Adjust Line Spacing

The **Line Space** property in the **Paragraph** panel controls the amount of space between the lines of text in your paragraphs. The default value for line spacing is 2 points. To change the spacing, enter a new point value in the **Line Space** field of the **Paragraph** panel. Negative numbers will decrease the spacing between lines.

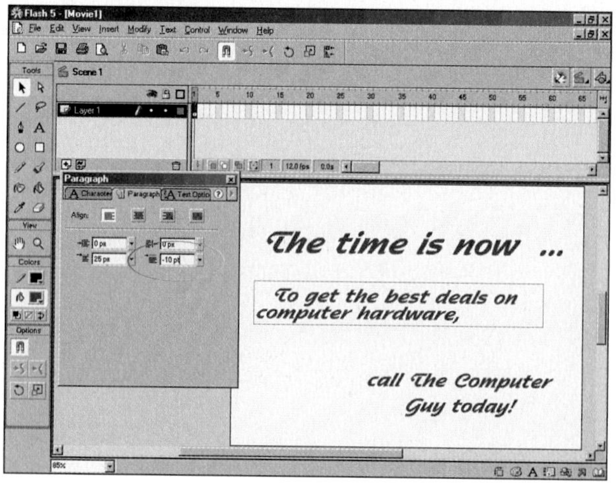

4 Create Superscript or Subscript Text

Choose **Window**, **Panels**, **Character** to open the **Character** panel. Here, the **Baseline Shift** drop-down enables you to create superscript or subscript text. First, select the text you want to change. Then choose **Superscript** or **Subscript** from the Baseline Shift drop-down menu.

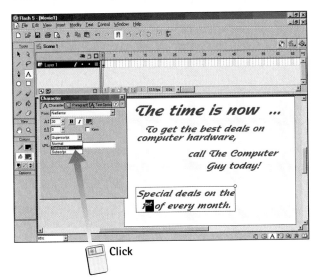

Click

5 Change Letter Spacing

To manually increase or decrease the amount of spacing between letters, use the **Tracking** field in the **Character** panel. Click on the arrow to use the **Tracking** slider. Move the slider up to increase the amount of space, or down to decrease the amount of space between the letters. Alternatively, you can enter a number in the **Tracking** field.

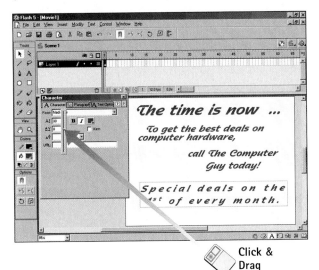

Click &
Drag

6 Enable and Disable Kerning

Enabling and disabling kerning controls the amount of space between certain pairs of letters. You might want to disable kerning for smaller text because it can sometimes be hard to read kerned letters when the font size is small. To disable kerning, uncheck the **Kern** option in the **Character** panel.

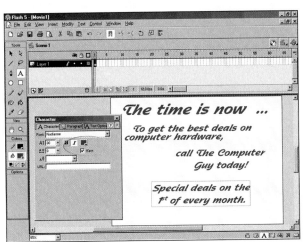

How-To Hints

Make a Statement

Line spacing, letter spacing, and kerning can make a difference in the way your text appears. Adding wide spaces between bold, dark letters can sometimes add an air of distinction and lighten up the look of your Flash movies. Play with different settings to discover the best look for your site.

End

How to Convert and Reshape Text

When you must use a font that will not export with your movie, or if you want to apply special fills to text, you can convert any TrueType and PostScript font to shapes. Windows TrueType fonts can be broken apart to lines and fills that you can reshape. For Macintosh users systems, PostScript fonts can be broken apart only if you are running Adobe Type Manager.

Begin

1 Convert Text to Shapes

Use the **Character** panel to select a nice, bold font (such as Arial Black or something similar) in a large text size (48 points or higher). Type your name in a text field. To convert the text to shapes that consist of lines and fills, select the text field with the Arrow tool. Then, choose **Modify, Break Apart**. Alternatively, press **Ctrl+B** (Windows) or **Cmmd+B** (Macintosh). The text is now converted to shapes.

Click

2 Change Stroke Properties

After text is broken into shapes, you can choose a different color and width for the stroke. Choose the Ink Bottle tool from the toolbox. Choose **Window, Panels, Stroke** to open the **Stroke** panel. Select a new color for the stroke, and change the width as desired. In this example, a red stroke, one pixel in width, is selected. Click on each letter to change its stroke to the new color and width.

Click

Click

3 Change the Fill

Choose **Window, Panels, Fill** to open the **Fill** panel. Use the Arrow tool to marquee around all the letters in your text if they are not still selected. Then, choose **Radial Gradient** from the **Fill** panel. Click each color pointer to select a new start and end color for your gradient (such as yellow and orange, as shown in this example). The text becomes filled with the gradient you design in the **Fill** panel.

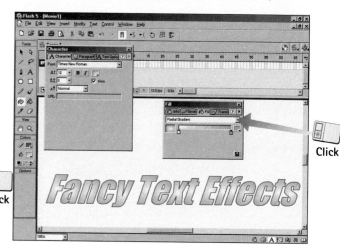

Click

4 Reshape Text Shapes

To reshape text, select the Arrow tool. Click away from the selected text to deselect it. Then, drag the outline of the text to reshape the curves. As you drag the outline, the fill adjusts to fill the new shape of the text.

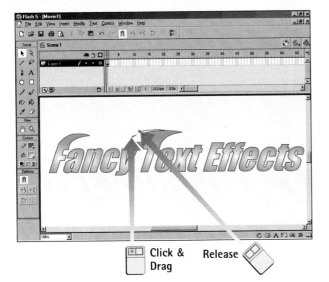

Click & Drag   Release

5 Group Text Shapes

After you break text apart, it exists as several individual shapes in your Flash movie. It is generally a good idea to group the individual letters back into the word or phrase that you originally broke apart because doing so makes it easier to move as a group. Select all the letters and choose **Modify, Group** to combine the letters into a group.

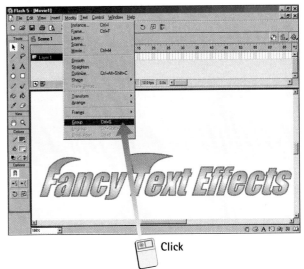

Click

End

How-To Hints

Ungrouping Grouped Text Symbols

To ungroup text symbols after you have grouped them, choose **Modify, Ungroup.** The text becomes separate objects again.

Convert to a Symbol

After you break apart your text, it no longer responds to effects such as adjusting tint or alpha. To make it respond to these types of effects, you have to convert it into a symbol. After you group your text, choose **Insert, Convert to Symbol** or press **F8** to convert the text to a Movie Clip, Button, or Graphic symbol. Then choose **Window, Panels, Effect** to add effects.

Watch File Size

It is generally not advisable to convert large blocks of text—such as paragraphs—into shapes because the size of your movie will increase considerably.

Task

6

Using Layers

*I*magine a high-rise office building. Each floor of the building contains offices arranged in a specific, yet unique layout. If the layout of the offices on the fifth floor require rearrangement, none of the offices on the floors above or below need be affected.

The same holds true in building a Flash project. Flash enables you to use multiple layers. Using this method, your project is extremely efficient and flexible. If you find that you need to make a change on the fifth layer, you can do so without affecting the layers above or below it.

No one has ever been sorry about creating a Flash project with too many layers. But many artists have lamented that they used too few. Use a new layer every time you create an element in your project that you want—or think that you might later want—to keep separate from the other elements of your project.

There is a difference between Flash layers and the floors of an office building. When you look down on a building from the top, you see only the roof. But when you look at a Flash project with multiple layers, it is like looking down on the top of a stack of clear acetate sheets. You see every object on each sheet, except those obscured by objects on a higher layer. Further, you can rearrange the order of your layers. For a feature that holds so much importance and power, mastering layers is quite easy, as shown in this part.

How to Create Layers

Create a new layer in your project whenever you add an object to your movie that would benefit from being separate from another object such as an animated instance. Prudent use of new layers keeps things flexible and organized. This task discusses the basic steps involved in creating a layer. In addition, it identifies the key features of every layer.

Begin

1 Use the Insert Menu

The first method of creating a layer in Flash involves accessing the **Insert** menu. To add a layer using this method, choose **Insert, Layer**.

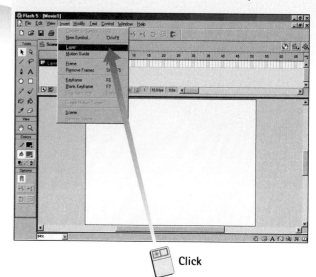

Click

2 Click on the Insert Layer Button

You can also use the **Insert Layer** button to create a new layer. To do so, simply click on the **Insert Layer** button.

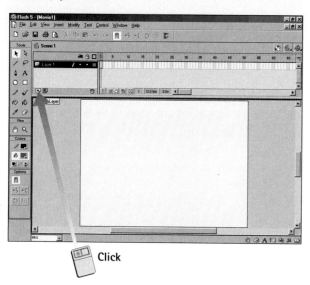

Click

3 Right-Click on an Existing Layer

As a third method of creating a new layer, right-click (Windows) or **Ctrl+**click (Macintosh) on the name of an existing layer, and choose **Insert Layer** from the menu.

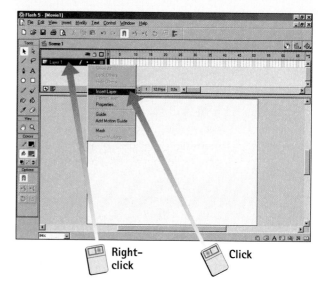

Right-click

Click

4 Name the New Layer

Every layer has a name. Flash automatically names the first layer in each project Layer 1. Subsequent layers have progressively higher numbers as their default names. Organize your project by renaming your layers. To rename a layer, double-click on its current name, and type the new name. Press the **Enter** key or click away from the layer name to make the name change permanent. The names you give your layers remain independent of the order of those layers on the Timeline.

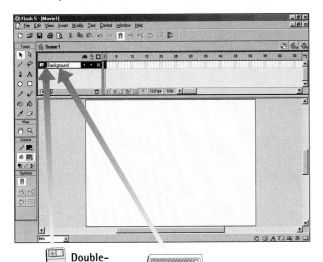

Double-click

5 Change the Layer Order

You can easily reorder your layers at any time. To do so, click on the layer you want to move, and drag and drop it to its new location in the Timeline. Release the mouse button to drop the layer into its new location. Reordering your layers determines how the contents of your layers will be shown on the stage. Objects on the lowest layer in the Timeline appear underneath objects on higher layers.

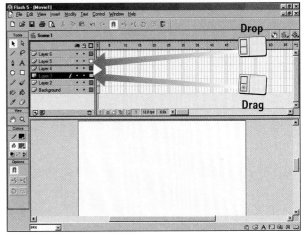

End

How-To Hints

Layer Order

Whenever you create a new layer, Flash places it directly above the currently selected layer. This holds true regardless of the method you use to create the new layer. As mentioned earlier, you can always reorder your layers according to your needs.

Layer Properties

You can use the **Layer Properties** dialog to change many of the attributes of layers, including the layer name. To access the **Layer Properties** dialog, choose **Modify, Layer.** Alternatively, right-click on the layer name (or **Ctrl**+click on a Mac), and choose **Properties** from the menu. Finally, you can access the **Layer Properties** dialog by double-clicking on the layer icon to the left of the current layer name.

How to Select One or More Layers

Before you can reposition a layer or multiple layers, you must first select the layer or layers you want to move. Flash provides several methods for selecting layers.

Begin

1 Click on the Layer Name

Click on a layer's name to select that layer. This also selects everything on the stage that is associated with the chosen layer.

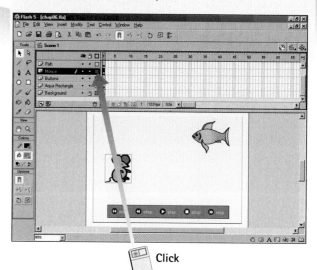

Click

2 Click on a Frame

You can also click on a frame in the Timeline to automatically select the layer that holds that frame. If you select a frame that is beyond the length of your movie, items on the stage remain unselected. However, when you select a frame from your movie, you also automatically select all items in that layer as defined by the previous keyframe.

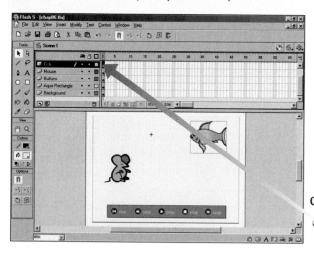

Click

3 Click on an Object on the Stage

When you select an object on the stage, you automatically select the layer that holds that object. All other objects on the stage remain unselected, even if they reside on the same layer as the object on which you click.

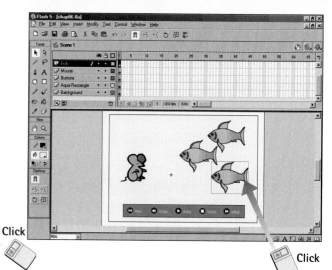

Click

4 Select a Range of Layers

Flash provides a couple different ways to select more than one layer at a time. The first method enables you to select a range of adjacent layers. To do this, click on the name of the first layer in the range. Then hold down the **Shift** key while clicking on the name of the last layer in the range. This selects not only these two layers, but also every layer in between the two.

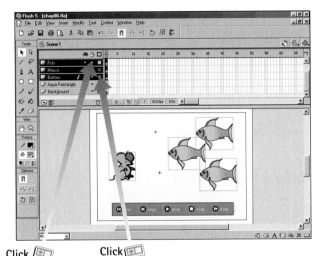

Click [keyboard] Click [keyboard]
↑Shift

5 Select Nonadjacent Layers

To select multiple layers that are not adjacent in the Timeline, first click on the name of one of the desired layers. Then, hold down the **Control** key (**Command** on the Mac) while clicking on the names of additional layers. These layers are added to the selection. If you change your mind about including a layer, continue holding down the **Control** key and click on the layer a second time. This action removes the layer from the selection group.

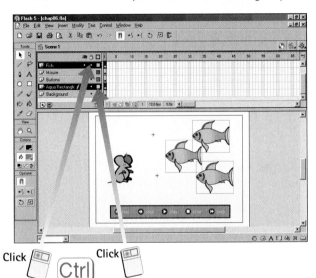

Click [keyboard] Ctrl Click [keyboard]

End

How-To Hints

Which Layer Has Focus?

The layer that currently has focus contains the pencil icon to the right of its name. Objects you add to the stage reside on the layer that has focus when you add them. Remember, the act of selecting a layer does not necessarily give that layer focus. Only one layer can have focus at a time. Selecting a single layer automatically gives that layer focus and the pencil icon moves to that layer. However, if you select multiple layers, you create a situation where several layers are selected, but only the last layer you select receives focus.

How to Cut, Copy, Delete, and Paste Layers

Of the familiar cut, copy, paste, and delete functions, Flash only provides a direct method of performing delete on layers. Interestingly, no method exists for placing a copy of a layer on the clipboard through a cut or copy operation, so you can't directly paste a layer, either. However, the other functions can be emulated by working with the frames of layers in conjunction with the layers themselves. This task shows how to perform these functions.

Begin

1 Delete a Layer

To delete the selected layer or layers from your Flash project, click the **Delete Layer** button. The **Delete Layer** button is represented by the trash can icon below the layer names list.

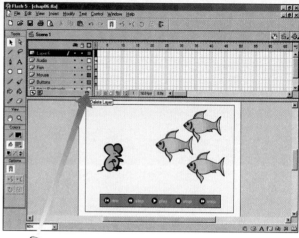

 Click

2 Delete a Layer in an Alternate Way

As an alternative to the method described in step 1, right-click (or **Ctrl**+click on the Mac) on the layer you want to delete, and choose **Delete Layer** from the menu.

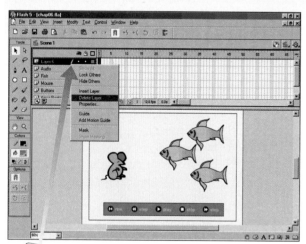

 Right-click

3 Copy a Layer to the Clipboard

To copy a layer to the clipboard, click on the name of the layer you want to copy. This selects the layer and all its frames. Choose **Edit, Copy Frames,** or right-click on the selected frames, and choose **Copy Frames.** You now have the original layer intact, and a copy of all of that layer's frames on the clipboard.

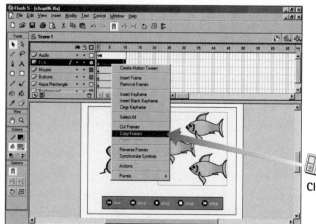

Click

4 Cut a Layer

To cut a layer you must, in essence, perform a two-step operation. First, click on the name of the layer you want to cut. This selects the layer and all its frames. Choose **Edit, Cut Frames,** or right-click (or **Ctrl**+click for the Macintosh) on the selected frames, and choose **Cut Frames.** Finally, click on the **Delete Layer** button to remove the layer from the project. The frames that you cut from the layer remain in the clipboard until you copy or cut other objects.

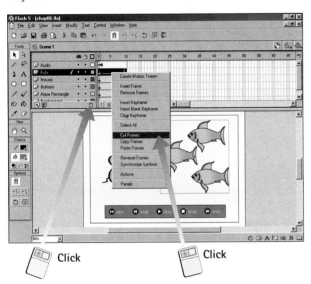

☐ Click   ☐ Click

5 Paste a Layer

By following step 3 earlier in this task, you have a copy of a layer's frames on your clipboard. To emulate pasting a layer, click on the **New Layer** button to create a new layer. Then click on the new layer's name, and choose **Edit, Paste Frames** to paste the contents of the clipboard into the new layer. Alternatively, right-click (or **Ctrl**+Click on the Macintosh) on the layer name and choose **Paste Frames** from the menu that appears.

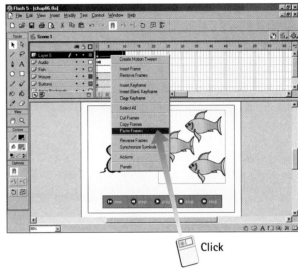

☐ Click

End

How-To Hints

Delete Means Forever

Keep in mind that when you delete a layer (just as when you delete any object) it is not placed on the clipboard. Because the clipboard does not hold a copy of the layer, a copy cannot be pasted back into your project (or any other project). After the layer is deleted, the only way to get it back is to undo the delete operation before saving the project. If you have done any work since deleting the layer, performing multiple undo operations will lose it. Further, if the project is saved after the layer is deleted, the layer is gone for good. To avoid problems, ensure that you really want to remove the layer before following step 1 or step 2 and saving your project!

TASK 4

How to Lock and Unlock Layers

Flash enables you to lock any layer that you want to protect from accidental modification. Because it's often confusing which layer contains an object on the stage, especially in complex projects, modification of the wrong layer can be very common. As an effective safety measure, lock any layer that you feel is finished, or close to finished. In fact, consider locking every layer except the currently selected layer. This task describes how to lock and unlock layers.

Begin

1 Lock a Layer

To lock a specific layer, click on the dot in the Lock/Unlock All Layers column to the right of the layer's name. Alternatively, double-click on the layer type icon to the left of the layer name to access the **Layer Properties** dialog. Then click in the **Lock** check box, and choose **OK.** When the locked layer is selected as the current layer, the pencil icon has a slash through it indicating that you can no longer edit this layer.

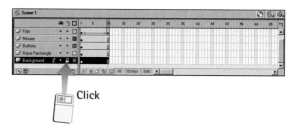

Click

2 Unlock a Layer

When a layer is locked, a lock icon appears in the Lock/Unlock All Layers column to the right of the layer name. Click on the lock icon to unlock the layer. Or, double-click the layer name, and uncheck the **Lock** option in the **Layer Properties** dialog as shown here.

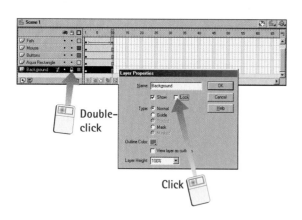

Double-click

Click

3 Lock and Unlock All Layers

There might be times when you want to lock all the layers in a project. To do so, click on the lock icon in the heading of the Lock/Unlock All Layers column. Click on the icon again to unlock all layers.

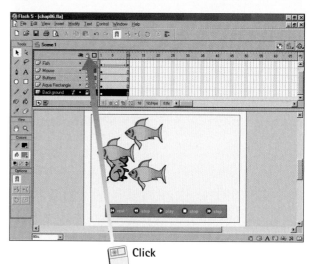

Click

4 Lock and Unlock a Range of Layers

If you want to lock a range of layers without locking all the layers in your project, click on the dot in the Lock/Unlock All Layers column of the first layer in the range. Now drag through the Lock/Unlock All Layers columns of all the layers in the range until you reach the last layer in the range. As you drag through each layer, it locks. Repeat the process to unlock the layers.

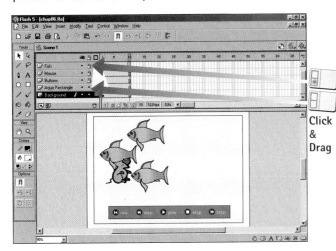

Click & Drag

5 Lock and Unlock All but One Layer

Flash gives you the option to lock all the layers in your project except one. To accomplish this, hold down the **Alt** key and click on the dot in the Lock/Unlock All Layers column of the desired layer. This locks all other layers. To unlock them, hold down the **Alt** key, and click on the dot in the Lock/Unlock All Layers column of the unlocked layer.

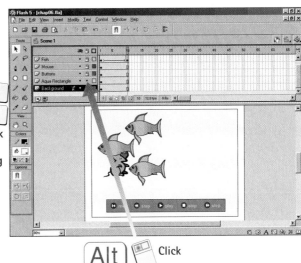

[Alt] Click

End

How-To Hints

Work with Only One Layer Unlocked

To avoid making accidental modifications to the wrong layer, consider working with just one unlocked layer at all times. Develop the habit of using the technique described in step 5: selecting the target layer by holding the **Alt** key and clicking in the desired layer's Lock/Unlock All Layers column. This action unlocks the layer you select, while locking all other layers in the project. By consistently using this method to select your layers, you protect yourself from inadvertent modification of the layers in your project.

How to View Layers

Flash provides three layer view possibilities. Layers can be hidden, viewed as outline, and visible. This provides a great deal of flexibility in how you view your project while working on it. This task explains how to hide and view layers, and to view a layer in Outline view.

Begin

1 Hide and View a Layer

To hide or view a layer, click on the dot under the Show/Hide All Layers icon to the right of the layer name. When you do so, a visible layer will be hidden, and a hidden layer will be made visible.

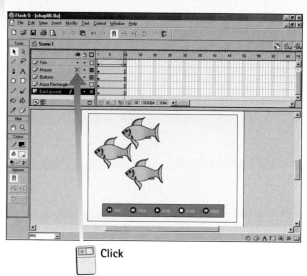

Click

2 Hide and View All Layers

Click on the eye icon at the top of the Show/Hide All Layers column to either hide all layers, or make them visible again.

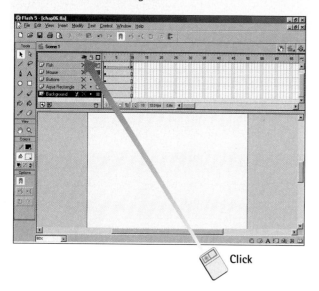

Click

3 Hide and Show a Range of Layers

To hide or show a range of layers, click in the Show/Hide All Layers column of the first layer in the range, and drag to the last.

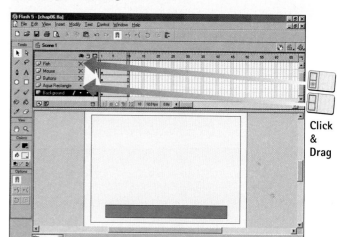

Click & Drag

4 View a Layer as Outlines

Many times you want to see the location of objects on a layer, without seeing the complex details. Flash enables you to view the contents of a layer as outlines. To toggle outline mode on and off, click on the colored square that appears in the Show All Layers as Outlines column to the right of the layer name. The colored square indicates the outline color used for each layer.

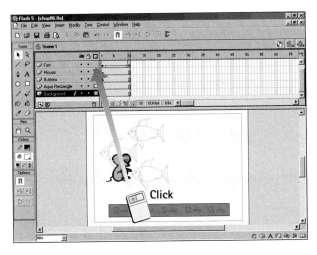

Click

5 View All Layers as Outlines

To turn on or off Outline view for all layers in the project, click on the **Outline** icon at the top of the Show All Layers as Outlines column.

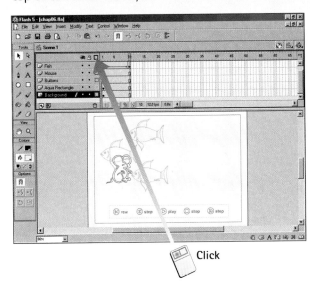

Click

6 View a Range of Layers as Outlines

To turn Outline view on and off for a range of adjacent layers, click on the dot in the Show All Layers as Outlines column for the first layer in the range, and drag to the last desired layer.

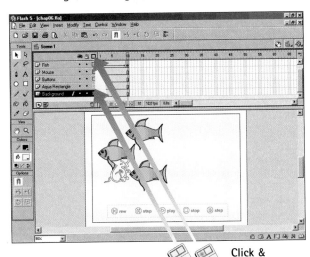

Click &
Drag

7 Hide All but One Layer

To hide all layers except for the selected layer, hold down the **Alt** key and click in the Show/Hide All Layers column of the selected layer. To make all the layers visible again, hold down the **Alt** key and click in the Show/Hide All Layers column of the selected layer again. Similarly, to toggle outlines on and off for all layers other than the selected layer (as shown here), hold down the **Alt** key and click the selected layer in the Show All Layers as Outlines column.

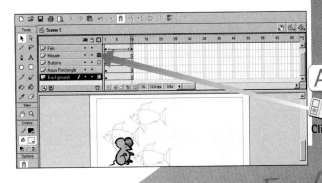

Alt

Click

End

How to Use Guide Layers

Flash enables you to create a special layer, called a *Guide layer*, into which you can place imported artwork, shapes, symbols, or text to help you draw and position objects on the stage. Any layer can be transformed into a Guide layer, and any Guide layer can be reverted back to a regular layer. Guide layers are not published with your final movie. This task explains how to use Guide layers.

Begin

1 Create the Guide Layer

Click on the **Insert Layer** button to create a new layer. This layer starts out as a normal layer. Right-click (**Ctrl**+click on the Macintosh) on the name of the new layer, and choose **Guide** from the menu. The layer icon changes to a horizontal line intersecting with a vertical line to identify this layer as a Guide layer.

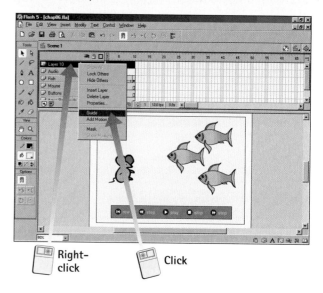

Right-click   Click

2 Name the Guide Layer

Double-click on the name of the new layer. Then enter a new name that identifies this layer as a Guide layer.

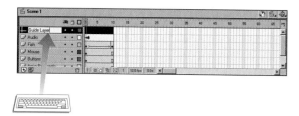

3 Reorder the Layers

Click on the Guide layer, and drag it so that it is the bottom layer in your project. This way, any artwork that you create or import into the Guide layer always appears below the actual artwork in your movie.

Click & Drag

Drop

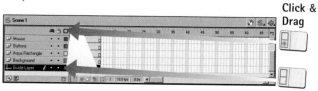

4 Create or Import the Guide Artwork

To use ruler lines as guides, choose **View, Rulers** to display the rulers at the top and left of the stage. Drag horizontal guides from the top ruler, and drag vertical guides from the left ruler. You can also use the drawing tools to create artwork for use as a guide when working with your active layers, or choose **File, Import** to import a graphic for use as your guide.

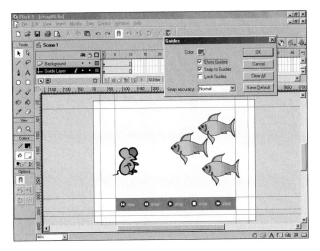

5 Lock the Guide Layer

After you have the graphics that you want to use as your guides, lock the Guide layer just as you would a normal layer so that you do not accidentally alter the graphics. Click on the dot in the Lock/Unlock All Layers column to the right of the guide name.

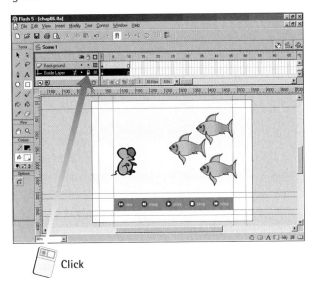

Click

6 Create Artwork on a Normal Layer

Use the Guide layer to help you create the artwork for your final movie on one or more normal layers. Because the Guide layer is locked, you need not worry about altering its contents while working on your normal layers.

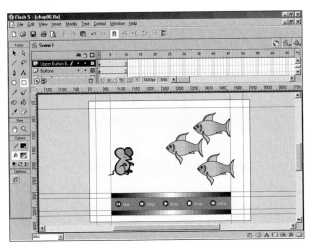

7 Convert to a Normal Layer

If you decide that you want your Guide layer to behave as a normal layer, Flash enables you to convert it back. Right-click (**Ctrl**+click on the Mac) on the Guide layer's name. Notice that the menu choice **Guide** has a check mark next to it. Choose **Guide** again to convert this layer back to a normal layer. You can also convert the layer by accessing the **Layer Properties** dialog.

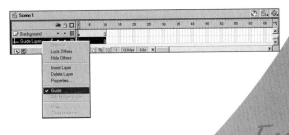

End

How to Use Mask Layers

Use a Mask layer to cover all parts of every layer linked to it, with the exception of a predefined area. A Mask layer can contain only one filled object, and that object acts as the "hole" in the mask that allows artwork on linked layers to show through. Use any of Flash's animation techniques to give the mask motion.

Begin

1 Create the Artwork to Be Masked

Use one or more normal layers to create or import the artwork that will be affected by the Mask layer.

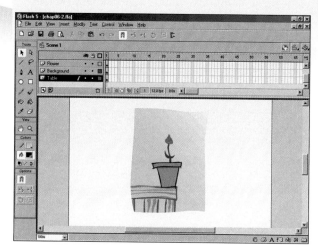

2 Create a New Layer

With the top layer created in step 1 selected, click on the **Insert Layer** button to create a new layer. This layer starts out as a normal layer, but will be transformed into a Mask layer in step 4. It is important to add the new layer on top of the previous layer because a Mask layer always masks the layer directly beneath it. Rename the layer to indicate that it is a mask.

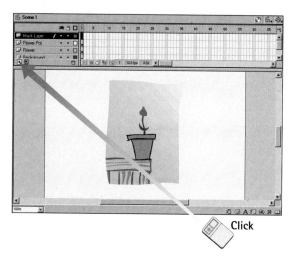

Click

3 Create the Mask Artwork

Draw a filled shape on the new layer. This shape represents the area where layers linked to the Mask layer will show through. Flash type and instances of a Flash symbol also make acceptable mask objects. Filled areas of the object will be completely transparent, allowing objects on linked layers to show through. Unfilled areas of the Mask layer will completely obscure objects on the linked layers.

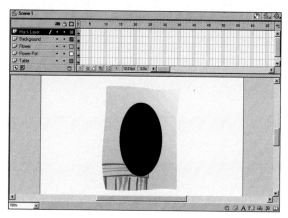

4 Apply the Mask

Right-click (Control+click on the Macintosh) on the name of the Mask layer, and choose **Mask** from the menu. You can also use the **Layer Properties** dialog. Because the mask effect shows only when the layers are locked, Flash automatically locks both the Mask layer and the layer directly below it (which is automatically linked to it). Unlock the layers to temporarily disable the mask, and edit the layers. Lock them again to reactivate the mask. To view the effect of the Mask layer, right-click on the Mask layer and choose **Show Masking** from the menu that appears.

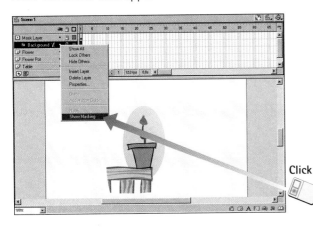

Click

5 Link Multiple Layers to the Mask

You can link multiple layers to the mask so that it affects all of them. Do so by dragging an existing layer to the position directly below the layer. After it is linked, lock and reorder this and any other linked layers until the desired effect is achieved. You can also use the **Layer Properties** dialog to link a layer to the mask, or hold down the **Alt** key while clicking on the layers you want to link to the Mask layer.

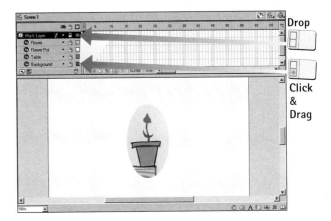

Drop

Click & Drag

6 Unlink a Layer from the Mask

If you decide that you no longer want a layer to be linked to the mask, unlink it by clicking and dragging it to a position above the Mask layer. Then reorder it for the desired effect, if necessary. You can also use the **Layer Properties** dialog.

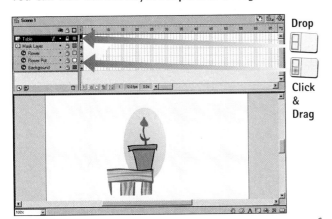

Drop

Click & Drag

How-To Hints

Layers That Are Not Linked to the Mask

Layers that are not linked to the mask behave normally. The presence of a Mask layer has no unusual effect at all on normal layers. A layer below the Mask layer, but not linked to it, will be visible everywhere except for the area under the visible portion of the mask. Although the mask concept might seem confusing at first, after you master it, you possess a very effective tool capable of creating extremely interesting effects.

End

Task

Selecting and Modifying Objects

This is probably no surprise, but if you want to do something to anything in Flash, you must first select it. Everyone basically knows how to select things. To an extent, selecting something in Flash is just the same as selecting something in a hundred other software programs. First you point to it, and then you click on it. You've selected it. End of chapter? Not quite.

There are other ways to select things in Flash. Even the simple point-and-click might not always work out the way you think it will. Therefore, in this part we first spend a little time talking about how to select objects.

After you select an object, what can you do with it? Move it, copy it, paste it, delete it, stack it, rotate it, flip it, scale it, skew it, align it, move its registration point, restore it, and inspect it. We talk about all these things in this part, and that's a lot to cover. No sleep for you tonight! So grab a cup of coffee, sit up straight, and let's get to it.

How to Select Objects with the Arrow Tool

Most of the time you'll use the Arrow tool to make your selections in Flash. In fact, you'll use it so often that our friends at Macromedia have supplied short-cuts to get to this tool quickly. A couple of different techniques exist for using this tool, and this task discusses those.

Begin

1 Click to Make a Selection

First, the basics: Use the Rectangle tool to create a filled rectangle with an outline. Click on it with the Arrow tool to select it. But be careful. Flash treats the fill and the stroke as two separate selectable items unless the object is grouped or an instance. Therefore, click on the fill once to select it, or click on the stroke to select it.

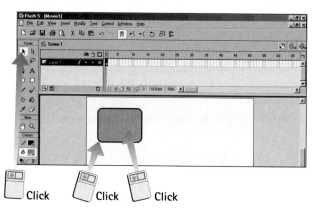

Click   Click   Click

2 Select a Shape's Fill and Stroke

Click away from the object to deselect it. Now, double-click on the object's fill with the Arrow tool. This selects both the stroke and fill simultaneously.

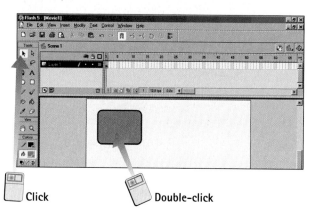

Click   Double-click

3 Add to a Selection

Deselect the objects again. Using the Arrow tool, double-click on the object's stroke to select the entire stroke. (If you single click on a stroke, you might select only a portion of it.) To add the fill to the selected stroke, hold down the **Shift** key, and click on the fill. To remove the fill from the selection, continue to hold down the **Shift** key, and click on the fill. You can continue adding to and removing from the selection with this method.

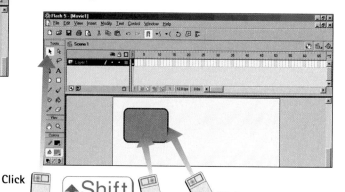

Click   [⬆Shift]   Click
Click

4 Draw a Rectangular Selection Area

Click outside the rectangle to deselect it. Now, click and drag with the Arrow tool to make a rectangular selection area around the entire object. This selects both the fill and stroke. Deselect it again. This time, include only part of the object in the selection box. This selects only the portion of the fill and stroke that fall within the box. For groups and instances, the selection box must encompass the entire instance or group for it to be selected.

Click & Drag   Release

6 Make Special Selections

Use the Arrow tool to make a few special selections. With the Arrow tool, choose **Edit, Select All** to select everything in a scene that is not on a locked or hidden layer. Choose **Edit, Deselect All** to deselect everything in the scene. Click between two keyframes in the Timeline to select everything on the layer that appears on the Stage between the keyframes.

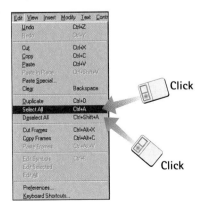

5 Select Connected Lines

Use the Line tool to draw two or more intersecting lines on the Stage. Click on one of the lines with the Arrow tool. This selects only the line segment between the end of the line and the point of intersection (or two points of intersection, depending upon how you drew the lines). Now, double-click on one of the lines. This selects all the intersecting lines in their entirety.

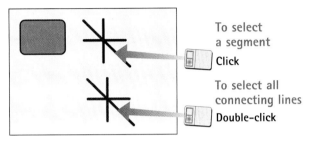

To select
a segment
Click

To select all
connecting lines
Double-click

How-To Hints

Select with the Subselect Tool

The Subselect tool enables you to select the individual points that make up the stroke of an ungrouped object. You can then modify the object by manipulating these points. This tool has no effect when you click on the fill of an object. When you use the Subselect tool on instances or grouped objects, it behaves the same as the Arrow tool.

Hide Selection Highlights

You've certainly noticed that when you select an item in Flash, a selection highlight appears. Often this highlight makes it impossible to see what the highlighted object really looks like. Most of the time, that isn't really a problem. However, sometimes you want to be able to see the details of the object even when it's selected. Toggle the highlights on and off by choosing **View, Hide Edges.**

End

How to Select Objects with the Lasso Tool

The Lasso tool enables you to draw a freehand selection area around the object or objects you want to select. You can also use the **Polygon Mode** modifier if you want to make a selection that has straight edges. This task discusses the Lasso tool and shows how to use it to make selections.

Begin

1 Position Three Objects on the Stage

Use the Rectangle tool to create a rectangle on the Stage. Change the fill color, and then use the Oval tool to draw a different colored oval that overlaps the rectangle. Finally, choose another fill color. Draw a second rectangle that overlaps both of the other objects. Arrange the objects so that it would be nearly impossible to select them individually using the selection method discussed in Task 1, step 4. (Note: These objects are not grouped. When you move the objects that appear at the top of the stack, they will "cut away" portions of the underlying objects.)

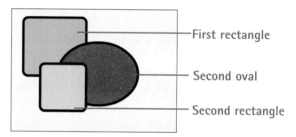

First rectangle
Second oval
Second rectangle

2 Begin a Freehand Selection Area

Click on the Lasso tool to select it. Begin drawing a freehand selection area around one of the objects, so that it completely encloses the object. Notice that the Lasso tool enables you to create a selection area in any shape you need in order to select an item.

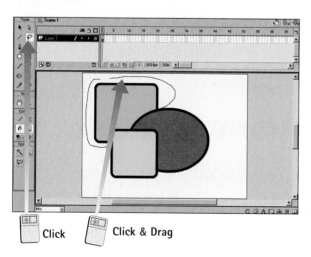

Click   Click & Drag

3 Select Two of the Objects

Continue drawing a freehand selection area around two of the objects on the Stage. Be careful not to touch any part of the third object with the Lasso tool, or you will inadvertently select part of the third object along with the two you want to select.

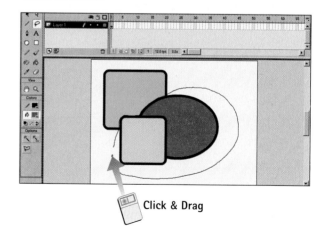

Click & Drag

4 Begin Straight-Edged Selection

To draw straight-line segments using the Lasso tool, select the **Polygon Mode** modifier. Click once to establish the starting point of the selection area, and drag the tool to the next point that requires a change of direction. Click again to establish the first line segment. Now drag in a new direction, and click when you reach the next point of direction change.

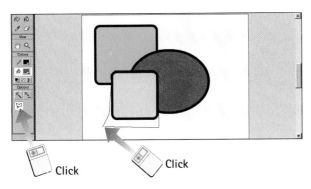

Click

Click

5 Select Two of the Objects

Continue making straight-line segments as in step 4 until you have drawn almost entirely around two of the objects. Double-click to close the selection area, and select the objects within.

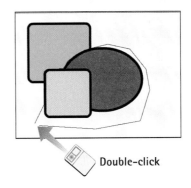

Double-click

6 Combine Freehand and Straight Selection

Click on the **Polygon Mode** modifier to turn it off. Click and drag to begin making a freehand selection area around the areas that are easy to draw around. Where freehand drawing gets difficult, hold down the **Alt** key. Release the left mouse button, and click around the tight areas to create polygonal segments. After you pass the rough spots, release the **Alt** key, and immediately click and drag the mouse to return to freehand mode.

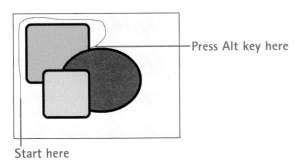

Press Alt key here

Start here

7 Close the Selection Area

Close the selection area by releasing the mouse button if currently drawing in freehand mode, or double-clicking if in polygon mode.

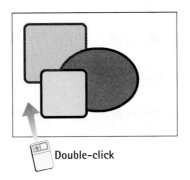

Double-click

End

How to Move Objects

Several methods exist to move objects about the Stage. This task explores those methods.

Begin

1 Select an Object

Draw several objects on Stage. Make sure that none of the objects touches any other. Use any of the methods discussed in tasks 1 and 2 to select an object on the Stage.

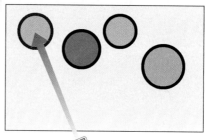

 Double-click

2 Drag the Object to a New Position

With the Arrow tool, click and drag the selected object to a new location on the Stage. Hold down the **Shift** key, and drag the item again. This constrains the object's movement to 45-degree and 90-degree angles.

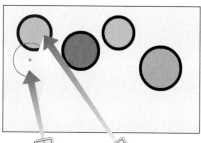

 Release   Click & Drag

3 Nudge an Object

With the object still selected, press the **right-arrow** key several times to nudge the object to the right. Use the **up-arrow** key to move the object up. The **down-arrow** and **left-arrow** keys work the same way.

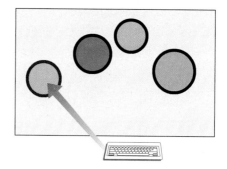

4 Open the Info Panel

Choose **Window, Panels, Info** to open the **Info** panel. This panel enables you to move and scale the selected item.

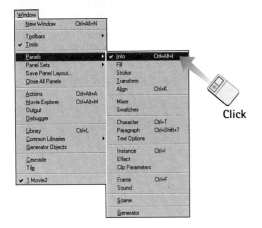

Click

5 Use the Info Panel

Enter new values for either or both the **X** and **Y** fields. To move the object toward the left, lower the X coordinate, and to move the object toward the right, raise the X coordinate. To move the object up, lower the Y coordinate, and to move the object down, raise the Y coordinate. Press **Enter** on your keyboard to finalize your choices. The object moves to the new coordinates you entered.

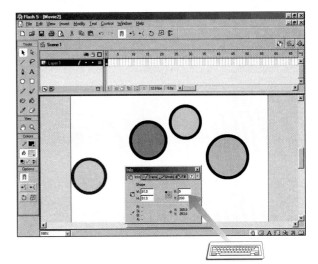

End

How-To Hints

Adding Objects to a Selection

By default, you must hold down the **Shift** key while you click to add additional objects to a selection. You can change this so that you simply click on additional items to add them to a selection. To change the setting, choose **Edit, Preferences.** The **General** tab contains a **Selection Options** section. Uncheck the **Shift Select** option to set Flash such that you can add additional items with a click rather than a **Shift**+click.

The Info Panel

The **Info** panel, discussed in the previous step, comes in handy when you are moving and scaling objects while you animate them. Use the **Info** panel to enter precise coordinates for location of objects. You can also use the **W** (width) and **H** (height) fields to scale objects to a specific size.

How to Cut, Copy, and Delete an Object

Flash contains the standard cut, copy, and delete (or clear) functions. This task discusses these functions.

1 Select an Object on the Stage

Use any of the methods discussed in tasks 1 and 2 to select an object on the Stage.

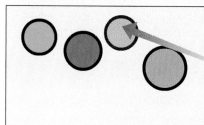

Double-click

2 Cut the Object onto the Clipboard

Choose **Edit, Cut** or use the keyboard shortcut **Ctrl+X** (Windows) or **Cmmd+X** (Macintosh) to cut the object from the Stage, and place it on the clipboard. Alternatively, you can click on the **Cut** button to achieve the same result.

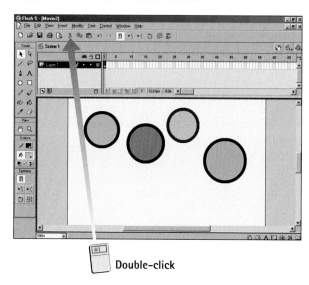

Double-click

3 Copy the Object to the Clipboard

Choose **Edit, Copy,** or use the keyboard shortcut **Ctrl+C** (Windows) or **Cmmd+C** (Macintosh) to copy the object and place it onto the clipboard. This leaves the original object in place on the Stage. Alternatively, you can click on the **Copy** button to achieve the same result.

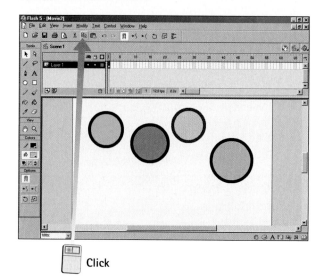

Click

4 Clear the Object

Choose **Edit, Clear** to remove the object from the Stage without placing it on the clipboard. Alternatively, use the **Delete** key or the **Backspace** key on your keyboard to execute this step. Remember that the **Clear** command does not place a copy of the cleared object onto the clipboard, so you will not be able to paste it back into your project later.

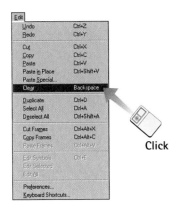

Click

5 Copy from the Transform Panel

Select another object, and choose **Window, Panels, Transform** to bring up the **Transform** panel. Click on the **Copy** button in the **Transform** panel. This places a copy of the selected object directly on top of the original. In fact, it's impossible to tell at this point that there are two objects present. While the top object is still selected, click and drag it to a new location.

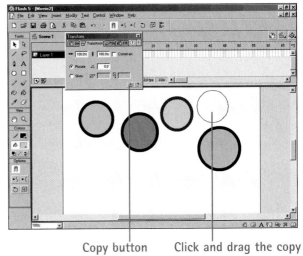

Copy button   Click and drag the copy

End

How-To Hints

A Shortcut to Copying

Here's a quick way to place a copy of an object on the Stage. First, select an item. Then drag and drop it to a new location while holding down the **Ctrl** key (Windows) or the **Cmmd** key (Macintosh). This makes an instant copy of the object, and both the original and new copy appear on the Stage.

Placing Items on the Clipboard

Although the **Cut** and **Clear** (or **Delete**) options might look like they achieve the same results, an important difference exists. When you clear an object, it's gone...*really* gone. On the other hand, when you *cut* an object, it's not really gone. The **Cut** command places the object onto the clipboard. You can add it back to the project by using the **Paste** command. Make sure that when you choose **Clear,** you really want to permanently remove the object!

How to Paste Objects into Flash

After you've cut or copied an object, the object resides on the clipboard. Flash provides a few different methods for pasting the object back into your project. This task explores those methods.

Begin

1 Cut an Object to the Clipboard

Use any of the methods discussed in previous tasks to select one or more objects on the Stage. Then, click on the **Cut** button in the toolbar to place the object or objects onto the clipboard.

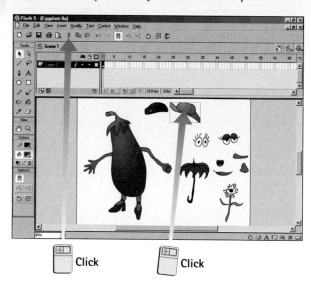

Click   Click

2 Select the Target Layer

If you want to paste the object into a new layer, click the **Add Layer** button in the Timeline and choose the correct frame. To add the object into an existing layer, click on the layer name to select it.

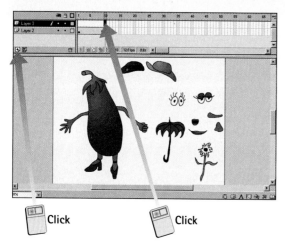

Click   Click

3 Use the Paste Command

To paste the object, choose **Edit, Paste** or use the keyboard shortcut **Ctrl+V** (Windows) or **Cmmd+V** (Macintosh). Alternatively, click on the **Paste** button on the toolbar. Flash pastes the object to the center of the Stage.

Click

4 Use the Paste in Place Command

Whereas the **Paste** command places the item directly in the center of the Stage, you can use the **Edit, Paste in Place** command to paste the item into the new layer at the same coordinates at which it originally occupied. Alternatively, you can use the shortcut **Ctrl+Shift+V** for Windows or **Cmmd+Shift+V** for Mac.

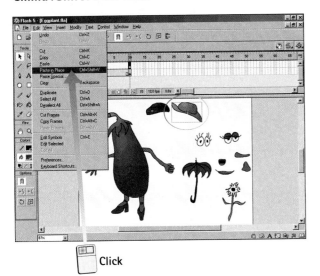

Click

5 Paste from Another Program

The clipboard is a function of both the Windows and the Macintosh operating systems. As a result, you can use the **Edit, Copy** command in another program to copy text or graphics onto the clipboard. Then, switch to Flash and use the **Edit, Paste** command to paste the object onto the Stage.

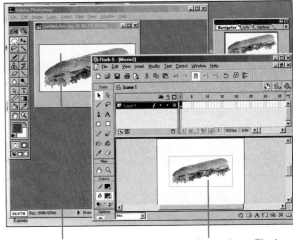

Copy from another application   Paste into Flash

6 Paste into Another Program

Conversely, you can use Flash to copy or cut any object to the clipboard. Then, you can paste the object into another program. Cut or copy the artwork in Flash. Switch to the other program, and follow its procedures for pasting.

Paste into another application   Copy from Flash

7 Combine Copy and Paste

Select the object. Hold down the **Ctrl** key while you drag and drop the object to a new location on the Stage. Flash instantly adds a copy of the artwork to the Stage without having to choose **Copy** or **Paste.**

Control   Release

Click & drag

End

How to Group Objects and Edit Grouped Objects

Often you want several objects on the Stage to act as a group in all operations. You can use the **Group** command to accomplish this. When you move one object of a group, you move all the objects of that group. When an object in the same layer is stacked on top of a group, the group maintains its integrity instead of being edited. Grouping is a valuable tool for maintaining the relationship between objects as you work on your overall movie design.

Begin

1 Select Two or More Objects

Use the methods in Tasks 1 and 2 to select two or more objects on the Stage. To become members of a group, the objects must be on the same layer. When you draw a shape, the outline and the fill of the shape are actually two separate objects, and you might want to group them at some point. In this example, both the fill and the outline of the circle are selected for grouping.

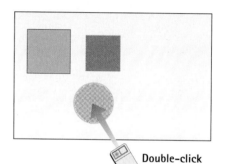

Double-click

2 Group the Objects

Choose **Modify, Group** to group the selected objects. Alternatively, press the keyboard shortcut, **Ctrl+G** (Windows) or **Cmmd+G** (Macintosh). Now, instead of each object having an individual bounding box, one bounding box surrounds the entire group.

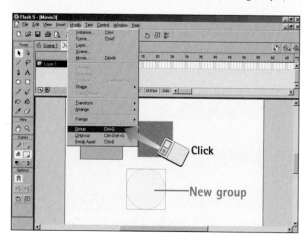

Click

New group

3 Choose a Group to Edit

Click away from the newly created group to deselect it. To reselect it, or to select a different group, use any of the selection techniques discussed in Tasks 1 and 2. For example, the easiest selection method is to click on any object in the group to select the entire group.

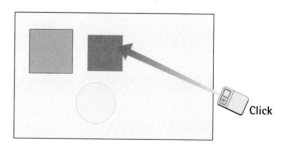

Click

4 Edit the Group

With the group selected, you can now manipulate it. For instance, click and drag one object of the group to a new position, and the entire group moves as one unit. Use the **Transform** panel (**Window, Panels, Transform**) to perform any transformation on the group. Scale it, rotate it, resize it, cut it, copy it, paste it, or skew it, as shown here.

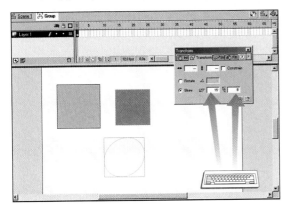

5 Edit an Object in the Group

Steps 3 and 4 might lead you to believe that you cannot select and edit an individual item in a group, but you can. To edit a grouped object, first choose **Edit, Edit Selected** (or double-click on the group). Everything on the Stage that is not part of the group appears dim, and undimmed items are temporarily ungrouped. Now use the selection techniques you know well by now to select and edit an individual item from the group.

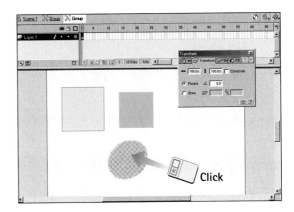

Click

6 Re-establish the Group

After you edit the individual item, choose **Edit, Edit All** (or double-click off the group) to reestablish the group relationship. The group again behaves as a normal group, and you can select and edit any other object on the Stage.

Click

7 Lock a Group

To avoid inadvertently modifying a group, you can lock it so that it cannot be selected or edited. Select the group, and choose **Modify, Arrange, Lock,** or select **Ctrl+Alt+L** (Windows) or **Opt+Cmmd+L** (Macintosh). To unlock all locked groups, choose **Modify, Arrange, Unlock All.** When you unlock items, they remain selected. To remove a group from the selection, hold down the **Shift** key and click on the group. You can then relock the remaining items that were unlocked.

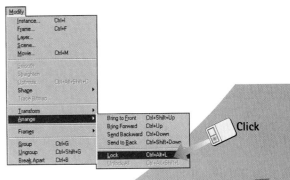

Click

End

When to Group Objects

When you draw strokes and fills of different colors above one another, you'll find that Flash uses the topmost shapes to "cut out" areas of underlying strokes. Topmost shapes act much like a "cookie cutter" in this regard. When placed on the same layer, any stroke of a different color affects underlying shapes unless you group them. This task demonstrates how to use grouping on the same layer to prevent overlapping objects from affecting one another.

Begin

1 Overlap Some Paint Strokes

To demonstrate how the "cookie cutter" strokes work, choose the **Brush** tool from the toolbox, or use the keyboard shortcut **B**. Select a wide brush width from the **Options** panel. Then, choose **Red** for a fill color. Draw a solid area on the Stage. Then, select **Yellow** for a fill color, and draw an area that overlaps the red fill.

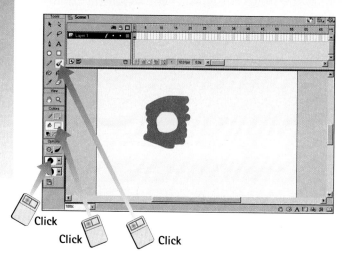

Click
Click
Click

2 Select and Move the Top Object

Choose the Arrow tool. Click and drag the yellow fill. Notice how the yellow fill "cut out" areas from the red fill. In some cases, this helps you create some interesting artwork. In cases when you don't want this to happen, you can use grouping to control how your artwork behaves on the same layer.

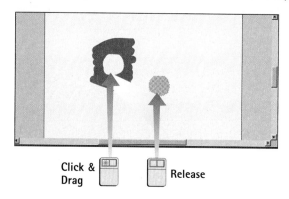

Click & Drag
Release

3 Draw an Object

Now to demonstrate how you can group objects as you draw. Let's say you're drawing a face. Start with an oval that is outlined in black. To prevent the "cut out" after you create this object, use the **Modify, Group** command or the keyboard shortcut **Ctrl+G** (Windows) or **Cmmd+G** (Macintosh) to group the stroke and fill together as one object.

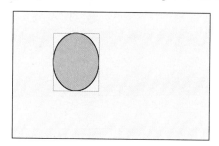

4 Draw More Objects

Next, you'll draw the eyes, nose, and mouth. However, you don't want to draw these items over the previous group because they will appear beneath the grouped oval. Instead, draw the features off to the side, and group them together. Then, move the group to position them over the face.

Release   Click & Drag

5 Draw Another Object

Now, draw the neck off to the side of the face. Group the stroke and the fill together as one object, and move it over the head. Then, use the **Modify, Arrange, Send to Back** command to place the neck behind the other items on the layer. (You'll learn more about the **Arrange** command in the next task.)

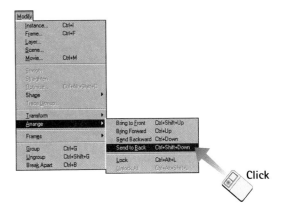

Click

6 Grouping the Groups

Now that your face is complete, you can group all the items together as one object. Use the Arrow tool to select all the items on the Stage. Then, choose the **Modify, Group** command to group them together as a single unit.

End

How-To Hints

Groups or Symbols?

We've stressed in several sections of this book that you should convert objects to symbols whenever you can. However, you don't have to convert *everything* you draw into symbols as you develop them. Symbols can contain groups. After you develop your objects as outlined in the previous task, convert the group into a symbol that you can place anywhere in your movie. In this case, there is no need to make each individual piece of the face a symbol.

How Strokes and Fills Relate to Groups

Notice that until you group a stroke and its fill, it appears beneath any groups that exist on the Stage. Strokes and fills always appear below groups and instances. Group strokes and fills to place them above other groups on the Stage.

How to Stack or Rearrange Objects

Two methods exist for determining the order of objects on the Flash Stage. In Part 6, "Using Layers," you learned how to use layers to control which object appears on top of other objects. You can also control the stacking order of objects that reside on the same layer. The stacking order determines which objects overlay others when they occupy the same position on a single layer. Let's take a close look at how to stack objects on the same layer.

Begin

1 Add Several Objects

Use what you learned in the previous task to create several objects on the same layer and in the same frame. Remember that you can select fills and strokes, and choose **Modify, Group** to group them together as a single entity. Position the objects so that they all overlap—the first group you created appears on the bottom, the last one on the top.

Click

2 Select the Bottommost Object

Click on the object at the very bottom of the stacking order to select it.

Click

3 Bring the Object to the Front

Choose **Modify, Arrange, Bring to Front** to rearrange the stacking order so that the selected object overlays the others as shown here. Alternatively, use the keyboard shortcut **Ctrl+Shift+up-arrow** to achieve the same results.

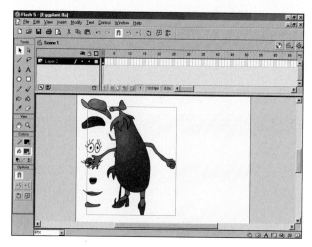

4 Send the Object to the Back

Choose **Modify, Arrange, Send to Back** to rearrange the stacking order so that the selected object once again lies under all the others as shown here. Alternatively, use the keyboard shortcut **Ctrl+Shift+down-arrow** to achieve the same results.

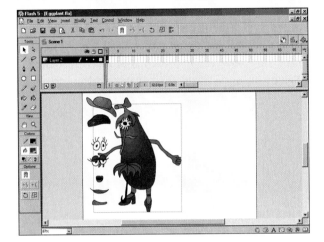

5 Move the Object Forward

Choose **Modify, Arrange, Bring Forward** to move the selected object up in the stacking order one position at a time. Alternatively, use the keyboard shortcut **Ctrl+up-arrow** to achieve the same results.

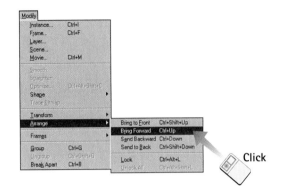

Click

6 Move the Object Backward

Choose **Modify, Arrange, Send Backward** to move the selected object down in the stacking order one position at a time. Alternatively, use the keyboard shortcut **Ctrl+down-arrow** to achieve the same results.

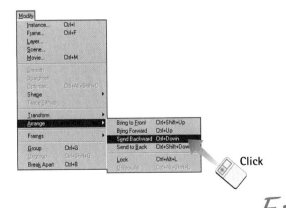

Click

End

How-To Hints

Should I Layer or Stack?

Sometimes it's a little confusing to decide whether you should stack objects on the same layer or place them on different layers. Whenever you intend to animate objects as a group, develop all the objects on the same layer, stack them as you learned in this task, and group them. Then, place the group on a separate layer so that you can animate it without affecting other objects. See Part 6 for a complete discussion of layers.

How to Scale an Object

Scaling an object changes its size. You will find many uses for the scaling capabilities of Flash. For example, you can use tweens (discussed in Part 12, "Animation") to animate an object so that it appears to grow or shrink. You can also use scaling to simply increase or decrease the size of an object that doesn't fit well at its natural size. Because Flash uses vector graphics, you can scale them up many times their original size without losing clarity or quality. This task shows you how to scale your Flash objects.

Begin

1 Select the Scale Modifier

Use any of the methods discussed in Tasks 1 and 2 to select an object on the Stage. Here, the character's hat is selected. Choose the Arrow tool from the toolbox. Click on the **Scale** modifier in the toolbar. A bounding box with handles appears around the object. Use these handles to resize the object.

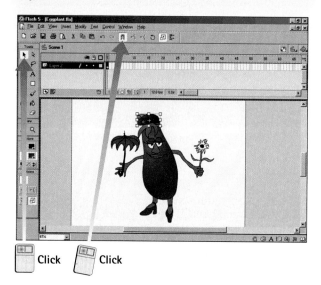

Click   Click

2 Scale an Object Horizontally

Click and drag either of the middle handles on the right or left to scale the object horizontally. Notice that you distort the shape of the object when you do so.

 Click & Drag

3 Scale an Object Vertically

Click and drag either middle handle on the top or bottom to scale the object vertically. Again, notice that you distort the shape of the object when you do so.

 Click & Drag

4 Scale an Object in Proportion

Click and drag any of the corner handles to scale the object both vertically and horizontally simultaneously. Notice that the aspect ratio (the relationship of the width and height) of the object stays unchanged. This resizes the object but does not distort it.

Click & Drag

5 Scale Using the Transform Panel

The **Transform** panel enables you to change the scale of an object. Choose **Window, Panel, Transform** to open the **Transform** panel. Enter new percentage values in the **Horizontal** and **Vertical** text fields. If the **Horizontal** and **Vertical** percentage values are different, you distort the image. Click on the **Constrain** box to prevent this from occurring.

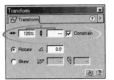

6 Scale Using the Info Panel

The **Info** panel enables you to change an object's pixel dimensions. Choose **Windows, Panels, Info.** Enter new values in the **W** (width) and **H** (height) fields. Notice that there is no **Constrain** button here, so be careful!

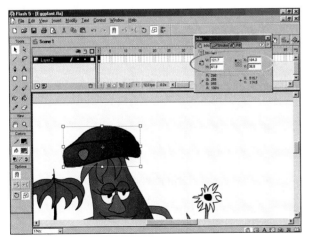

End

How-To Hints

Tearing Panels from Home Windows

Normally, the **Transform** panel and the **Info** panel open in the same window, and you can use the tabs to select between them. You can also tear off a panel from a window to place it separately on the Stage as shown in step 6. To do this, click on the tab that is associated with the panel you want to tear off. Then drag the panel from its tab to a new location on the Stage. To place the panel back in its home window, drag the panel from its tab and release it in the window that you want to place it into.

Distorting an Image

Keep in mind that when you scale an object in only the horizontal or the vertical direction, you distort the shape of that object. Give this careful consideration when you rescale photographic images. If that's the effect you're going for, great...in some cases, it can create striking artwork. However, you might want to think twice before you widen that picture of the boss!

How to Rotate and Flip Objects

The ability to rotate and flip objects in Flash opens up a world of animation possibilities. Tires that spin, clock hands that move around the face of the clock, pendulums that swing, and mirrors that actually reflect an image represent but a few of the possibilities opened up by the rotation and flipping. This task shows how to rotate and flip your Flash objects.

Begin

1 Select an Object

Use any of the methods discussed in Tasks 1 and 2 to select an object on the Stage.

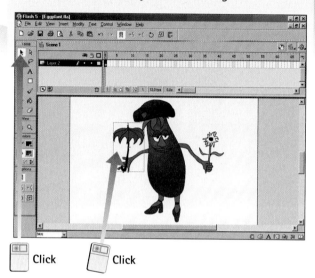

Click   Click

2 Use the Rotate Command

Choose **Modify, Transform, Rotate.** Handles appear on the edges of the object's bounding box. Click away from the object to deselect it. The handles disappear. Choose **Modify, Transform, Rotate 90 degrees CW** (clockwise), or **Modify, Transform, Rotate 90 degrees CCW** (counterclockwise). These options automatically rotate the object 90 degrees without requiring you to drag the handles.

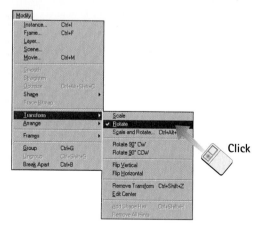

Click

3 Select the Rotate Modifier

You can also use the Rotate modifier to rotate an object. Click on the **Rotate** modifier in the toolbar.

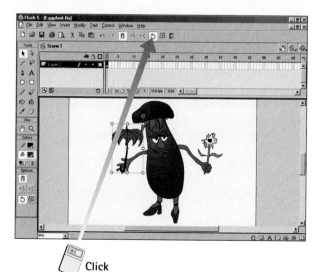

Click

4 Click and Drag a Handle

Hover the mouse over any of the corner handles, and notice that the cursor changes to the rotate cursor. Click and drag the mouse to rotate the object in response to your movements. Notice that, by default, the object rotates around its center registration point. You'll learn how to change this registration point in Task 13.

Click & Drag

5 Open the Transform Panel

Choose **Window, Panels, Transform** to open the **Transform** panel. Click on the **Rotate** radio button to select it if it is not already selected.

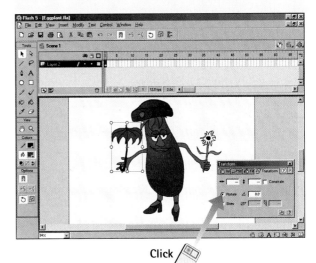

Click

6 Enter a Rotation Value

Double-click in the **Rotate** angle field, and type in an angle of rotation to apply to the object. Press **Enter** to rotate the object in accordance with the value you entered. Negative values, such as shown here, rotate the object counterclockwise. Positive values rotate the object clockwise.

7 Flip an Object

You can also flip an object horizontally or vertically. Choose **Modify, Transform, Flip Vertical** or **Flip Horizontal** to flip the object horizontally or vertically, based on its center registration point.

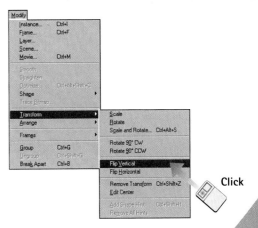

Click

End

How to Skew an Object

When you skew an object, you slant it along the X (horizontal) or Y (vertical) axis. You can also skew it along both axes at the same time. When you skew an object, you add perspective and achieve special effects or looks. Explore the technique of skewing an object in this task.

Begin

1 Select an Object

Use any of the methods discussed in Tasks 1 and 2 to select an object on the Stage.

Click

2 Click on the Rotate Modifier

Select the Arrow tool from the toolbox. Then, click on the **Rotate** modifier in the toolbar. The familiar handles appear along the edges of the object's bounding box.

Click

3 Drag a Handle

The Skew cursor appears as a bi-directional arrow when you position the cursor over the middle handle at the top, bottom, left, or right. Click and drag the middle handle at the top or bottom to skew the object along the horizontal axis. Click and drag the middle handle at the right or left to skew the object along the vertical axis.

Click & Drag

4 Skew with the Transform Panel

You can also skew objects horizontally, vertically, or both by using the **Transform** panel. Choose **Window, Panels, Transform** to open the **Transform** panel. The **Skew** radio button might already be selected, and the skew fields might already contain values. If so, these values reflect the skews you created in step 3.

Click

5 Enter the Skew Angles

To skew an object from the **Transform** panel, click on the **Skew** radio button. The left skew field slants an object along the horizontal axis. The right skew field slants an object along the vertical axis. To change a value, double-click in the field and type the desired angles for your skew. Press **Enter** to finalize your choices. The object immediately reacts to the changes.

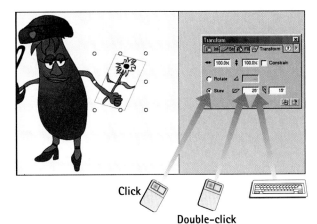

Click   Double-click

End

How-To Hints

Unskewing an Object

Use the **Transform** panel to remove skewing from an object. Click with the Arrow tool to select the object you want to unskew. Choose **Window, Panels, Transform** to open the **Transform** panel. Then, enter **0** in both the horizontal and vertical skew angle fields. You can return all settings in the **Transform** panel to their original positions by clicking on the **Reset** button, located in the lower-right.

Creating a Transformed Copy

If you want to create a copy of the transformed object, click on the **Transform Copy** button, located in the lower-right corner of the **Transform** panel. Then, click and drag the copy to a new location on the Stage.

How to Align Objects

The **Align** panel will often be your best friend. It enables you to line up objects on the Stage—quickly, easily, and exactly—to bring cohesiveness and order to your movie design. You can use it to evenly space objects, or resize selected objects so that they all match in size. You can even perform all these operations at once. Here we discuss the techniques used in aligning objects.

Begin

1 Open the Align Panel

Use the techniques discussed in tasks one and two to select multiple objects on the Stage. The objects you select can be on the same or different layers. Next, choose **Window, Panels, Align** or click on the **Align Panel** button on the toolbar to open the **Align** panel.

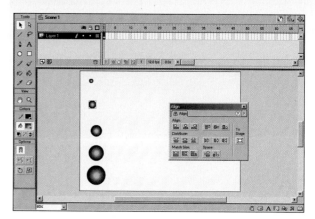

2 Select an Align Option

The **Align** panel provides six alignment options that can be applied to selected objects. Three of the options align the objects vertically according to their left edges, center, or right edges. The other three options align the objects horizontally according to their top, middle, or bottom. Click on the desired button, and Flash repositions one or more of the objects to align them. In this example, the **Align Center** button aligns the circles vertically at their center points.

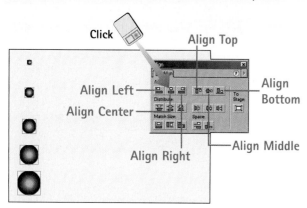

3 Select a Distribute Option

The six different **Distribute** options automatically distribut the objects evenly across the space they consume. The first three options distribute vertically, spacing the tops, middles, or bottoms of the objects evenly. The last three options distribute horizontally, placing the left, center, or right sides of the objects evenly. The example shown here is distributed based on the bottom of each object.

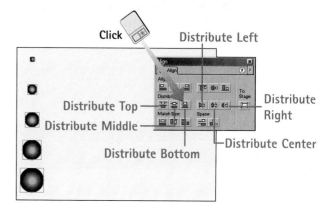

4 Select a Match Size Option

The **Match Size** option in the **Align** panel resizes smaller objects to be equal in size to the largest object. You can match horizontal size, vertical size, or both using one of the three **Match Size** options. Click on the desired option to resize the smaller objects to the exact size of the largest object. In this example, the **Match Horizontal Size** button is clicked. All objects resize to the same width as the widest object.

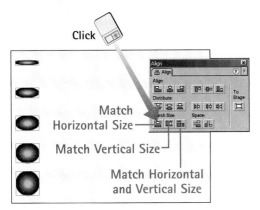

Click

Match Horizontal Size

Match Vertical Size

Match Horizontal and Vertical Size

5 Select a Space Option

Two **Space** options move the objects so that an equal amount of space exists between their edges. The first option creates an even amount of space between vertically placed objects (as shown here), and the second option creates an even amount of space between horizontally placed objects. Click on the desired button, and Flash repositions the selected objects so that they are evenly spaced.

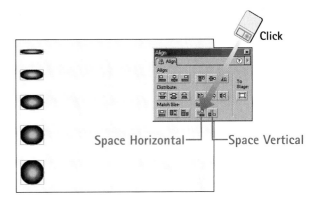

Click

Space Horizontal — — Space Vertical

6 Align Relative to Stage

When the **To Stage** button option is pressed, all the alignment options that you choose are aligned to fit the dimensions of the Stage. For example, with the **To Stage** button engaged, the **Align Left Edges** button aligns the left edges of the objects to the left edge of the Stage, and the **Space Horizontal** button evenly spaces the objects to touch the top and bottom of the Stage. Disengage the button to align and distribute the objects as shown in previous steps.

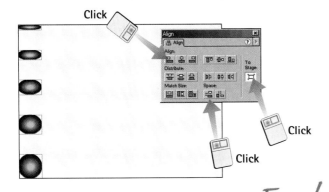

Click

Click

Click

End

How-To Hints

Align to What?

How does Flash know which point in the curve to use when it aligns the left side of one object to another? Flash determines alignment by a bounding box that surrounds the objects. Bounding boxes are always rectangular, so Flash never has trouble finding an edge to align to!

Distribute? Space?

At first glance, the **Distribute** and **Space** options might appear to do the same thing, but a slight difference exists. The **Distribute** options put an equal distance between the edges being used to make the distribution. In other words, distributing them vertically by their top edges puts an equal distance between the top edges of the objects. On the other hand, the **Space** options equalize the actual distance from any object to its neighbor so that it is the same as the distance between any other two adjacent objects.

TASK

13

How to Move an Object's Registration Point

Every group, instance, text block, and bitmap in your Flash project has a registration point. Operations such as scaling, rotating, and skew use this point as an "anchor." By default, the registration point lies in the center of an object, but this task shows how to move the registration point to achieve different results.

Begin

1 Select an Object

This example demonstrates how to change the registration point of a pendulum on a clock. Each object that makes up the clock appears in a separate layer. Zoom in to the pendulum so that you can see the object more clearly. Then click with the Arrow tool to select the pendulum.

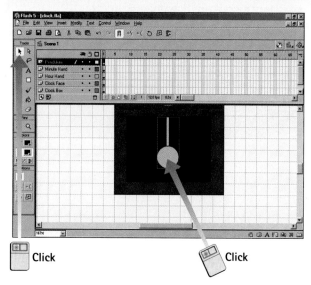

Click   Click

2 Rotate the Object

Rotate the object using the rotate modifier of the Arrow tool. As the object rotates, notice that its registration point (represented by a hollow circle) lies at the object's center. This registration point acts as an anchor point from which the rotation occurs. If you animate the pendulum with the registration point in the center, it won't look very natural!

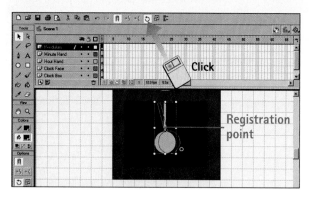

Click

Registration point

3 Make the Registration Point Moveable

Choose **Modify, Transform, Edit Center** to make the registration point moveable. A white crosshair appears at the object's registration point.

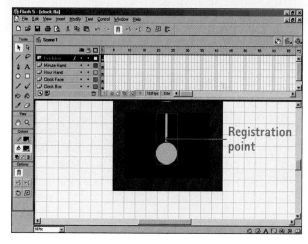

Registration point

138 PART 7: SELECTING AND MODIFYING OBJECTS

4 Move the Crosshair

To help you position the registration point more accurately, use the Zoom tool to move in closer to the object. Then, use the Arrow tool to drag and drop the white crosshair to a new location. Note that you can move the registration point anywhere you want—even outside of the object and its bounding box, or off the Stage and onto the work area. In this case, we want to move it to the top center of the pendulum.

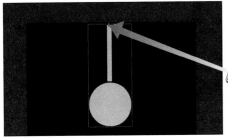

Click & Drag

5 Deselect the Crosshair

Choose **Modify, Transform, Edit Center** to disable this feature. Note that the **Edit Center** command functions as a toggle switch. Choose it once to turn on the feature, and choose it a second time to turn the feature back off.

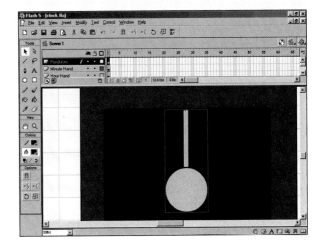

6 Rotate the Object Again

Click on the **Rotate** modifier once again. Again, handles appear around the bounding box of the object. Click and drag one of the corner handles to rotate the object. Notice that the object now rotates in a much more natural manner because you changed the registration point.

Click

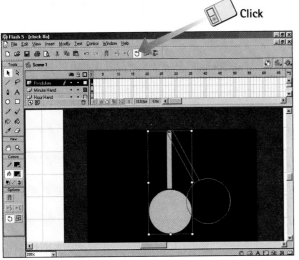

How-To Hints

What Uses the Registration Point?

Although the example in this task uses rotation to demonstrate moving the registration point, Flash uses the registration point as a reference for all types of transformations and positioning. Experiment with different operations, and various registration point locations to see what effects you can come up with.

If You're Having Trouble...

If you're having trouble positioning the registration point, check to see what snapping options you're using. If **Snap to Grid, Snap to Rulers,** or **Snap to Objects** is enabled, you might have difficulty getting the registration point to move exactly where you want it. Disable snapping options to move the registration point freely.

End

Task

Frames and Keyframes

An animation is nothing more than a series of still images played one after another, each in its own cell or frame. To build an animation in Flash or in the traditional sense, you develop a series of frames, each slightly different than the next. Then you play the frames rapidly to give the illusion of movement. The more frames there are in your movie, the longer the movie plays.

A *keyframe* is a special type of frame that defines when an action or event is to occur, or that marks the start or end of an animation sequence. Think of a keyframe as a snapshot of what you want your movie layer to look like at a specific point in time. Use keyframes to define start and end points of an animated sequence.

When you create a new Flash movie, Flash places a blank keyframe in the first frame of Layer 1. Blank keyframes appear as small hollow dots in the Timeline. After you add an object to a keyframe, the keyframe appears as a filled black dot. The contents of a keyframe remain on Stage through every frame that follows, until it reaches a new keyframe with new contents. When you place a blank keyframe into a frame that already contains content, the blank keyframe removes the existing content and replaces it with a blank screen.

You can make a keyframe of any frame in your project. In fact, for frame-by-frame animation, you make a keyframe of every frame, following traditional animation techniques in which the artist creates every frame individually. Most often in Flash, however, you create tweened animations. In a tweened animation, only the first and last frames of the sequence are keyframes, and Flash interpolates between the two to create the intermediary frames. We'll cover this in depth in Part 12, "Animation."

Mastering Flash requires a thorough understanding of the keyframe concept because so much power lies there. Combining keyframes with tweening techniques enables you to create complicated animation sequences quickly and easily without drawing each frame one by one.

How to Add, Clear, and Delete Keyframes

As stated, the complicated process of creating animation can be broken down into the simple mechanics of building frames and keyframes. In the same way, the seemingly daunting task of creating keyframes can be readily understood by breaking down the techniques for manipulating them.

Begin

1 Enable Flash 4 Frame Drawing

To display keyframes as shown in the examples in this part, choose **Edit, Preferences**. The **Preferences** dialog opens to the **General** tab shown here. Check the **Flash 4 Frame Drawing** option in the **Timeline Options** section. This option displays blank keyframes as hollow circles in the Timeline, and makes it easier to see where keyframes occur.

2 Add a Blank Keyframe

To add a blank keyframe to any frame on any layer, place the cursor in the target frame on the Timeline. Choose **Insert, Blank Keyframe**. Alternatively, right-click (**Ctrl+**click on the Mac) on the target frame, and choose **Insert Blank Keyframe**. The blank keyframe removes any content that previously appeared in the frame. From the new keyframe on, that information no longer appears on the Stage.

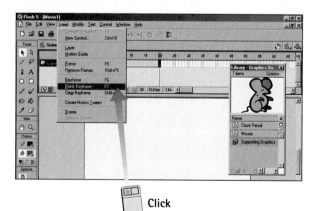

Click

3 Add a Keyframe

When you add a new nonblank keyframe, anything on the Stage still appears at this new keyframe. You can then adjust the contents of the keyframe to achieve the desired effect. For example, assume that an object appears at the left of the screen on the first frame, but you want to move it to the right of the screen in frame 20. Place the cursor in frame 20 on the Timeline, and choose **Insert, Keyframe (F6)**. Move the object to its new location in frame 20.

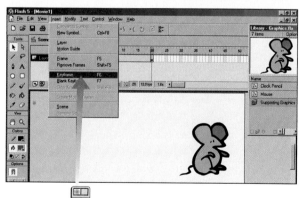

Click

4 Clear a Keyframe

If you decide you no longer want a change to occur in a specific frame, you can clear the keyframe. To clear a keyframe, right-click on it and choose **Clear Keyframe**. Or, select the frame and press the keyboard shortcut **Shift+F6.** Clearing the keyframe removes any information on the Stage. However, the action does not delete the frame, it merely transforms it from a keyframe to a regular frame. Your project maintains the same total number of frames.

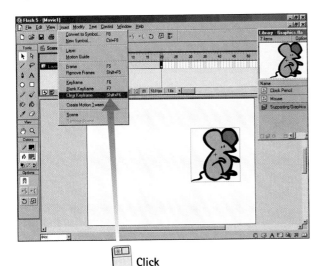

Click

5 Delete a Keyframe

You can delete a keyframe only if it is the last frame of the layer. Right-click on the keyframe, and choose **Remove Frames** (note that this command also removes multiple frames when more than one frame is selected). Or, press the keyboard shortcut **Shift+F5.** This both clears the frame—removing any information on the Stage—and deletes the frame. Your project now contains one fewer frames.

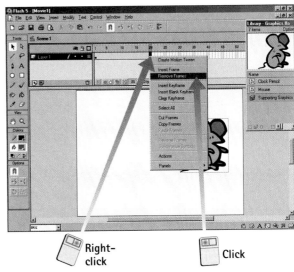

Right-
click

Click

End

How-To Hints

Keyframe Quirkiness

Beware of quirks when working with keyframes. For instance, if you add a keyframe beyond the last frame of the current layer, Flash adds extra frames to the layer's Timeline to fill in between the first keyframe and the new keyframe. However, if you insert a keyframe on an already exist-ing frame, Flash simply converts the existing frame to a keyframe without adding frames. Another example: If you choose **Delete Frame** when on a keyframe that is not the last frame of the layer, Flash removes one frame from your project, but not the keyframe. To remove such a keyframe, you must first use the **Clear Keyframe** command, and then delete the frame in a sepa-rate operation.

Adding and Deleting Regular Frames

To add and delete regular frames, select the target frame, and choose the appropriate option under the **Insert** menu.

How to Select and Move Keyframes

As you synchronize your movie to sounds or other actions within the project, you sometimes need to adjust the timing of your keyframes. In this task, you learn how to select and move keyframes forward or backward in your Timeline.

1 Select a Keyframe

To select a keyframe, click on the keyframe dot in the Timeline. Flash highlights the selected keyframe by filling the frame in the Timeline with black and changing the color of the keyframe dot to white. Flash also selects all the contents on the Stage at that keyframe.

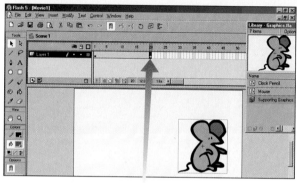

 Click

2 Move a Keyframe Forward

To move a keyframe forward in the Timeline, click on the keyframe dot in the Timeline to select it. Next, click and drag the keyframe dot to a different frame in the Timeline.

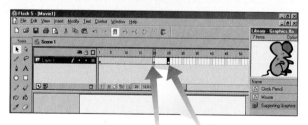

Click & Drag   Release

3 Extend the Segment Forward

When you move a keyframe that is preceded by a segment of frames, you have to extend that segment to the new location of the keyframe. To do this, click the frame that formerly appeared before the keyframe before you relocated it (it now appears immediately before a new keyframe). Next, drag the frame to the frame immediately before the new location of your keyframe.

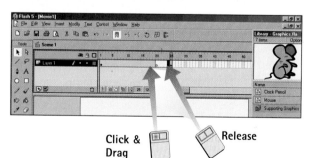

Click & Drag   Release

4 Move Backward

To move a keyframe backward in the Timeline, you must first move the frame immediately before the keyframe. After you move the frame, a new keyframe appears immediately after the frame you moved. A series of frames appear between it and the original keyframe.

5 Reposition the Keyframe

Now, move the original keyframe (the one at the end of the Timeline in this figure) to the frame immediately after the segment that you moved. The frame to which you want to move the keyframe currently contains a new keyframe, which will be replaced with the keyframe you're moving.

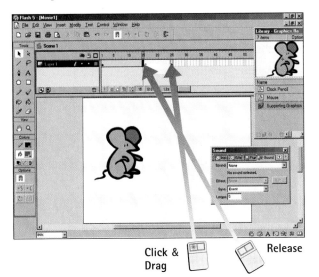

Click & Drag

Release

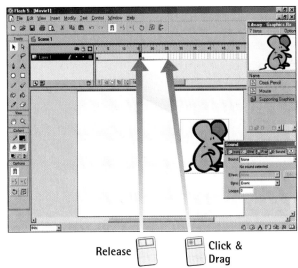

Release

Click & Drag

End

How-To Hints

More Keyframe Quirkiness

Moving the ending keyframes of a tween is slightly different than moving the ending keyframe of a range of static frames. When you move the ending keyframe of a tween out in the Timeline, Flash creates a new keyframe at the old location, and a range of static frames between the old location and the new one. You then move the ending tweened frame (not keyframe) to the frame before the newly moved keyframe. If you move the ending keyframe of a range of static frames, Flash creates a blank keyframe at the old location, and all the frames between the old location and the new location are blank.

When you move the frame before the ending keyframe after a range of static frames to a position earlier in the Timeline, Flash inserts a blank keyframe immediately after it. The blank keyframe and the frames that follow it are empty. After you've moved the final keyframe to its new location, you can add additional content to the empty frames or delete them, if you prefer. If you move the frame before the ending keyframe of a tween to an earlier position, Flash adds a new keyframe and static frames that range all the way to the old location of the keyframe.

TASK 3

How to Assign Actions to a Frame

Actions allow your Flash animation to break beyond the linear path of the Timeline. You can use actions to cause specific events to take place. Frame Actions are always added at a keyframe. If you try to apply an action to a frame that is not a keyframe, Flash will move the action to the last previous keyframe. Frames that contain actions will have a small "a" in them in the Timeline. Keep your Timeline more organized and easier to work with by adding your actions to a dedicated actions layer. In this example, you'll add a simple Go To action to a keyframe.

Begin

1 Open the Frame Actions Panel

To add actions to a keyframe, you must first access the **Frame Actions** panel for the target frame. There are several techniques for accessing the **Frame Actions** panel. First, select the target frame by clicking on it. Then choose **Window, Actions**.

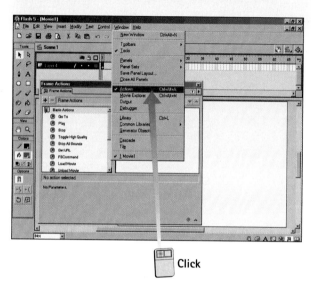

Click

2 Right-Click on the Target Frame

Another method of accessing the **Frame Actions** panel is to right-click (**Ctrl+click** on Macintosh) on the target frame, and choose **Actions**.

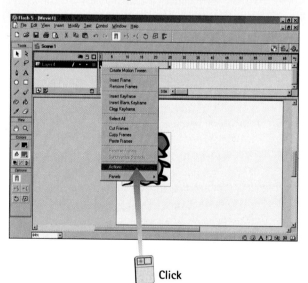

Click

3 Double-Click on the Target Frame

The third method used for accessing the **Frame Actions** panel is to double-click on the target frame.

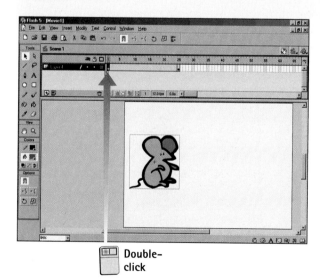

Double-click

4 Choose Action Type

When in the **Frame Actions** panel, click on the **Basic Actions** icon to access all the basic actions that you can assign to frames. You now have full access to all of the various action choices, as well as the controls and parameter of the actions.

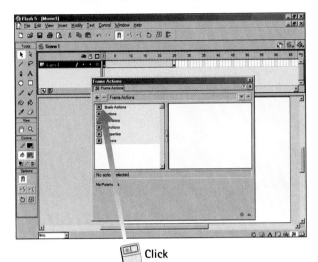

Click

5 Choose an Action from the List

To add an action, double-click the desired action in the list. The parameters section that appears at the bottom of the panel offers different choices depending upon which action you choose from the list. Choose **Go To** from the list. The default in the Parameters section is **Go To frame one of the current scene**. Press **OK** to accept this default Go To setting.

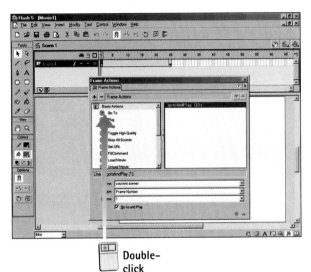

Double-click

6 Preview the Action

To make sure that the action has the desired effect, choose **Control, Enable Simple Frame Actions,** and then play the movie. Verify that when the movie reaches the frame to which you added the action, the playhead is instantly moved to frame one of your movie. If this does not happen, verify that **Enable Simple Frame Actions** is turned on, and check to make sure the action is properly constructed to go to frame one.

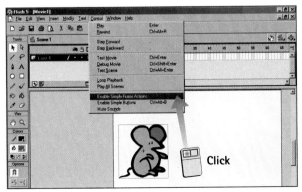

Click

How-To Hints

Frame Actions Mean Power

Frame actions represent one of the areas of hidden robustness in Flash. Although detailed discussion of actions is beyond the scope of this book, here is a small taste of what you can do with actions. You can build complex action lists into a keyframe by adding additional actions as needed. Multiple actions can easily be rearranged depending upon the desired effect. If you know a little bit about programming, you can write expressions that Flash will execute on-the-fly to execute desired tasks. Using if...then statements and loop structures that are familiar to programmers, actions quickly become extremely powerful tools.

End

Task

9

Symbols and Instances

*F*lash movies are more compact when you create or convert all your objects to *symbols*. Flash stores the information about a symbol only one time in your project file. Every time you use a copy, or instance, of that symbol, Flash refers back to the original symbol. As a result, your file sizes remain smaller than when you use objects that are simply drawn and placed on the Stage.

There are three types of symbols in Flash. *Graphic symbols* are used for static images. *Movie Clips* are reusable pieces of animation that play independently of the main movie, somewhat like a movie within a movie. Movie Clips can animate in a single frame, making them perfect for use in animated buttons. *Buttons*, discussed in more detail in Part 10, "Buttons and Actions," are symbols that cause an action to take place when a user hovers over or clicks on it.

Flash enables you to create symbols in two ways: by starting with an empty symbol and building shapes upon it, or by converting existing objects to symbols. When you create a symbol using either method, Flash stores it in your movie's library.

When you drag a symbol from the library and place it into your movie, Flash creates an *instance* of the symbol. The instance links back to the original master symbol. You can make instances look vastly different—by applying effects to their color, brightness, and opacity, and by changing their scale, rotation, or skew—without affecting the master symbol or any other instances of that symbol. However, when you edit a symbol in symbol-editing mode, you are actually editing the master symbol and so the changes are applied to every other instance that links to the same master symbol.

With wise planning and use of symbols, you can make movies that download and stream much faster. Use instances whenever you can. The key here is to *economize* on the elements that make up your movie.

How to Create a New Symbol

Use the **Insert, New Symbol** command to create an empty symbol. Build the symbol in symbol-editing mode as you draw the objects on the Stage. In many ways, it's best to create your symbols in this manner. When you create a symbol while working in symbol-editing mode, your symbol can contain multiple layers and frames.

Begin

1 Select Insert, New Symbol

If you already have other objects on the Stage, make sure that none of them are selected. Then, choose **Insert, New Symbol** or use the keyboard shortcut **Ctrl+F8** (Windows) or **Cmmd+F8** (Macintosh).

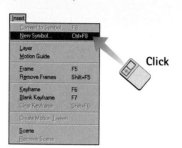

Click

2 Name the Symbol

In the **Symbol Properties** dialog, enter a unique name for your symbol. It's important to use a logical name that you'll remember. If you enter a symbol name that already appears in your movie library, Flash prompts you to use a different name.

3 Choose a Behavior Type

To specify a behavior type, choose **Movie Clip** if you want to create an animated symbol. Choose **Button** if you want your symbol to perform an action when it is hovered over or clicked. (Buttons are discussed in more detail in Part 10.) Select **Graphic** if your symbol will consist of a single, static frame.

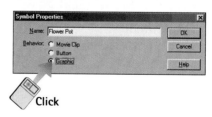

Click

4 Enter Symbol-Editing Mode

Choose **OK** to exit the **Symbol Properties** dialog and enter symbol-editing mode. The Timeline displays a new tab for your symbol, which tells you that you are in symbol-editing mode, and thus editing the master symbol. The Timeline displays one layer named Layer 1. A crosshair, which marks the registration (or center) point of the symbol, appears on the Stage. Remember from Part 7, Task 13 that operations such as scaling, rotating, and skew use the registration point as an "anchor."

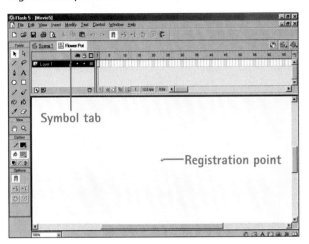

Symbol tab

Registration point

5 Develop Your Symbol

Develop your symbol using drawing and text tools, imported objects, or other symbols from your library. Use multiple layers if desired. Insert frames and keyframes to add animation to your Movie Clip symbols.

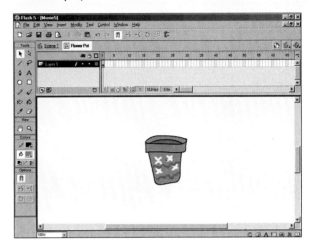

6 Exit Symbol-Editing Mode

To exit symbol-editing mode, click on the **Scene** tab above the Timeline; choose **Edit, Edit Movie**; or use the shortcut **Ctrl+E** (Windows) or **Cmmd+E** (Macintosh).

How-To Hints

Where Did Your New Symbol Go?

You might be alarmed after you spend a lot of time creating a new symbol, only to find that it doesn't appear on your Stage when you exit symbol-editing mode. Not to worry—you'll find the symbol in your movie library and can add it to the Stage as outlined in Task 5.

End

How to Convert an Object to a Symbol

You can convert any object that appears on your Stage to a symbol. Note that when you build symbols this way, Flash places all the different layers on one layer when you create the symbol.

Begin

1 Select Several Objects at Once

To select several objects on the Stage, use the Arrow tool to click and drag a rectangular area around the objects you want to select.

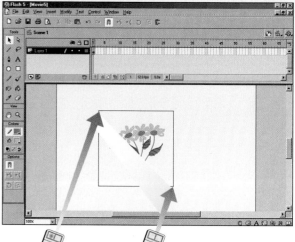

Click & Drag　　Release

2 Select Objects One at a Time

Click on an object with the Arrow tool to select a single object. Choose **Edit, Preferences** and verify the status of the **Shift Select** option in the **General** tab. This determines how additional objects are selected. When **Shift Select** is not checked (disabled), you can left-click to select additional objects. If **Shift Select** is checked, use **Shift**+click to add items to the selection.

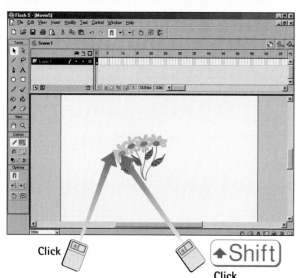

Click　　　　　　　　(⬆Shift)
　　　　　　　　　　　　Click

3 Convert the Objects to a Symbol

After you select the object or objects that you want to convert, choose **Insert, Convert to Symbol**, or press F8 on your keyboard. The **Symbol Properties** dialog appears.

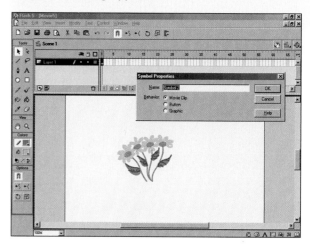

4 Name the Symbol and Choose Its Behavior

Enter a name for the symbol in the **Name** field. Next, select the radio button that corresponds to the behavior you want (**Graphic, Button,** or **Movie Clip**).

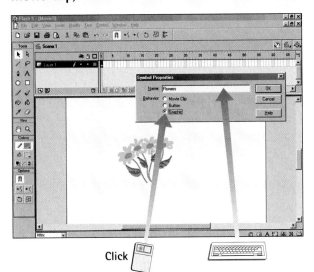

Click 📱   ⌨️

5 Complete the Symbol

Click on **OK** to convert the selected object or objects to a symbol. Flash places the master symbol in your project library. The objects that you initially selected on the Stage are converted to an instance of the symbol.

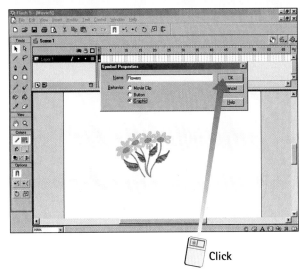

📱 Click

End

3

How to Create a Movie Clip

The Movie Clip is a very special type of symbol that is somewhat like a Flash mini-movie itself. Movie Clips can contain animation, other symbols, text, imported artwork, and interactive buttons. You can place Movie Clips anywhere in your project... the Movie Clip animates independently of the movie, even on a single frame.

Begin

1 Create a New Symbol

With nothing selected on the Stage, choose **Insert, New Symbol**. The **Symbol Properties** dialog appears. Enter a name for the symbol in the **Name** field, and choose **Movie Clip** for the behavior. Click on **OK** to enter symbol-editing mode.

Click   Click

2 Develop Your Frames

Your Movie Clip should contain multiple frames because it is animated. In the example shown here, the wings flap back and forth through the use of tweens, which you'll learn more about in Part 12, "Animation."

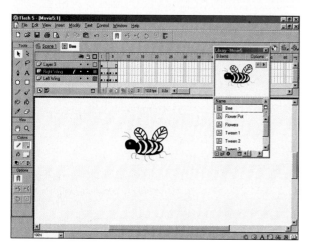

3 Add the Movie Clip to Your Main Movie

When your symbol is completed to your satisfaction, choose **Edit, Movie,** or click on the **Scene** tab to return to movie-editing mode. Click on the **Insert Layer** button at the lower-left corner of the Timeline to create a new layer for your Movie Clip. Then click and drag your new symbol from the movie library onto the new layer.

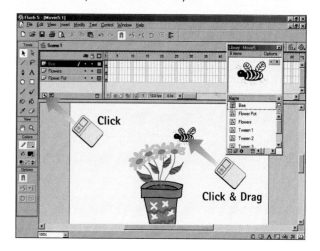

Click

Click & Drag

4 Test the Movie

Choose **Control, Test Movie,** or use the keyboard shortcut **Ctrl+Enter** to watch your Movie Clip play in the movie. Even though your main movie contains one frame, the movie animates within it. Close the new window to return to editing your movie.

End

How-To Hints

Animated Buttons!

Because Movie Clips animate in a single frame, it makes them ideal to use for creating animated buttons. Use a Movie Clip as the Over state of a button. When your mouse hovers over the mouse, the button displays an animation. This will be covered in Part 10.

How to Convert Symbol Behaviors

Occasionally, you might need to convert between symbol behaviors. For example, you might initially create a Graphic symbol, and find later that you want to convert it to a Movie Clip or to a Button. This task shows you how to convert between symbol behaviors.

Begin

1 Open the Movie's Library

Open the project that contains the symbol you want to change. If your movie library is not open, choose **Window, Library,** or use the keyboard shortcut **Ctrl+L** to open it.

Click

2 Select a Symbol from the Library

Click on the symbol name in the library to highlight the symbol that you want to change. A picture of the symbol appears in the preview pane.

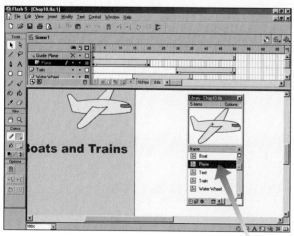

Click

3 Select a New Behavior (Method 1)

Right-click (or **Ctrl+**click on the Mac) on the symbol name to open the **Library options** menu. Choose **Behavior** from the menu that appears, and drag the mouse to the right to select a new symbol behavior. Any instances already on Stage will retain their original behavior. All new instances dragged from the library will change to reflect this new behavior.

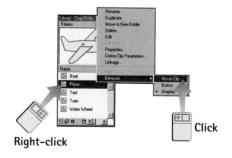

Right-click   Click

4 Select a New Behavior (Method 2)

Alternatively, you can use another method to select a new behavior. This method also enables you to change the name of the symbol. Right-click (**Ctrl**+click on the Mac) on the symbol in the library and choose **Properties** from the menu that appears. Enter a new name for the symbol in the **Symbol Properties** dialog. Then select a new behavior type, and click on **OK** to apply the changes. Any instances already on Stage will retain their original behavior. All new instances dragged from the library will change to reflect this new behavior.

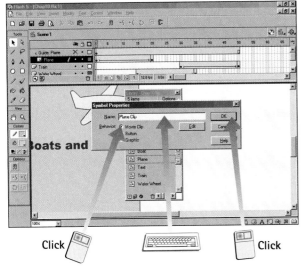

Click   Click

End

How to Edit Symbols

Occasionally, you need to change the color or art-work of a symbol after you create it. There are a number of ways that you can change a symbol that is already on the Stage. When you edit a master symbol it updates all instances of the symbol that link back to the same master symbol. As a result, you don't have to change the symbol in every location in which it appears. The following task demonstrates the many ways that you can edit a symbol.

Begin

1 Open the Symbol from the Library

One way you can edit a symbol is to access it from the movie library. Right-click (**Ctrl**+click on the Mac) on the name of the symbol you want to change, and choose **Edit** from the menu that appears. The symbol opens in symbol-editing mode. After you make changes to the symbol, choose **Edit, Edit Movie** or use the keyboard shortcut **Ctrl+E** to return to your movie Stage. Any instances on the Stage that are linked to the symbol will reflect the changes you made.

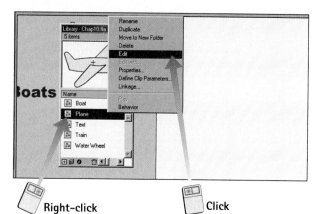

Right-click   Click

2 Open a Symbol from the Stage

Alternatively, you can enter symbol-editing mode from the Stage. Right-click (**Ctrl**+click) on the symbol you want to change, and choose **Edit** from the menu that appears. The symbol opens in symbol-editing mode. Choose **Edit, Edit Movie** to return to your movie Stage after you finish editing.

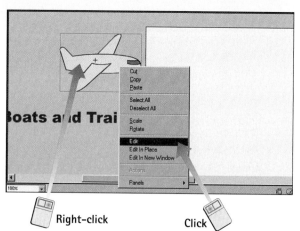

Right-click   Click

3 Edit a Symbol in Place

Sometimes, you need to make changes to a symbol while you also see the other objects that surround it. To do this, right-click (**Ctrl**+click) on any symbol on the Stage, and choose **Edit In Place** from the menu. Alternatively, double-click on the symbol. The surrounding artwork dims behind the symbol you are editing.

Double-click

4 Edit in a New Window

You can also edit a symbol in a window that is totally separate from the Stage. To do this, right-click (**Ctrl**+click) on a symbol on the Stage and choose **Edit In New Window**. The symbol opens in a separate window that you can display in conjunction with the movie on the Stage. Click on the **Close** button in the upper-right corner of the symbol window when your edits are complete.

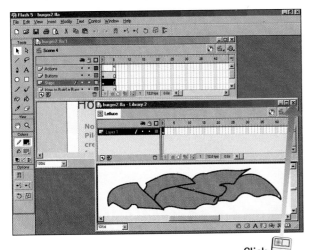

Click

End

How-To Hints

Editing Symbols Saves Time!

As your collection of original Flash movies increases, you will soon discover the value of making changes to existing symbols. As you'll learn in Task 6, you can use symbols from other Flash movies. If you already have a symbol in another movie that is close in appearance to the new symbol that you want to create, by all means, use it! After you add the symbol to your current project, you can treat it the same way as any other symbol in your movie.

How to Add Symbols to Your Movie

After you create a symbol, it's a relatively easy process to add it to your movie. Every symbol that you create is stored in your movie library. To add a symbol, simply drag it from the library onto the Stage.

2 Copy and Paste Symbols

You can also use the **Copy** and **Paste** commands to create a new instance of a symbol that you have already placed on the Stage. Select the symbol that you want to copy, and choose **Edit, Copy** (or click on the **Copy** button on the toolbar) to copy it into the clipboard. Then, choose **Edit, Paste** (or click on the **Paste** button on the toolbar) to paste the symbol into the center of the Stage. Click and drag the copy to move it to its proper location on the Stage.

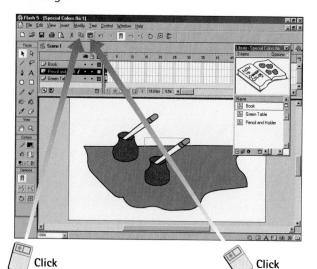

Click   Click

Begin

1 Insert a Symbol from the Library

To open the library that is associated with your movie, choose **Window, Library.** Alternatively, use the shortcut **Ctrl+L** (Windows) or **Cmmd+L** (Macintosh). As you click on the symbols in the library, a preview appears in the preview window. Drag the selected symbol to the Stage and release the mouse button.

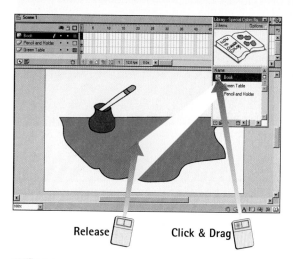

Release   Click & Drag

3 Move Symbols to Another Layer

You can easily move an object from one layer to another. First, select the symbol or symbols that you want to move. Then, choose **Edit, Cut** (or click on the **Cut** button on the toolbar) to remove it from the current layer and place it into the clipboard. Switch to another layer, and choose **Edit, Paste in Place.** The symbol appears in the new layer exactly where it appeared on the original layer.

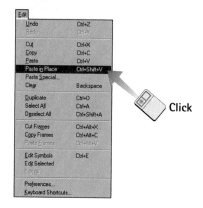

Click

4 Use Symbols from Other Movies

As we already mentioned, you can use symbols from other Flash movies that you have already created. Choose **File, Open as Library** to display the **Open as Library** dialog. Use the **Look in** box to locate the movie that contains the symbols you want to use in your current movie. Choose **Open** to display the library for that project. Click and drag symbols from this library onto your Stage.

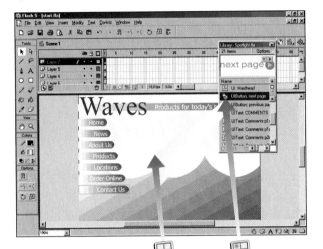

Release

Click & Drag

5 Use Symbols from Shared Libraries

Shared libraries let you use symbols from other movies in multiple projects. This is really a timesaver because when you edit any master symbol in a shared library, the symbol is updated in every project in which the symbol appears. To use symbols from a shared library, choose **File, Open as Shared Library**. Use the **Open as Library** dialog to locate the movie that contains the symbols you want to share. Click and drag symbols from this library onto your Stage.

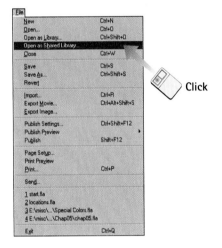

Click

End

How-To Hints

Naming and Saving Your Shared Libraries

Shared libraries are a feature that is new to Flash 5, and they will save you copious amounts of time. It makes sense, in this case, to name your shared library movies and locate them in special folders so that you can easily recognize them as shared libraries. For example, use Windows Explorer to create a folder named Shared Libraries in your Flash 5 installation folder. Store all your shared libraries there, using movie names such as Buttons.fla, Movie Clips.fla, and so on.

How to Change Instance Properties

Any time you drag a symbol from the library onto the Stage, you create an *instance* of that symbol. The **Instance Properties** dialog enables you to convert the behavior of an instance to another behavior without affecting the other instances on the stage or the master symbol in the Library. The **Effect** panel offers several options that change the appearance of an instance. You can adjust the brightness, tint, or transparency of an instance without affecting the other instances on the stage. Refer to Task 8 to learn how to implement special color changes.

Begin

1 Open the Effect Panel

Click on the Stage with the Arrow tool to select the instance you want to change. Choose **Window, Panels, Effect** to open the **Effect** panel.

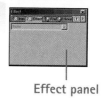

Effect panel

2 Change the Brightness of an Instance

To change the brightness of an instance, choose **Brightness** from the **Effect** drop-down list. Move the **Brightness** slider down to darken the color or up to brighten the color. Alternatively, enter a numerical value between **–100** (black) and **+100** (white) in the **Brightness** field. A brightness setting of **0** returns the symbol to its original level.

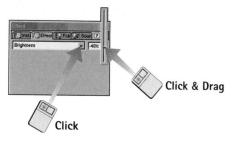

Click & Drag

Click

3 Change the Tint of an Instance

To change the color of an instance, select **Tint** from the **Effect** drop-down list. Use the crosshair cursor to select a new color from the color selector at the bottom of the dialog; or enter numerical values in the **R, G,** and **B** fields; or click on the small color square to choose a new color from the current color set. Use the slider at the right of the **Effect** drop-down to adjust the brightness of the color.

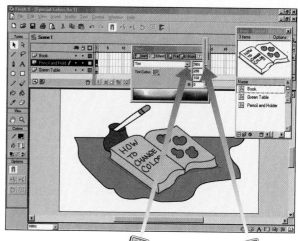

Click   Click & Drag

4 Change the Transparency of an Instance

To change the transparency of an instance, select **Alpha** from the **Effect** drop-down list. The default setting of **100%** displays the symbol at full opacity. To make the symbol more transparent, move the **Alpha** slider down, or enter a value between **0** and **99** in the **Alpha** field. An **Alpha** setting of **0** makes the instance completely transparent.

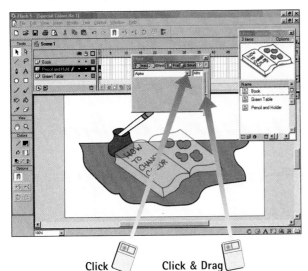

Click

Click & Drag

End

How-To Hints

Animating Color and Transparency

You can animate the preceding effects changes over time. See Part 12, "Animation," to learn how to use tweens to create color changes over time.

How to Create Advanced Color Effects

The fields and sliders on the left side of the **Advanced** option of the **Effect Panel** enable you to adjust red, green, blue, and alpha values wherever they appear in a symbol. The sliders on the right side of the panel enable you to control the percentages of red, green, blue, and alpha that are used in the entire symbol, similar to an overall tint. The following example helps illustrate the differences between these two sets of sliders.

Begin

1 Select the Symbol

Choose a symbol from your movie library and position it on the Stage. Right-click (**Ctrl**+click) on the symbol and choose **Panels, Effect** from the menu that appears. Choose **Advanced** from the **Effect** drop-down.

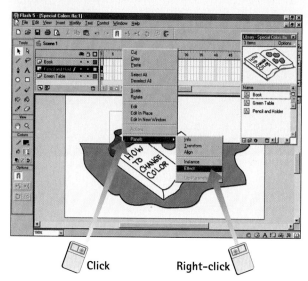

Click   Right-click

2 Adjust Colors Selectively

Double-click on a numerical value to enter a new value, or use the associated slider to adjust the amount of red, green, blue, or alpha in the instance. Here, the **Green** slider is adjusted to **60%**. Compare the symbol in the library to the adjusted symbol on the Stage. The yellow pencil is affected because green is used in part to compose the color yellow.

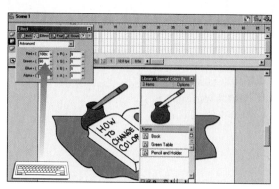

3 Adjust Overall Tint

Use the **R, G, B,** and **A** sliders in the right half of the dialog box to adjust the entire symbol as a whole. Here, the **R** slider is increased to **128**. This affects the amount of red in the entire symbol, rather than confining the change to areas where red appeared in whole or in part.

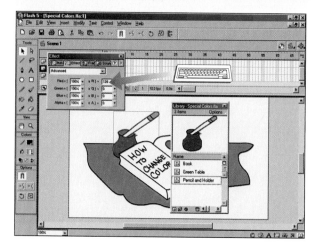

4 Close the Effect Panel

To close the **Effect** panel, choose **Window, Panels, Effect** to toggle off the panel. Alternatively, click on the **Close** button in the upper-right corner of the **Effect** panel.

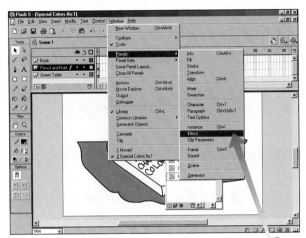

Click

End

How-To Hints

When to Use Advanced Color Changes

It's not always easy to predict how advanced color adjustments affect the colors in an instance because every color you use in your movie is created with varying combinations of red, green, and blue light. If you want to change the color of only one or two areas in an instance, use the Ink Bottle tool or the Paint Bucket tool to apply a new stroke or fill color to the areas you want to change. Advanced color effects are best used when you want to animate a color change over time.

9

How to Break Apart Instances

Normally, when you edit an instance in symbol-editing mode, the changes you make affect every instance that links back to the same master symbol. This could also affect symbols in other movies if you use shared symbol libraries. When you break apart an instance, it breaks the connection to the original master symbol. After you break apart the instance, you can edit it without affecting the instances that are still linked to the master. Then you can convert the new version into a new master symbol. These points are illustrated in the steps that follow.

Begin

1 Place the Instance on the Stage

Drag several instances of a symbol from your library to create multiple copies on the Stage.

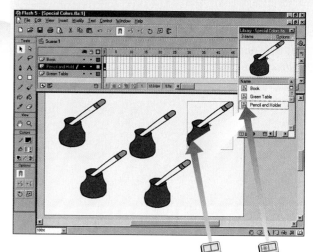

Release   Click & Drag

2 Select the Instance

Select the Arrow tool from the toolbox. Click on one of the instances on the Stage to select it.

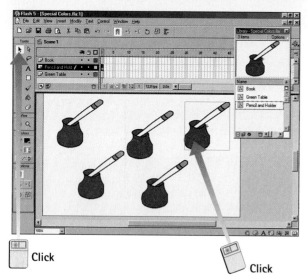

Click

Click

3 Apply the Break Apart Command

Choose **Modify, Break Apart,** or use the keyboard shortcut **Ctrl+B** (Windows) or **Option+B** (Macintosh). Flash breaks apart the symbol and selects all the components that make up the symbol.

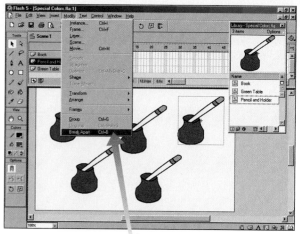

Click

4 Edit the Objects

The link to the master symbol is now broken, so you can edit the instance without affecting the other instances that you placed on the Stage.

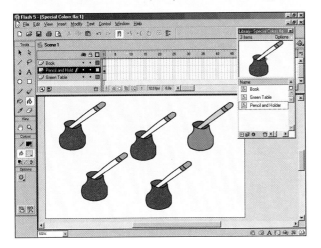

5 Convert Back into a Symbol

Use the Arrow tool to draw a rectangular selection around all the objects that you edited. Choose **Insert, Convert to Symbol** or use the keyboard shortcut **F8** to open the **Symbol Properties** dialog.

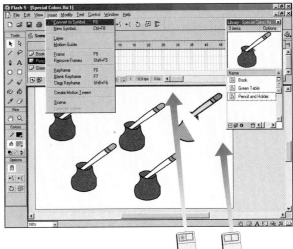

Click & Drag   Release

6 Name the New Symbol

Enter a new name for the symbol in the **Name** field, and select one of the **Behavior** types (**Graphic, Button,** or **Movie Clip**). Click on **OK** to add the new symbol to your movie library.

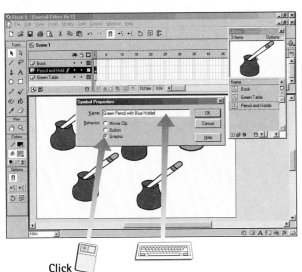

Click

How-To Hints

Break Apart with Caution!

Be careful when you break apart symbols ...especially symbols that are animated or very complex. For example, when you break apart an animated symbol, Flash discards all frames but the current frame and your symbol will no longer animate.

End

Task

10

Buttons and Actions

*B*uttons and actions make your Flash movie really come alive with interactivity. A button is a clickable "hot spot" that typically has four states: Up, Over, Down, and Hit. The actions that you assign to a button determine how the button functions.

Think of your Flash-animated Web site as a series of doors through which your Web visitors can pass. Each door leads down a specific path that you provide, and presents different material that your visitor can experience. Without buttons and actions in your Flash movies, your visitor follows one path. He or she moves through new doors only when you decide it is time to do so. This defeats the purpose of the Web's hyperlink functionality.

The beauty of a well-designed Web site is that visitors can follow whatever links they desire, and view the information according to their own whims. Buttons and actions provide users the freedom to open the doors that interest them, and to follow the paths that interest them when they so choose.

In theory, this is no different than providing hyperlinks in a traditional HTML-based Web page. However, Flash gives you the potential to present a wonderland of information in a way that is far more pleasing and effective than a traditional HTML Web page. Buttons and actions are critical pieces of the complete Flash picture. ●

How to Create Buttons

Buttons consist of four consecutive frames that represent the various states of the button: Up, Over, Down, and Hit. The Up state represents how the button looks before the user hovers over or clicks on it. The Over state represents how the button looks when the mouse hovers over it. The Down state represents how the button looks when the user clicks on the button. The Hit state defines the shape and size of the area that responds to mouse actions. This task discusses the construction of a new button.

Begin

1 Create a New Symbol

With nothing selected on the Stage, choose **Insert, New Symbol**. Alternatively, use the keyboard shortcut **Ctrl+F8** (Windows) or **Cmmd+F8** (Macintosh) to access the **Symbol Properties** dialog.

Click

2 Choose Button Behavior

In the **Symbol Properties** dialog, enter a name for the new button in the **Name** field. In the **Behavior** section, click to select the **Button** radio button. Choose **OK** to enter symbol-editing mode.

Click

Click

3 Create the Up State

Flash now switches to symbol-editing mode, and the name of your button appears on a tab above the Timeline. You see four frames marked **Up, Over, Down,** and **Hit,** with **Up** being the current frame. Use the drawing tools, import a graphic, or place an instance of another symbol on the Stage to create the button's Up state. Two layers are used in the example shown: one for the shape and one for the text.

4 Create the Over State

Click on the **Over** state tab in the Timeline, and choose **Insert, Keyframe**, or press **F6** to create a keyframe on each layer that you want to repeat in the Over frame. Modify or change the button artwork so that the Over state is different from the Up state; for example, change the color. The keyframe in Layer 2 copies the white text into the Over state.

Click

5 Define the Down and Hit States

In a similar manner, repeat step 4 for the Down and Hit states. In the example shown here, the background of the button remains blue in the Down state, but the text changes to yellow. The keyframe in Layer 1 of the Hit state copies the button background to define the active button area.

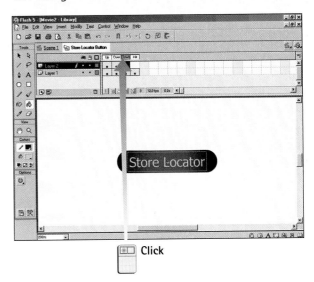

Click

6 Use the New Button

When your button artwork is complete, choose **Edit, Edit Movie**, or click on the **Scene 1** tab to return to normal editing mode. Choose **Window, Library** to open your movie library, and drag an instance of the new button onto the Stage.

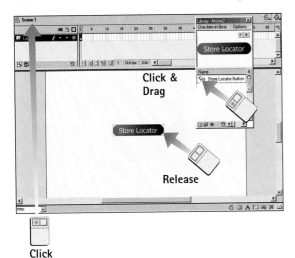

Click & Drag

Release

Click

How-To Hints

The Hit State

The Hit state of a button defines the area that responds to the mouse click. The artwork that you place in the Hit state is invisible in your movie. Just make sure that the artwork on the Hit state is a solid area that covers the area you want to respond to the mouse click. It does not have to be the exact size of the button. In fact, if your button is very small, you might want to make the Hit state larger.

Nudging the Down State

To make a button appear as though it is pressed down as the user clicks it, in the Down state, use the arrow keys on the keyboard to nudge the button down and to the right by a few pixels.

End

How to Enable, Select, and Test Buttons

Now that you have defined the various states of the button, you should test to make sure that the button states work as intended. Normally, you should disable buttons while you are working on your animation so that you can select them, move them, and so on. Enable your buttons when you want the buttons to react to your mouse movements as they would in the final animation. This task shows how to make sure the visible behavior of the button works according to your design.

Begin

1 Select a Disabled Button

A button acts like any other instance on the Stage until you enable it. To select a button, click on it with the Arrow tool, or drag a selection box around the button to select it.

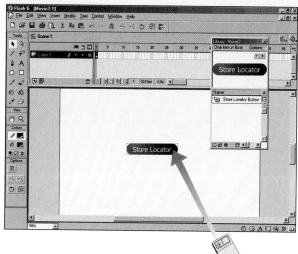

Click

2 Enable Button Behavior

To test the states of the button and to make sure that it acts as you expect, you need to enable button actions. Choose **Control, Enable Simple Buttons**. A check mark appears next to this option when button actions are enabled. Alternatively, use the keyboard shortcut **Ctrl+Alt+B** (Windows) or **Cmmd+Opt+B** (Macintosh).

Click

3 Select an Enabled Button

If you click on a button while button actions are enabled, it will respond by changing to the Down state that you created. To select a button while the **Enable Simple Buttons** option is on, you must use the Arrow tool to draw a selection area around the button. You can then move the button by using the arrow keys on your keyboard.

Click & Drag

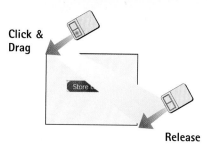

Release

4 Test a Button

While the **Enable Simple Buttons** option is on, you can verify that your button artwork is correct. The Up state displays on the Stage as long as the mouse does not hover over or click on the button. Next, hover the mouse over the button to verify that the **Over** artwork is correct. Click on the button to verify that the **Down** artwork is correct, as shown in this example.

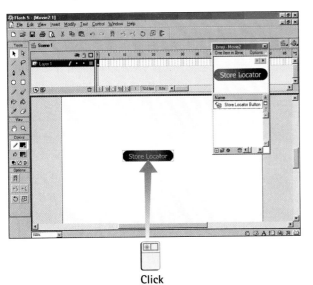

Click

5 Disable Buttons

After you verify the behavior of the button, switch back to Buttons Disabled mode. To do this, repeat the **Control, Enable Simple Buttons** command, or type the keyboard shortcut **Ctrl+Alt+B** (Windows) or **Cmmd+Opt+B** (Macintosh). The check mark disappears when the buttons are disabled.

Click

End

How-To Hints

To Enable or Not to Enable

Most of the time, you will find it much easier and more practical to work with your buttons disabled. After you verify that the buttons behave as intended, there is no need to keep the **Enable Simple Buttons** option on. In fact, doing so can quickly become quite distracting.

As you add actions to buttons, this becomes even more of an issue. When you click on a button that is enabled, Flash executes the action that you assigned to the button. This can lead to much confusion and aggravation as you work on your movie. It is much more practical to design your project while buttons are disabled. Enable them when you want to test operation.

How to Assign Actions to Buttons

Buttons become very useful when you assign actions to them. Actions can quickly become complex, but this introduction to actions remains relatively basic. This task shows an example of a movie that uses buttons to jump to different frames. As an example, we've created a movie that shows an example of how to build a burger in five steps. Each step is five frames long, with a Stop action appearing in the last frame of each step. Each step also includes a button that jumps to the first frame of the next step. Even though you don't have this exact movie to follow along with, you can apply the task to any movie.

Begin

1 Add Stop Actions to Frames

By default, a movie plays through all frames and then it loops continuously. But, in our example, we need to stop the movie on frame 5 so that the viewer can use the button to jump to frame 6. Notice that the Timeline includes an Actions layer that displays a small "a" in frames 5, 10, 15, 20, and 21. In each of these frames, an action stops the movie. Refer to Part 8, "Frames and Keyframes," and add Stop actions to the appropriate frames.

Add Stop actions to frames 5, 10, 15, 20, and 21

2 Open the Instance Panel

Choose **Control, Enable Simple Buttons** to turn off (uncheck) the option. Then click on the button to which you want to assign the action (in this example, the button on frames 16 through 20), and choose **Modify, Instance**.

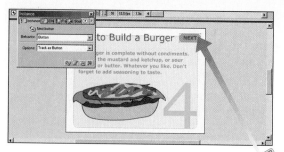

Click

3 Open the Object Actions Panel

To open the **Object Actions** panel, click on the **Edit Actions** button, located at the bottom-right corner of the **Instance** panel.

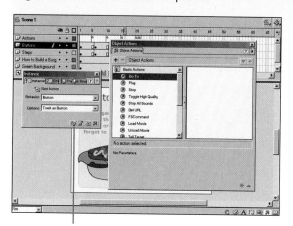

Edit Actions button

4 Choose the Desired Action

Click on the + (plus sign) button in the Object Actions panel. Then, click on Basic Actions to expand the menu, and click on Go To for the action. Alternatively, expand the Basic Actions list in the left section of the panel and double-click on Go To (you can see these items in the preceding figure). Initial properties appear at the bottom of the panel and in the script window.

Click

5 Specify the Go To Destination

Notice that the first line in the script reads on (release) {. This causes the action to occur when the user releases the mouse button *after* he or she clicks on the button. The second line reads gotoAndPlay(1);. By default, Go To actions jump to the first frame and play the animation. To change this value to frame 21, enter 21 in the Frame field located at the bottom of the panel. The second line in the script should now read gotoAndPlay(21);. Click on the X in the upper-right corner of the Object Actions panel to close it.

Script

6 Test the Button

Repeat steps 3 through 5 to configure the remaining buttons. To test the buttons, choose Control, Test Movie. When you click on the button in the fourth step of the movie, you jump to the fifth step of the movie, shown here.

How to Build a Burger

Complete your burger with the top of your sesame seed bun .... and enjoy!!!

5

End

How-To Hints

Getting Fancy with Actions

You can fine-tune your actions to achieve the exact results you want. Experiment with the different parameters for not only the action itself, but also for the event that triggers the action. Click on the on (release) { line of the script shown in step 5 to see other mouse actions that can trigger events. Experiment with your buttons, and note how the button behavior changes when you fine-tune button actions.

How to Make a Button Jump to a New Scene

Jumping to another frame of your movie is just the beginning of the fun. Actions assigned to buttons serve many purposes that are more far-reaching. This task teaches you how to assign an action to a button that causes the movie to jump to a completely different scene. In this case, the project is similar to the one shown in the previous task. The only difference is that each step of the "burger building" movie now appears in a different scene in the movie. To learn more about using scenes, refer to Part 11, "Using Scenes."

Begin

1 Select the Button

First, choose **Window, Panels, Scene** to display the **Scene** panel. This enables you to jump quickly from scene to scene in your movie. Select Scene 4, for example. With the **Control, Enable Simple Buttons** option turned off, click on the button in Scene 4 to select it.

Click

2 Open the Object Actions Panel

Choose **Modify, Instance** to open the **Instance** panel. Then click on the **Edit Actions** button, located at the bottom-right corner of the **Instance** panel. The **Object Actions** panel appears.

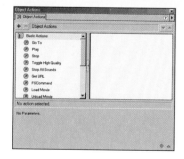

3 Add to the Go To Action

Click to expand the **Basic Actions** list in the left section of the panel, and then double-click on **Go To** to select the action. Initial properties appear at the bottom of the panel and in the script window.

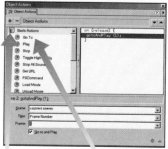

Click   Double-click

4 Specify the Go To Destination

Click on the **Scene** drop-down arrow to expand the menu selection. Among the several choices are **<previous scene>** and **<next scene>**, the latter of which you can certainly use in this example. In movies that are more complex, you can specify the scene number by selecting it from the bottom of the drop-down list. Here, we choose **Scene 5** from the list. Leave the **Type** field set at its default of **Frame Number**, and verify that the **Frame** field displays **1**. Close the **Object Actions panel.**

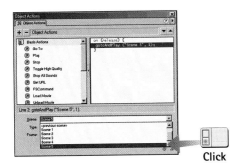

Click

5 Test the Button and Its Actions

Repeat steps 2 through 4 to configure the remaining buttons in your movie. To test the buttons, choose **Control, Test Movie.** When you click on the button in the fourth scene of the burger-building movie, you jump to the fifth scene (shown here).

End

How-To Hints

Make Sure That Your Movie Contains the Scenes!

If you're following along with these instructions as you work with your own Flash movie, make sure that the scene that you are jumping to exists in your movie. If you don't see the scene in the **Scene** drop-down list, exit the **Object Actions** panel and create the new scene. The new scene will appear in the **Scene** drop-down the next time you open the **Object Actions** panel.

Be More Specific

You can be more specific when you jump to another scene. Use the **Frame Number** field discussed in step 4 to specify a frame other than the first frame in the target scene. This enables you to hone in on the exact spot anywhere in your movie when you create a **Go To** action.

Go To and Stop

By default, the Go To action enables the **Go to and Play** option that appears at the bottom of the **Object Actions** panel in step 3. To go to a scene and stop the movie at that scene, uncheck the **Go to and Play** option.

How to Create a Button That Jumps to a URL

As you build your Flash-enhanced Web site, you will eventually need to provide hyperlinks to other Web pages, either within your own Web site or to other pages on an intranet or on the Internet. In such cases, you need to configure your button to jump to a specific URL. For example, the **Press Releases, Product News,** and **Customer Views** buttons shown in the examples that follow can link to appropriate Web pages on your site. The following task explains how to configure a button for this purpose.

Begin

1 Add Buttons to the Stage

Develop your buttons as outlined in Task 1. Then, choose **Window, Library** to open the movie's Library. Drag your buttons from the Library and drop instances of the buttons on the Stage. Three buttons appear in this example.

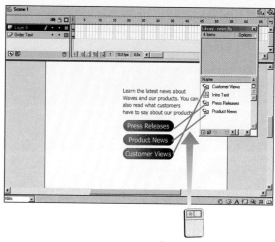

Drag & Drop

2 Access the Object Actions Panel

With the **Control, Enable Simple Buttons** option off, click on the button that you want to change. Choose **Modify, Instance** to open the **Instance** panel. Then click on the **Edit Actions** button, located at the bottom-right corner of the **Instance** panel. The **Object Actions** panel appears.

3 Choose the Get URL Command

Click to expand the **Basic Actions** list in the left section of the panel, and then double-click on **Get URL** to select the action. Initial properties appear at the bottom of the panel and in the script window.

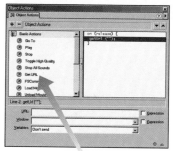

Double-click

4 Specify the URL to Go To

In the **URL** field at the bottom of the **Object Actions** panel, enter the absolute or relative URL to which you are linking. In the example shown here, the button jumps to a page named **product-news.html,** which is located in the same Web folder as the Flash movie. Notice that the URL also appears in the script at the right side of the panel.

5 Specify How the Web Page Opens

Click on the **Window** drop-down list to choose how you want the browser to load the target URL. For example, choose **_blank** to open the specified Web page in a new browser window. If you leave the **Window** field blank, the new URL will load in the same browser window. Close the **Object Actions** panel to assign the action to the button.

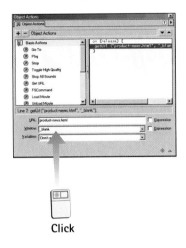

Click

End

How-To Hints

Handling Variables

The **Object Actions** panel also includes a **Variables** option, shown in the figure in step 5. Variables are used in advanced scripting and in creating interactive forms, which are beyond the scope of this book. In this simple example, there are no variables to send. Therefore, keep the default option of **Don't Send** from the **Variables** drop-down list.

Creating a Button That Sends Email

You can also use the **Go to URL** command to create a button that sends email to a valid email address. Follow the procedures outlined in this task to create the button. When you enter the URL in step 4, type **mailto:** followed by the email address to which you want to direct the mail (for example: **mailto:myemail@myprovider.com**).

How to Load One Movie into Another

Flash movies can become quite large. In fact, if your Flash movie is larger than 300KB, you might want to split it into multiple sections and use buttons to load additional movies that the user selects. Although the Flash Player typically plays one movie at a time, the **Load Movie** command can be used to "superimpose" one movie on top of another. This makes it possible to break your movies into smaller, more manageable sections that load much faster. You learn this technique in the following task, which loads one movie for common navigation and symbols, and plays movies that display related content when the user clicks on a button.

Begin

1 Create the Container Movie

Create a movie that includes the common elements that appear in all the movies, such as the navigation buttons in this example. This is referred to as a *container movie*. Our example is named start.fla and it publishes a Web page and animation named start.html and start.swf, respectively. The resulting Flash movie is only 5KB in size, making it very quick to load.

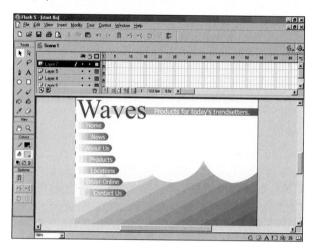

2 Develop Additional Movies

Develop additional movies that will be superimposed over the container movie when the buttons are selected. Here, six additional movies are made: one each for **Home**, **News**, **About Us**, **Products** (shown here), **Locations**, **Order Online**, and **Contact Us**.

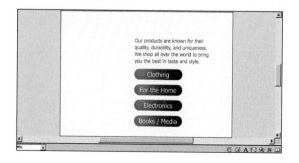

3 Configure the Container Movie

Open the container movie (in our example, start.fla) for editing. Click on one of the buttons to select it for editing (such as the **Products** button shown here). Then, immediately right-click (Ctrl+click on the Macintosh) on the same button to gain quick access to the **Object Actions** panel.

4 Choose the LoadMovie Option

Click to expand the **Basic Actions** list in the left section of the panel, and then double-click on **LoadMovie** to select the action. Initial properties appear at the bottom of the panel and in the script window.

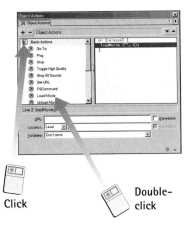

Click

Double-click

5 Set the URL for the New Movie

In the **URL** parameter field, type the URL of the movie you want to load (**products.swf**, as shown in this example). For location, select **Level** from the drop-down, and enter 1 in the adjacent field. This loads the new movie one level, or layer, higher than the container movie. Leave the **Variables** option set at its default setting of **Don't send.** Then close the **Object Actions** panel to assign the settings.

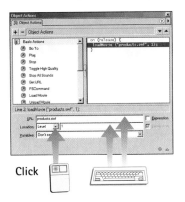

Click

6 Test Your Container Movie

After you configure the remaining buttons as outlined in steps 3 through 5, publish all the movies using the same publish settings. Choose the **Control, Test Movie** command to test your movies. Alternatively, use your Web browser to open the HTML page that contains the container movie. Click on each button to verify that all movies load properly, and are attractively positioned within the container movie.

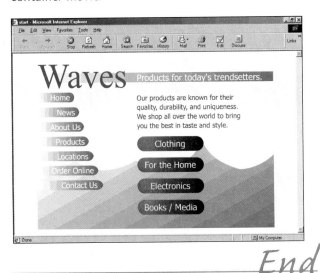

How-To Hints

Great Byte Savings!

Although this is a very simple example of how to superimpose movies, it illustrates a very important technique. Building all these screens as scenes in the same movie results in a Flash movie of 27KB or more in size. By loading the individual movies separately, the worst-case scenario drops to a tiny 9KB (5KB for the container, and 4KB for the superimposed movie). Your visitors will enjoy pages that download much faster.

About Movie Levels

In step 5, you configured the new movie to load in Level 1. Your container movie is placed on Level 0. By specifying Level 1 for the new movie, you place it one level or layer higher than the container movie so that it appears over it. You can also load additional movies over these, and assign them higher level numbers. The highest number appears at the top.

End

How to Play and Stop Movies

Now that you are becoming familiar with buttons and actions, creating buttons to start and stop your movies will be easy. The following task modifies the Spotlight Mask.fla movie that was installed with your Flash product. The example adds two buttons to this movie: one button starts the movie, and the other stops the movie.

Begin

1 Create Play and Stop Buttons

Use the **Insert, New Symbol** command to create **Play** and **Stop** buttons for the Spotlight Mask movie, using the steps outlined in Task 1. Label one button **Play** and the other **Stop**. Create a new layer in the movie, and in the first frame place one button on each side of the Stage as shown here.

Play button   Stop button

2 Assign the Play Action

Click on the **Play** button to select it. Then immediately right-click (**Ctrl**+click on the Macintosh) on the button and choose **Actions** from the menu that appears. Expand the **Basic Actions** list on the left side of the **Object Actions** panel. Then, double-click on **Play** in the options list to assign this action to the button. Because there are no additional parameters to assign to this button, close the **Object Actions** panel to assign the action to the button.

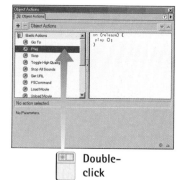

Double-click

3 Assign the Stop Action

Click on the **Stop** button to select it. Use the same procedure outlined in step 2 to assign the **Stop** action to this button. Close the **Object Actions** panel to assign the action to the button.

Double-click

4 Add a Frame Stop Action

To prevent the movie from starting until the user selects the **Play** button, add a Stop action to the first frame of the movie. Refer to Part 8 for a review of how to assign actions to frames.

Add Stop action to first frame

5 Test the Buttons

Choose **Control, Test Movie.** Click on the **Play** button to start the movie. Click on the **Stop** button to discontinue playback.

End

How-To Hints

Basic Navigation

Play and **Stop** buttons are probably the easiest buttons to understand because the actions they perform are self-explanatory—the Play action plays a movie, and the Stop action stops it. Unlike the other actions you learned about in this section, the Play and Stop actions do not require any additional work to add parameters. It doesn't get any easier than that!

How to Edit Actions

As you make more use of buttons and actions, you sometimes realize that the first action you use does not achieve the desired result. You can easily edit your frame actions. This task shows some of the basic edits that are possible.

Begin

1 Open the Object Actions Panel

Click on the button that you want to edit, and then right-click (**Ctrl**+click on the Macintosh) to choose **Actions** from the menu that appears. The **Object Actions** panel appears, and the existing parameter settings appear in the panel.

2 Change or Add Button Events

You can assign more than one event to trigger a button's action. To add or change the event that triggers an action, highlight the line that begins with **on (**. This displays a menu of events that can trigger an action. Check one or more options in the list. In the example shown here, check the **Key Press** event to add this action to the event list, and enter **P** in the appropriate field. Now, the user can play the movie in two ways: by pressing the **Play** button and by entering **P** on the keyboard.

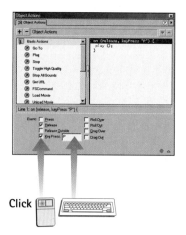

Click

3 Add One or More Actions

You can also assign more than one action to a button. To add another action, highlight the action that already appears in the action script, and double-click on another action in the **Object Actions** list. The example shown here adds the **Toggle High Quality** action to the list. Now, when the movie plays, it plays in the highest quality possible.

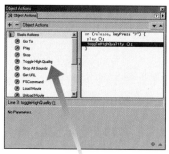

Double-click

4 Changing the Order of Actions

When you assign multiple actions to a button, you might find that the actions occur in the wrong order. If you need to change the order of the actions, it is easy to rearrange them. First, click to highlight the action that you want to move in the script. Then, click on the **Up-arrow** or **Down-arrow** button to shuffle that action to a new position in the list.

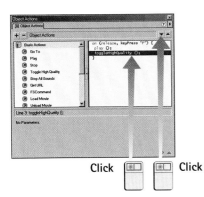

Click   Click

5 Adjust an Action's Parameters

Sometimes you'll discover that although an action in your list is correct, you incorrectly entered the action parameters. Highlight the action that you want to change, and edit the parameters as necessary. In the example shown here, the URL is changed to products.html and the **Window** drop-down menu displays additional choices to select.

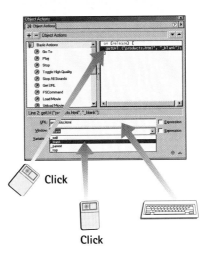

Click

Click

End

How-To Hints

Experiment with Actions

This discussion of actions only scratches the surface of their true potential for making Flash movies with complex functionality. Because you can edit actions so easily, you should feel free to experiment with all different types and combinations of actions, action orders, and parameters. If you make a decision that turns out to cause problems, edit the action until you achieve the desired results. The best way to learn the true potential of actions is to begin using them. Don't be afraid of them. They are not carved in stone. You can turn back if you need to!

Task

Using Scenes

n Hollywood, moviemakers break their movies into sections, called *scenes*. The content of each of these sections tells a piece of the overall story. By itself, an individual scene—although perhaps entertaining—does not give the viewer a complete picture of the movie as a whole. Stitched together one after another in a logical sequence, each scene plays its part in building the whole story.

Just as in your favorite Hollywood blockbuster, your Flash movies can contain scenes. You typically use scenes to organize your Flash content into small pieces with related subject material. For instance, you might use one scene for a Web site's home page, one for the products section, one for the news section, and so on.

By default, scenes in your Flash project play one after another according to the order in which they appear in the **Scene** panel (discussed fully here in Task 3). However, buttons and actions (described in Part 10) open up all kinds of possibilities for nonlinear navigation of your movie.

Using scenes can be a good idea because they help to divide your movie into more manageable sections. Nevertheless, there might be times when it is best not to use them. You might find that you simply prefer to organize your movie within one single scene. If your movie contains a large amount of information (for example, an extensive Web site), it might be more efficient to use separate movies instead of one movie with several scenes. Breaking large movies into scenes does not make the movie take less disk space, or necessarily play more efficiently. It really is mostly a matter of organizing your work.

How to Organize with Scenes

You can use scenes in any type of Flash movie. To determine whether you should use scenes in your movie, and how to use them, it helps to organize your thoughts and make an outline or storyboard of the movie. This task suggests one such process. Use this systematically, or use it as a guide toward building the process that works best for you.

Begin

1 State Your Movie's Overall Goals

Every Flash project starts with an organized plan. It helps to write your overarching goals for the movie. To begin, determine what you hope to accomplish with the movie you create. Assume, for example, that you want to create a site that includes an online store.

> Goal: Design an Easy-to-use interface for an online store

2 Construct a Rough Outline

After you define your goals, break them down into manageable chunks. Create an outline of the sections that are necessary to provide all the information that you want to impart. For instance, you need a home page for your store's site. Then you need sections such as News, Products, Contacts, and so forth. Plan to let these sections represent the scenes you use to organize your Flash movie.

> Goal: Design an Easy-to-use interface for an online store
>
> Scene 1 - Home Page
> Scene 2 - News
> Scene 3 - About the Store
> Scene 4 - Products
> Scene 5 - Locations
> Scene 6 - Order Online

3 Expand the Rough Outline

Now that you have the scenes generally mapped out, you must begin planning the details. If scene one represents your home page, you must make choices about what information needs to be present on that page. As a minimum, you need a button to take the user to each of the topics present in your rough outline. You must begin to make operational decisions, such as whether to use the same navigation bar in each scene, or create something new each time.

> Goal: Design an Easy-to-use interface for an online store
>
> Scene 1 - Home Page
>   Create an intro animation, 30 seconds or less
> Scene 2 - News
>   Create links to Press Release, Product News and
>   Customer Feedback pages
> Scene 3 - About the Store
>   Need links to info about founders and mission
> Scene 4 - Products
>   Link to products pages - Clothing, Books and Media,
>   For the Home, and Electronics
> Scene 5 - Locations
>   Link to Store Locator (online database)
> Scene 6 - Order Online
>   Link to Online Store

4 Create the New Scenes

You can proceed in one of two ways at this point. You can create the first scene and all the artwork in it before you add other scenes. Or, you can immediately assign names for all the scenes, and develop the artwork for each scene after you assign the names. Using the second method, your Flash project contains the basic scene structure from the beginning. Experiment with the working style that best suits you.

5 Construct the Scene Contents

Based on the details that you outlined in step 3, assemble each scene. Create artwork for the buttons that must appear. Position any required text fields. Place the artwork you want to use. Your scenes really begin to take shape at this point.

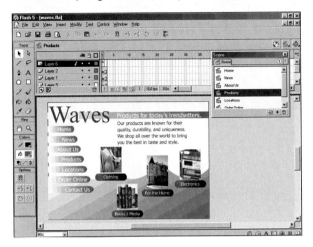

6 Add Actions to Build Functionality

After you add all your buttons, text, and artwork to all your scenes, your Web site is almost ready. Now you must construct the actions that provide the interactivity needed for the viewer to navigate from one scene to the next. Add buttons, assign actions to frames, or both to provide that interactivity.

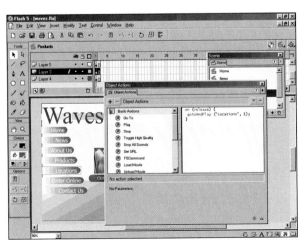

7 Test Your Movie

As a final step, choose **Control, Test Movie** to test the functionality of all your buttons and frame scripts. Verify that all the scenes perform as expected, and that the movie accomplishes the goals you defined in step 1.

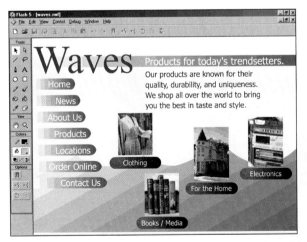

End

How to Add, Navigate Between, and Remove Scenes

Two basic methods exist to add a new scene, remove a scene, and navigate between existing scenes during the development process. When you add a new scene, Flash presents you with a fresh Timeline and Stage—a clean slate. Because scenes are independent from each other, one scene might have four layers, even though another scene contains only two layers. This task explores the add, remove, and navigation techniques for scenes.

Begin

1 Add a Scene with the Insert Menu

Notice that when you open a new movie, it contains one scene by default. Directly above the Timeline, the scene identifier shows the name of the current scene. In this case, the scene is named Scene 1. To add another scene, choose **Insert, Scene.** A new scene appears, as indicated by the change in the label to Scene 2 and the empty Stage and Timeline.

 Click

2 Add a Scene from the Scene Panel

You can also use the **Scene** panel to add a new scene. To do so, choose **Window, Panels, Scene.** The **Scene** panel opens. On the panel, click on the **Add Scene** button.

Click

3 Use the Edit Scene Button

The **Edit Scene** button sits at the top-right corner of the Flash window, just to the left of the **Edit Symbols** button. This button accesses a drop-down list of all the scenes currently in your movie. To navigate to the desired scene, click on the **Edit Scene** button. From the drop-down list, click on the name of the scene to which you want to navigate.

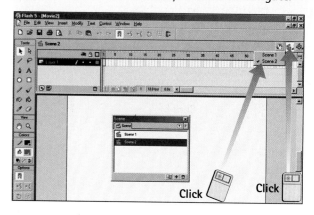
Click   Click

4 Use the Scene Panel to Navigate

To navigate to another scene using the **Scene** panel, choose **Window, Panels, Scene**. The **Scene** panel opens, and displays a list of all the scenes in the current movie. From the list of scenes, click on the name of the desired scene to activate it.

Click

5 Remove a Scene (Method 1)

To remove a scene using the **Insert** menu, choose **Insert, Remove Scene**. An alert box asks you to confirm that you really want to permanently remove the scene. Click on **OK** to complete the operation. The scene is removed.

Click

6 Remove a Scene (Method 2)

To remove a scene by using the **Scene** panel, choose **Window, Panels, Scene** to open the **Scene** panel. From the list in the panel, choose the name of the scene you want to remove from the movie. Click on the **Delete Scene** button. An alert box warns you that the operation cannot be undone. Click on **OK** to complete the operation.

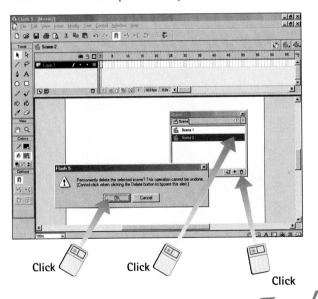
Click   Click   Click

How-To Hints

The Scene Panel

The **Scene** panel serves as a convenient tool for working with the scenes in your movie. Although we discuss some of its functions and capabilities here, the next task fully explores the **Scene** panel.

Back Up Your Scenes

You might have noticed that after you delete a scene, it's gone forever. Before you delete that scene, it is a good idea to save a backup copy of your project. To create a backup copy of your project, choose **File, Save As.** Use the **Save As** dialog to locate the drive and folder to which you want to save the file, and then enter a new name for your backup copy. Click **Save** to save the backup copy.

End

How to Use the Scene Panel

As the previous task shows, the **Scene** panel provides a convenient tool for managing the scenes in your movie. It enables you to quickly add, navigate to, remove, and reorder your scenes. It also provides a list of the scenes you have added to your project, and gives you quick access to scene-related help topics. In this task, we look at all the functions of the **Scene** panel.

Begin

1 Duplicate a Scene

You can duplicate a scene to use as a template, or starting point for another scene, thereby saving yourself the work of re-creating elements that are essentially the same from scene to scene. To duplicate a scene, choose **Window, Panels, Scene**, and click on the name of the scene you want to duplicate from the list. Now click on the **Duplicate Scene** button. An exact replica of the scene appears on the list as a new scene.

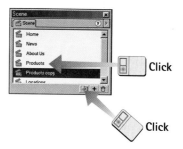

Click

Click

2 Add a New Scene

To add a new scene to your movie by using the **Scene** panel, choose **Window, Panels, Scene**. In the **Scene** panel, click on the **Add Scene** button.

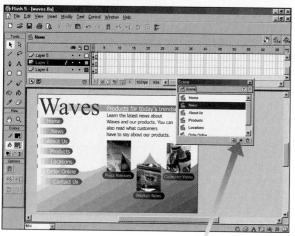

 Click

3 Remove a Scene

If you decide that a scene is not required in your movie, you can easily remove it. Choose **Window, Panels, Scene,** and in the **Scene** panel, click on the name of the scene you want to remove. Click on the **Delete Scene** button. An alert box appears to warn you that this action is permanent, and cannot be undone. Click on **OK** to remove the scene from the movie, and its name from the scene list.

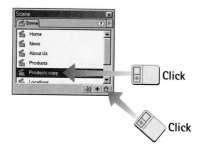

Click

Click

4 Reorder the Scenes in Your Movie

The scenes in your movie play in a linear fashion unless you add actions to control the playback order. You can easily reorder the scenes in your movie with the **Scene** panel. To do so, click on the name of the scene you want to move, and drag it to its new location in the scene list.

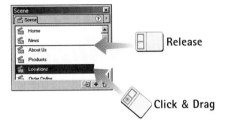

Release

Click & Drag

5 Rename a Scene

To rename a scene in your movie, double-click on the scene's name in the **Scene** panel's scene list. A text field appears with the current name of the scene highlighted. Type to remove the old name while adding the new name. If you want to modify only certain parts of the original name, click on the scene's name a third time before typing to place your insertion point. Use the **Delete** or **Backspace** key to remove unwanted letters, and type in the new ones. Press the **Enter** key when you are finished.

6 Access Scene-Related Help

To access help topics related specifically to scenes, click on the **Help** button (the circle with a question mark) on the top right of the **Scene** panel. Flash help opens, and presents you with a number of scene-related help topics.

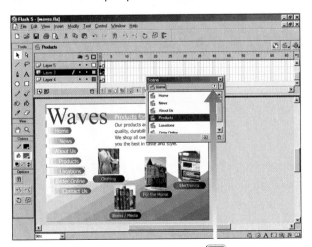

Click

7 Close the Scene Panel

To close the **Scene** panel, click on the **Close** button at the top right of the window. Alternatively, choose **Window, Panels, Scene**.

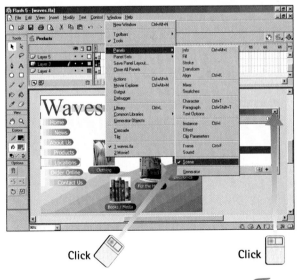

Click

Click

End

Task

PART *12*

Animation

*T*raditional animation techniques require a lot of time because the artist has to draw each frame individually. In Flash, you can animate one frame at a time to create subtle and complex animations, but you don't have to.

Flash helps you create impressive animations, without drawing each frame individually, using a technique called *tweening*. Tweening enables you to create complex animations in a fraction of the time required by the traditional method. Tweened animations also result in a smaller file size because Flash stores only the values for the actual changes between frames, not the complete set of values for every frame as with frame-by-frame animation.

When you create a tweened animation, you draw the artwork for the first frame in the sequence. You add a keyframe later in the Timeline that holds the artwork for the final frame of the animation sequence. Through the magic of tweening, Flash generates all the frames *in between* the first and last frames, regardless of how many frames exist between the two. That is the meaning of the term *tween*.

There are two types of tweens, each of which serves a different animation purpose. A *Motion Tween* enables you to change certain properties of a symbol instance (such as its size, color effect, rotation, or position on the Stage). A *Shape Tween* enables you to transform one shape to another. In this part, we take a close look at Flash's capability to help you create tweened animations. ●

How to Move an Object with Motion Tweening

In the most basic tweened animation, you move an object along a straight path from one position on the Stage to another over a range of frames. Motion Tween can be used with text, symbols, instances, or a single group of objects. This task shows how to scroll a line of text from the left of the Stage into the center of the Stage. The text pauses for a while, and then moves off the right side of the Stage at the end. You can apply the same techniques to any symbol in your movie library.

Begin

1 Add an Instance

Create a symbol of a line of text and add a layer named Text. Click on the **Show Library** button on the **Quick Launch Bar** to open the library. Drag the text symbol onto the work area to the left of the **Stage** in the first frame of the Text layer. Click inside the **Timeline** at frame 50, and press **F5**. You now have 50 frames in the **Timeline**, so your animation will be 50 frames long.

Click, and then press F5 on keyboard

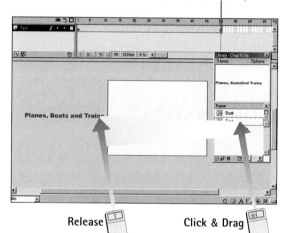

Release   Click & Drag

2 Create the Ending Keyframe

Click in the Timeline at the frame that represents where you want the scrolling text to pause (frame 20, in this example). Choose **Insert, Keyframe** or press **F6** on your keyboard to add a keyframe at this location. Notice that the frame that precedes this new keyframe contains a rectangular box, which identifies the frames between the two keyframes as *static frames* that contain no moving elements.

Click, and then press F6 on Keyboard

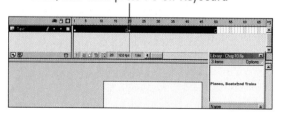

3 Move the Ending Keyframe's Text

Click to select the frame that contains the ending keyframe (frame 20 on the Text layer in this example). Then click and drag the object you want to move (the text symbol). Release the mouse when the object is in its new location.

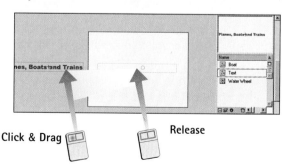

Click & Drag   Release

4 Transform into a Motion Tween

Right-click (**Ctrl+**click on the Macintosh) anywhere within the range of frames between the two keyframes, and choose **Create Motion Tween** from the menu that appears. The hollow, static rectangle disappears, and a solid arrow with blue background appears between the starting keyframe and the ending keyframe. If you click and drag the playhead (called *scrubbing*), you'll see the text move across the Stage. Congratulations, you have just created your first Motion Tween!

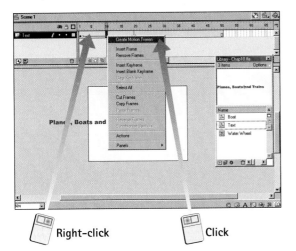

Right-click   Click

5 Add the Second Motion Tween

In this example, we want the text to pause until frame 30, where the second tween begins. The steps to create the second tween are similar to the first. Add keyframes at frames 30 and 50 for the start and end keyframes, respectively. With frame 50 active, move the text completely off the right side of the Stage. Finally, right-click any frame between frames 30 and 50, and choose **Create Motion Tween** from the menu that appears. Your second tween is complete.

Click, and then press F6 on keyboard

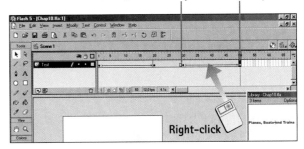

Right-click

6 Test Your Tweened Sequence

To make sure that your animation performs as you expect it to, click on the first frame of the sequence. Choose **Control, Test Movie** or press **Ctrl+Enter** (Windows) or **Cmmd+Enter** (Macintosh) to begin playback. If you completed the steps correctly, the object moves smoothly to the center of the Stage, pauses briefly, and then moves off the Stage.

Planes, Boats and Trains

How-To Hints

Moving the Tweened Frames

If you decide after creating the tweened sequence that it needs to occur at a different point on the Timeline, hover the mouse over it. When the arrow changes to the hand, click and drag the sequence to the desired location.

Animation Speed

When you create tweened sequences, keep in mind that you can control the speed at which the object moves from its start position to its end position. To do this, adjust the number of frames in the sequence. Fewer frames in the sequence result in a faster-moving object. Obviously, a longer tweened sequence creates a slower-moving animation. You can also adjust the speed of the animation by changing the movie frame rate. If you leave the number of frames constant, a higher frame rate results in a faster-moving animation.

End

How to Tween a Rotation

Now that you know how to create a basic Motion Tween, you can apply the same techniques to many other object properties. This task demonstrates how you create a tweened sequence that rotates an object on the Stage.

Begin

1 Create the First Keyframe

In the movie you animated in Task 1, click on the **Insert Layer (+)** button at the lower-left corner of the Timeline to create a new layer. Click again to create a second new layer. Name the first layer **Boat** and the second one **Water Wheel**. Create new artwork for these layers, and convert them to symbols. Click in frame 15 of each layer and choose **Insert, Keyframe** or press **F6** to create the starting keyframe. Initially, these keyframes are empty.

Click, and then press F6

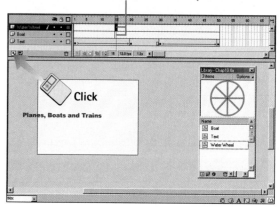

2 Add an Instance to the Stage

Click to select the keyframe in frame 15 of the Boat layer. Then drag an instance of the boat from the library onto the Stage. Finally, click and drag the last frame of the Boat layer from frame 50 to frame 35. Repeat these steps for the water wheel, placing it on frames 15 through 35 of its own layer.

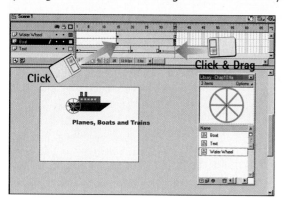

3 Create the Ending Keyframe

Click on the frame in the Timeline where you want your tweened sequence to end (in this case, frame 35 of the Water Wheel layer). Choose **Insert, Keyframe** or press **F6** to add a keyframe.

Click, and then press F6

4 Create the Tween

Right-click (**Ctrl**+click on the Macintosh) in the span of frames between the two keyframes in the Water Wheel layer, and choose **Create Motion Tween** from the menu that appears.

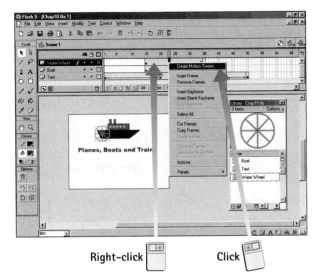

Right-click   Click

6 Test Your Tweened Sequence

Click on the first keyframe of your sequence, and choose **Control, Test Movie** to play the movie. Alternatively, press the **Ctrl+Enter** keys (Windows) or **Cmmd+Enter** (Macintosh) to begin playback. The boat appears between frames 15 and 35, while the water wheel rotates three times.

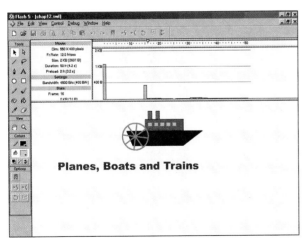

End

5 Add Rotation to the Object

Choose **Window, Panels, Frame** to open the **Frame** panel. From the **Rotate** drop-down, choose either **CW** for clockwise rotation (as in this example) or **CCW** to rotate counterclockwise. Double-click in the **times** text field, and enter the desired number of rotations (3 in this example). Press the **Tab** key to finalize the settings.

Click

How-To Hints

Rotating and Moving Simultaneously

This example shows how to create an object that rotates without changing positions on the Stage. To create an object that rotates while it moves from one position to another, combine the steps you learned in Task 1 with those you learned in this task. In fact, you can tween all the properties of an object during the same tweened sequence to achieve various effects.

None and Auto Options

When you expand the Rotate drop-down in the **Frame** panel, you also find **None** and **Auto** options. Use these options to define the behavior of an object that you rotate manually with the **Modify, Transform, Rotate** command while it moves to a new position on the Stage at the same time. Choose **Auto** to rotate the object from its start position to its end position over the course of the sequence. Choose **None** to move the object without rotating it. When the sequence reaches the last frame, the object immediately transforms to the rotated position.

How to Tween Scale

Tweening the scale of an object on the Stage helps to accomplish several animation effects. An object that grows equally in both the horizontal and vertical planes often appears to be flying toward the viewer. Adjust only the vertical measurement to give the illusion of an object growing taller, or adjust only the horizontal measurement to portray something growing fatter. This task shows how to tween size.

Begin

1 Create the Starting Keyframe

Click in the frame at which you want the animation to begin (frame 30 of a new Train layer, in this example). Choose **Insert, Keyframe** or use the keyboard shortcut **F6** to make the frame a keyframe. Click to make the keyframe the active frame, and click and drag an instance of a symbol (such as the train shown here) from the Library to the Stage.

Click, and then press F6

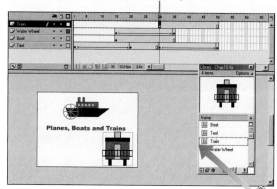

Click & Drag

2 Create the Ending Keyframe

Click on the frame in the Timeline that you want as the end of your tweened sequence. In the example shown here, the last frame in the Train layer ends the sequence. Choose **Insert, Keyframe** or press **F6** to add the ending keyframe.

Click, and then press F6

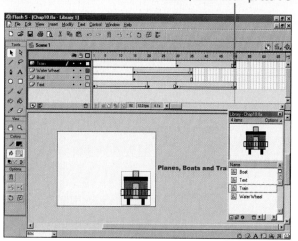

3 Scale the Object

Click to select the end keyframe on the appropriate layer. With the object that you want to scale selected, choose **Modify, Transform, Scale,** or press the **Scale** button in the toolbar. The object now contains several "handles." Click and drag a corner handle to scale an object uniformly. Click and drag the top or bottom handle to scale vertically. Click and drag a side handle to scale horizontally.

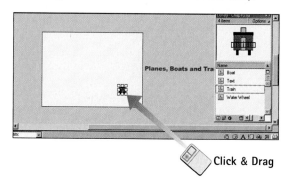

Click & Drag

4 Create the Tween

Right-click (**Ctrl**+click on the Macintosh) in the span of frames between the two keyframes, and choose **Create Motion Tween** from the menu that appears.

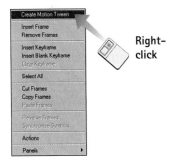

Right-click

5 Choose the Scaling Option

Click within the tweened sequence in the Timeline, and choose **Window, Panels, Frame**. The **Frame** panel enables you to view the parameters of the Motion Tween you created in step 4. For this task, check the **Scale** box to make the object grow gradually during the course of the tweened sequence. Uncheck this box to maintain the object at the same size until the movie enters the final frame of the sequence.

6 Test Your Tweened Sequence

Click on the first keyframe of your sequence, and choose **Control, Test Movie** to play the movie. Alternatively, press the **Ctrl+Enter** (Windows) or **Cmmd+Enter** (Macintosh) key on your keyboard to begin playback. In this example, the train appears in frame 30 and seems to move away as the movie continues.

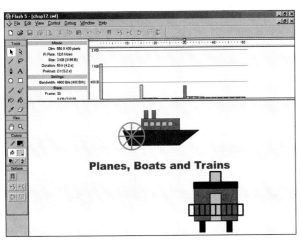

How-To Hints

Scaling and Rotating by Exact Values

Often you want to scale or rotate your object by using an exact value. Instead of choosing **Modify, Transform, Scale,** or **Modify, Transform, Rotate,** choose **Modify, Transform, Scale and Rotate.** This accesses a dialog in which you enter numerical values for these two operations, enabling you to be consistent over time with different objects.

End

How to Tween Color

You can also create a tween sequence that changes the color of an object over the course of time. This task presents the steps necessary to achieve this effect. At the same time, you'll learn how to create more than one tween by using the same keyframes. Here, you'll change the color of the text as it scrolls off the end of the Stage.

Begin

1 Create the Starting Keyframe

If a keyframe does not already exist in the frame at which you want a tween to begin, use the steps outlined in previous tasks to add a keyframe and associated artwork. For this example, we'll use the keyframe that already exists at frame 30 of the Text layer.

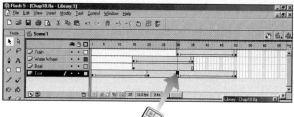

Click

2 Create the Ending Keyframe

Similarly, if a keyframe does not already exist in the frame at which you want the tween to end, click on the frame in the Timeline that you want as the end of your tweened sequence and add another keyframe as outlined in previous tasks. For this example, we will use the keyframe that already exists at frame 50 of the Text layer.

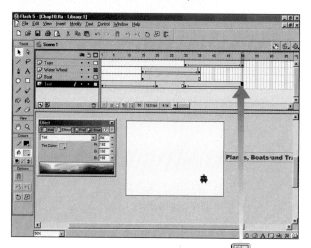

Click

3 Select Tint from the Effect Panel

Choose **Window, Panels, Effect** to open the **Effect** Panel. You can use the **Effect** Panel to change the color of the instance in the ending keyframe. Click to select the last keyframe of the sequence (frame 50 of the Text layer, in this case). From the drop-down list on the **Effect** panel, choose the color property you want to change. For this example, choose **Tint** from the list.

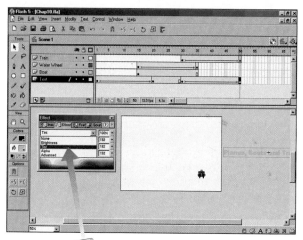

Click

4 Choose a New Instance Color

The **Tint** dialog provides several methods of choosing a new color for the instance. For example, click the **Tint Color** chooser box. Drag through the colors in the current palette, and release the mouse when you find a color you like. Use the **Percentage** slider at the right of the drop-down list to vary the amount of tint that is applied to the instance.

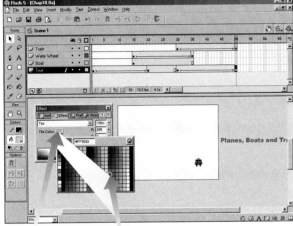

Click & Drag   Release

5 Create the Tween and Review it

In the example shown here, the existing Motion Tween changes color at the same time that the text moves across the screen. If a Motion Tween does not already exist, right-click (**Ctrl**+click on the Mac) in the span of frames between the beginning and ending keyframes. Choose **Create Motion Tween** from the menu that appears. Finally, click on the first keyframe of the sequence, and choose **Control, Play** or press **Enter** to view the tweened color change.

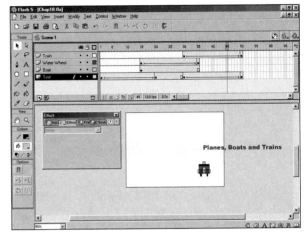

End

How-To Hints

Fading an Object In or Out

The steps to fade an object in or out are very similar to those you use to create a Color Tween. Follow the first two steps as outlined in the previous task. In step 3, choose **Alpha** from the drop-down list in the **Effect** panel. To create a fade-in, set the starting alpha value at 0% and the ending value at 100%. To create a fade-out, set the starting alpha value at 100% and the ending alpha value at 0%.

Using the Effect Panel

This task only scratches the surface of the power hidden within the **Effect** panel. Use the **Effect** panel to achieve many interesting and unique effects. In addition to the **Tint** and **Alpha** options that you learned about here, you can also tween the brightness of an object. Choose the **Advanced** option to tween any numerical combination of **Tint, Alpha,** and **Brightness.**

How to Move Objects Along a Path

In Task 1, you made a tween sequence in which an object moved along a straight line from one position to another. What if you don't want to move the object in a straight line? Flash provides a way for you to move the object along any path you want. This task explains how to accomplish this.

Begin

1 Create a Moving Object

Add an instance to the starting keyframe (in this example, frame 1 of the new Plane layer) and position it at the desired starting point on the Stage. Create a new keyframe at the ending frame (frame 20 of the Plane layer shown here) and move the instance to the desired ending position. Right-click in the range of frames between the first and last keyframe, and choose **Create Motion Tween**. Choose **Control, Play** to verify that you have correctly created the tween.

Start keyframe   Motion Tween   End keyframe

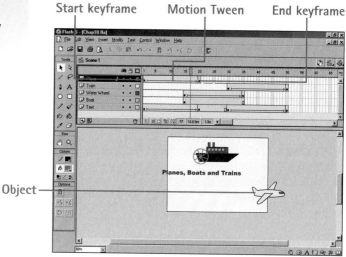

Object

2 Create a Motion Guide Layer

Make sure that the layer containing the tween you created in step 1 is selected. Choose **Insert, Motion Guide**. Flash creates a new layer that serves as the motion guide layer directly above the selected layer. Flash automatically names the layer Guide:*name* where *name* represents the name of the layer you clicked. Flash indents the original layer in the layers list to indicate that the Guide layer controls it.

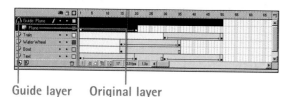

Guide layer   Original layer

3 Create the Motion Path

Click on the frame of the Guide layer that corresponds to the start of the tweened sequence. Use the Pen, Pencil, Line, Circle, Rectangle, or Brush tools to draw a motion path. For this example, the Pencil tool is used to draw a path that starts and ends at the desired positions on the Stage.

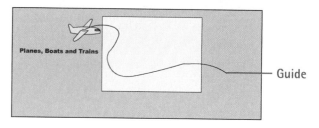

Guide

4 Snap the Object to the Path

Click on the start keyframe of the Motion Tween in the original object layer. Choose **Window, Panels, Frame,** and click in the **Snap** box if snapping is not already active. The registration (or center) point of the object snaps to the motion path automatically. To adjust the position, click the Arrow tool, then click and drag the object close to the beginning of the path. When you release the mouse button, the object snaps to the beginning of the path.

5 Snap to the End of the Path

Click in the ending keyframe of the object layer to select it. Next, click and drag the object to a location near the end of the motion path. The object's registration point should snap to the end of the path because you activated snapping in the last step.

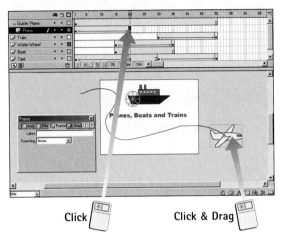

Click   Click & Drag

6 Lock and Hide the Motion Guide

To avoid inadvertently changing your motion guide, lock the Motion Guide layer by clicking on the dot under the **Lock** icon. To hide the motion guide so that it does not cause clutter on the Stage during editing, click on the black dot under the **Eye** icon. Choose **Control, Test Movie** to view your work.

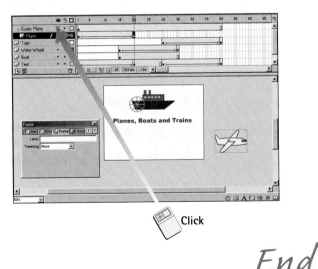

Click

End

How-To Hints

Orienting Your Object to the Path

To *orient the object to the motion path* means that the object's baseline shifts so that it always remains parallel to the motion path. In the case of the example shown in the previous task, this option would cause the plane to bank up and down as it moves along the path. To achieve this effect, click the **Orient to Path** box in the **Frame** panel.

Control Multiple Layers with One Guide

You can use one motion path to control objects on several different layers by dragging them directly underneath the Guide layer. After a layer is under the influence of a guide, you can reorder it with the other layers under the guide's influence. To remove a layer from the influence of a guide, drag it above the Guide layer and then reorder it appropriately.

How to Tween Shapes

Up to this point, our discussion has focused on how to create Motion Tweens. Flash also uses another type of tween that greatly aids you in developing animations. The *Shape Tween* enables you to "morph" one shape into another, and provides for some very interesting animation effects. Unlike Motion Tweens, which require instances, you can only Shape Tween non-symbols. This task shows you how to use Shape Tweens to change one shape into another.

Begin

1 Create the Beginning Artwork

Like Motion Tweens, Shape Tweens must start and end on keyframes. Choose or create a keyframe to use as the starting point of the tween sequence. Use any of the drawing tools to create an object on the Stage. We'll keep it simple for this example and use a red cross, with a small hole in its center, to represent the starting shape for the tween.

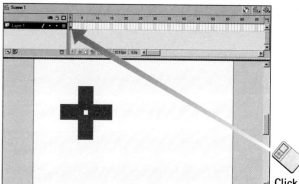

Click

2 Create the Ending Artwork

Click in the desired end frame (frame 30 in the example), and choose **Insert, Blank Keyframe** or use the keyboard shortcut **F7**. This creates a keyframe that contains no artwork. Use the drawing tools to create the desired artwork. The red square with the white center shown here represents the shape that the starting shape transforms into at the end of the animation sequence.

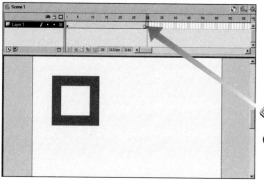

Click

Click

3 Create the Shape Tween

Now that you have the starting and ending artwork, you can use a Shape Tween to fill in the intermediary steps of the animation. Click on the first keyframe in the Timeline sequence to select it. If the **Frame** panel is not already active, choose **Window, Panels, Frame** to open it. Choose **Shape** from the **Tweening** drop-down list. The familiar solid arrow appears over a light green color to show that the tween is a Shape Tween.

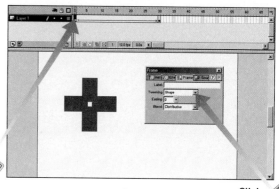

Click

4 Make Choices for Easing

The **Easing** text field and slider enables you to control the acceleration of the tween. Enter a positive value (from 1 to 100) to slow the animation down as it gets closer to the end of the sequence. Enter a negative value (from –1 to –100) to speed up the animation as it draws nearer the end. You can also click on the drop-down arrow next to the **Easing** text field to adjust the setting with a slider.

5 Make a Blend Choice

Two blend options enable you to control the Shape Tween. From the **Blend** drop-down, choose **Distributive** to create an animation with smoother and more irregular shapes during the intermediary steps. Choose **Angular** if the shapes in your animation have many straight lines and definite corners, such as the shapes in this example. The **Angular** option preserves these lines and corners during the intermediary steps of the tween. Test your animation by pressing **Ctrl+Enter**.

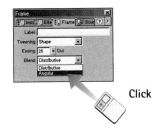

Click

End

How-To Hints

What Objects Can You Shape Tween?

The easier question to answer asks, "What objects cannot be used in a Shape Tween?" If you're accustomed to creating many Motion Tweens, this point causes much frustration, so take note! Unlike a Motion Tween, a Shape Tween cannot use symbols, groups, text blocks, or bitmap images. Users often develop the (normally good) habit of turning all artwork into symbols, and adding instances to the Stage to maximize performance and minimize file size. However, be careful! You can not Shape Tween an instance of a symbol.

Shape Tweening a Letter

The previous hint states that you cannot use text in a Shape Tween. Yet, many of us have seen Flash animations where a box or other object morphs into a letter. You can indeed morph a box into a letter, but you have to be a little tricky. Although you can't use a text block in your Shape Tween, you can use artwork that *looks* like text. To do this, add your letter to the Stage. Select it with the Arrow tool, and choose **Modify, Break Apart.** Now you've transformed the letter into artwork that *looks* like text and you can use it in your Shape Tween sequence. Life is good!

Tweening Size, Location, and Color

When using a Shape Tween, you can also cause the object to move across the Stage, change color, and grow or shrink in size while changing shapes. To do so, set these attributes to different values for the object on the first frame and the object on the last.

7

How to Use Shape Hints

We hope that you followed along with the previous example and played the Shape Tween after you created it. If so, you might have noticed that the beginning shape (the cross) seemed to almost disappear before it changed into the square. Sometimes intermediate frames of a Shape Tween contain unrecognizable shapes because of the way Flash interpolates each frame. Shape hints enable you to set points that link relationships between areas in the beginning and ending shapes. This task shows how to use shape hints to improve the appearance of a Shape Tween.

Begin

1 Add a New Shape Hint

Click on the beginning keyframe of a Shape Tweened sequence in the Timeline. Choose **Modify, Transform, Add Shape Hint,** or use the keyboard shortcut **Ctrl+Shift+H**. A red dot with the letter "a" appears in the middle of the object on this frame (we changed the shapes to blue so that you could see the dot better). This dot represents the new shape hint.

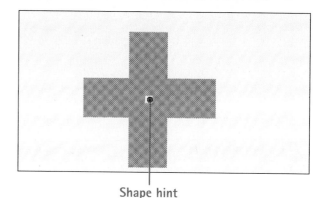

Shape hint

2 Reposition the Shape Hint

Click and drag the shape hint to the desired location on the artwork. For best results, position this first shape hint in the upper-left corner of the object. (Here, it is shown in the upper-left corner of the middle hole.)

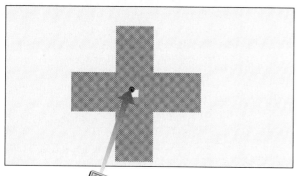

Click & Drag

3 Select the Ending Keyframe

Click to select the ending keyframe of the Shape Tween. You see a shape hint marked "a" here as well. Flash automatically generates a shape hint in the last frame when you create a shape hint in the first frame.

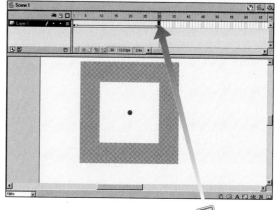

 Click

4 Position the Ending Shape Hint

Click and drag the shape hint in the ending keyframe to a position that corresponds to the one set for the beginning keyframe. After you position the start and end shape hints, the start shape hint changes to yellow, and the end shape hint changes to green.

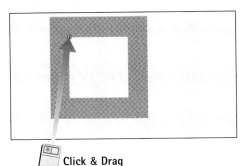

Click & Drag

6 Add More Shape Hints as Needed

One shape hint might not adequately control the tween. You can add up to 26 shape hints to your Shape Tween. The example here shows eight shape hints on each of the shapes. Arrange the hints in a counterclockwise fashion for the best results, and make sure to use corresponding positions for the related hints on the ending keyframe. Play the animation to evaluate the results of each newly added hint.

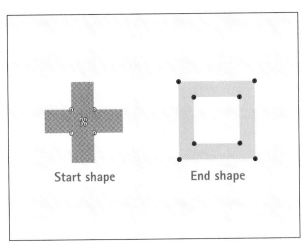

Start shape   End shape

5 Evaluate the Results

In the Timeline, click on the beginning keyframe of the sequence. Choose **Control, Play** and watch the Shape Tween. Pay special attention to how the tween reacts to the newly added shape hint. Reposition the shape hints on the beginning and ending frames to fine-tune the tween.

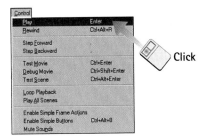

Click

How-To Hints

Hide and Show Your Shape Hints

Shape hints can add unnecessary visual clutter to your project. To solve this problem, choose **View, Show Shape Hints** to toggle them between visible and invisible. Be sure to click in one of the keyframes of the sequence that contains the shape hints, or the **Show Shape Hints** option will not be available.

Removing Shape Hints

You might decide that you placed one or more shape hints in error. To remove a single shape hint, click and drag it off the Stage. To remove all shape hints from a tweened sequence, click on the beginning keyframe in the Timeline. Then choose **Modify, Transform, Remove All Hints**.

Tweening Between Complex Shapes

When the Shape Tween you create involves complicated shapes, it might be very difficult to achieve the exact tween results you desire. In such a case, it might help to break up the sequence into several shorter tween sequences that, as a whole, make up the overall sequence you need.

End

How to Animate with Layers

Working with layers becomes critical when you create animated sequences. Part 6 explains using layers in detail. You will quickly become fond of layers when you create your first animation that contains several objects that tween simultaneously. This task looks at how to use layers in an animation that requires more than one tweened sequence to occur at the same time. It demonstrates that it is quite impossible to create a multifaceted animation without layers.

Begin

1 Create a Tweened Sequence

Use any of the tweening techniques discussed in the previous tasks in this part to create a tweened animation. Here, a text object scrolls from left to right.

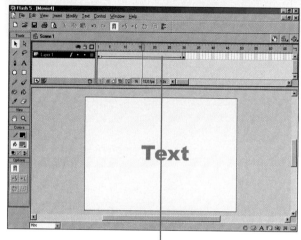

Motion Tween

2 Create a Simultaneous Tween

Click on any intermediary frame within the Motion Tween that you created in step 1. Attempt to create a second tweened sequence by choosing **Insert, Blank Keyframe.** You have now ruined the already existing tweened animation. This demonstrates that you cannot build two overlapping tweened sequences on the same layer.

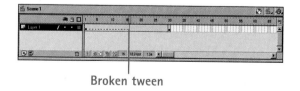

Broken tween

3 Create a New Layer

All is not lost! Layers spring to your rescue. Click once on the **Undo** button to restore your original tweened sequence. Next, click on the **Insert Layer** button in the lower-left corner of the Timeline to create a new layer.

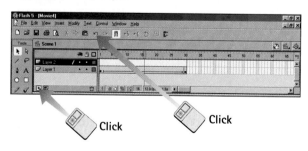

Click   Click

4 Create a Second Tween

Now, on the new layer in the Timeline, click on the same frame number as you did in step two. Choose **Insert, Blank Keyframe.** Your original tween remains unaffected. Now use the techniques you've learned in previous tasks to create a tweened animation that is shorter or longer than the first. You now have two tweened sequences in your movie, each of which appears to move at a different speed. The second tween appears above the first one.

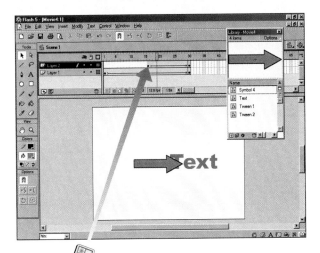

Click

5 Preview the Movie

Choose **Control, Rewind,** and then **Control, Play** to watch your animations. You now have two simultaneously moving, yet independent, tweened sequences in your movie. Hurray for layers!

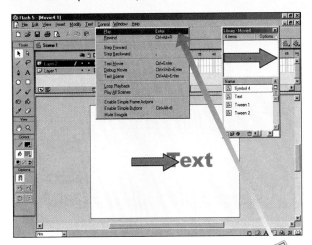

Click

End

How-To Hints

Reorder Your Layers

Layers enable you to control the order in which objects are stacked on the Stage. Change the order of layers to control which objects are "in front." For example, imagine an animation in which a blue car drives by going one way, and a red car drives by going the other way. If the blue car layer is the top layer, the movie shows the red car passing behind. If you place the blue car layer beneath the other, the red car appears in front.

To reorder the layers, click on a layer name. Drag it up or down to place it above or below its previous location.

Task

13

Adding and Using Sound

*T*he practice of using sound to enhance the movie experience is as old as movies themselves. Before the technology was in place to add a soundtrack to the film itself, live musicians accompanied the film to help set the mood for the onscreen action.

As moviemakers strive to achieve realism, the importance of well-placed, high-quality sound has grown. Your Flash movies are no different. They, too, benefit from the prudent use of sound. Dialog, music, and sound effects (also referred to as "audio sweetening") must all blend seamlessly to create a cohesive soundtrack that enhances the viewing experience, instead of detracting from it.

Flash provides several basic, yet powerful, tools for adding and manipulating sound in your movies. Becoming familiar with the techniques of working with audio in Flash will certainly help you to take your movies to the next level. ●

How to Import Sounds and Add Them to a Movie

To use sound in your animation, you must first import the sound into your Flash Library. Then you add it to the movie. It's always a good idea to keep the sounds you add to your animation on a separate layer. In fact, you might consider making a new layer for each sound that you add. Flash treats each sound layer as a separate track of audio, and mixes all sounds together in the final movie.

Begin

1 Import the Sound

To import a sound, choose **File, Import,** or use the keyboard shortcut **Ctrl+R** (Windows) or **Cmmd+R** (Mac).

Click

2 Locate the Desired Sound File

In the **Import** dialog (Windows) or Mac file chooser, navigate to the folder that contains the WAV (PC), AIFF (Mac), or MP3 (either platform) file on your system. Note that you can import both WAV and AIFF files in Windows if QuickTime 4 is installed on your Windows system. After you select the file, choose **Open** (Windows) or **Import** (Mac). The file is added to the Flash project, and appears in the Library just as any other imported media does.

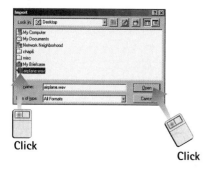

Click

Click

3 Create a New Layer for the Sound

To create the sound layer, click the **Insert Layer** button at the lower-left corner of the Timeline. Alternatively, right-click (**Ctrl+**click on the Macintosh) on an existing layer, and choose **Insert Layer** from the menu. The new layer appears directly above the currently selected layer. To label the layer with a descriptive name, double-click on the current layer name, and type the new name.

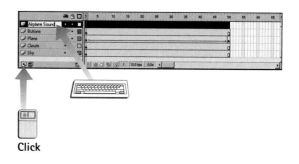

Click

4 Add the Sound to the Movie

If you want to start the sound in a frame other than the first frame, use the keyboard shortcut **F6** to add a keyframe to the desired frame. Then click to select the target keyframe. Choose **Window, Panels, Sound** to open the **Sound** panel.

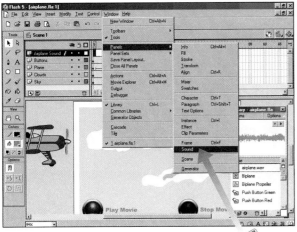

Click

5 Specify the Desired Sound

From the **Sound** drop-down in the **Sound** panel, choose the name of the sound you want to insert at the selected keyframe. This adds the sound to your project at the selected keyframe.

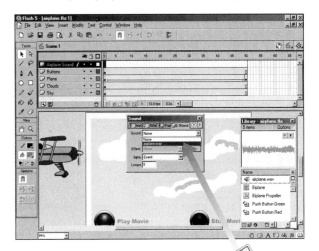

Click

6 Add Sound Using a Shortcut

A shortcut method exists for adding sound directly from the Library. After you select a target keyframe as in step 4, choose **Window, Library** to open the Library window. Click on the name of the sound in the list. Now, click and drag either the waveform of the sound or the name of the sound onto the Stage.

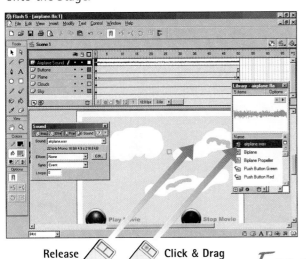

Release   Click & Drag

How-To Hints

Missing Sounds

If you don't see the sound you are looking for in the **Sound** drop-down or the Library, you have forgotten to import it. Importing the sound will always be the first step in the process.

Sounds from the Common Library

Even if you don't have any of your own, you can still add sounds to your movies. Flash provides a library of sounds you can use freely. To find them, choose **Window, Common Libraries, Sounds.** Use the same technique to add these sounds to your movie as discussed in step 6 above.

End

2

How to Adjust Sound Effects

After you add a sound, you must specify certain behaviors for the sound. You do this in the **Sound** panel. There are several preset sound effect options in the **Effect** drop-down list. This task explains these options.

1 Open the Sound Panel

Click on the keyframe, or frame, that holds the sound. Choose **Window, Panels, Sound** to open the **Sound** panel.

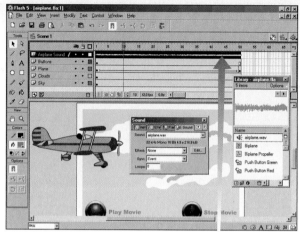

Click

2 Choose to Apply No Effect

From the **Effect** drop-down, choose the **None** option to leave the sound unaltered. Using this option, Flash plays the sound using the original audio properties.

Click

3 Choose a Channel

Stereo files have discrete right and left channels that, when played together, create a richer sound. Sometimes you want to use just the sound from one channel, but not the other. Choose the **Left Channel** or **Right Channel** option from the **Effect** drop-down to accomplish this.

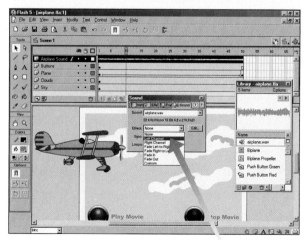

 Click

4 Pan a Sound

You can easily create the effect of a sound moving from one side of the room to the other. This is sometimes referred to as a *pan*. From the **Effect** drop-down, choose the **Fade Left to Right** or **Fade Right to Left** option, depending on the direction you want the illusion to emulate.

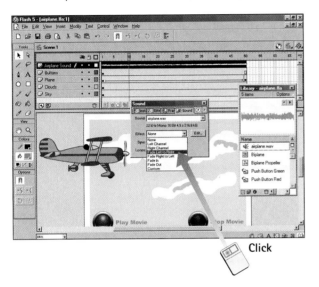

Click

5 Fade Sounds In or Out

The process of raising or lowering the volume of a sound over time is referred to as a *fade*. From the **Effect** drop-down, choose **Fade In** to create a sound that starts with a volume level of 0% and fades in to a volume level of 100%. Choose **Fade Out** to achieve the opposite effect.

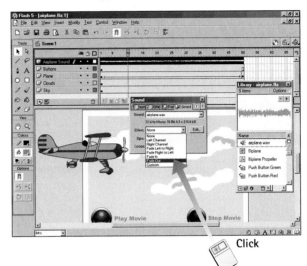

Click

6 Set the Loop Amount

Each time a sound is played, it is set to *loop*. A sound with a loop value of 1 will play only one time. Likewise, a loop value of 6 will cause the sound to play six times in a row. Set the loop amount by entering a value in the **Loops** field.

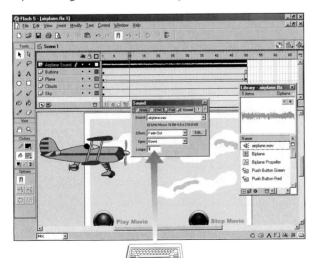

How-To Hints

Invisible Waveforms

After the sound has been added, its waveform appears in the Timeline. Note that the waveform does not appear on the Stage, even if you dropped the waveform directly from the Library onto the Stage. This is a potential source of confusion. Remember that the Stage holds only visible (or potentially visible) items.

Graphical Effect Representation

Each of the effects mentioned in this task has its own unique graphical representation. Click the **Edit** button in the **Sound** panel to view the graph for the chosen effect. You can also use this graph to create a custom effect, which you'll learn more about in Task 3.

End

3

How to Customize Sound Effects

In the previous task, you learned how to add effects to a sound. There is one special case in the **Effect** drop-down list in the **Sound** panel. That is the **Custom** option. In this task, you will learn how to create custom effects for your sounds.

1 Open the Sound Panel

After you add a sound to your movie, click on the keyframe or any frame that holds the sound. Choose **Window, Panels, Sound** to open the **Sound** panel.

Click

2 The Custom Effect

To create a custom effect for your sound, choose **Custom** from the **Effect** drop-down. Alternatively, select the effect that most closely matches the effect you want to achieve, and click the **Edit** button. The **Edit Envelope** dialog pops up with a waveform graphical interface that you will use to create your custom effect. Note that if you change the settings for any of the preset effects using the **Edit** button, you automatically switch to the custom effect.

Click

3 Mix of Left and Right Channels

When you choose None from the **Effect** drop-down, one node appears at the beginning of each channel in the audio file. You can adjust the volume of each channel individually by dragging this node up or down. Note that you can adjust the volume of the entire channel only when this first node is the only node that appears in the channel.

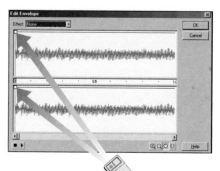

Click, Drag, & Release

4 Create Custom Volume Changes

To add more adjustment nodes (which are represented by squares), click at various spots on the volume lines. When you add a node to one channel, Flash automatically adds a corresponding node to the other channel. When you move a node forward or backward in time, the corresponding node in the other channel also moves forward or backward the same amount. Move the left and right channel nodes up or down independently to create custom volume adjustments for each channel.

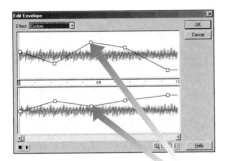

Click, Drag, & Release

5 Preview Your Custom Effects

For evaluation purposes, you can easily preview changes made to the sound's effects. Click on the **Play** button in the **Edit Envelope** dialog to preview the sound three times. Click on the **Stop** button to discontinue playback.

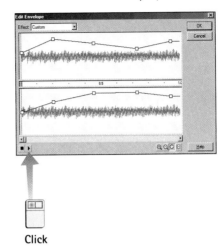

Click

6 Adjust the Sound's Length

The time ruler between the left and right channels indicates the sound's length with a white highlight. Sliders appear at the beginning and end of the time ruler. Use these sliders to adjust the start and end points of the sound. Move the start slider to the right to cut out the beginning portion of the sound, and the end slider to the left to cut out the end portion of the sound.

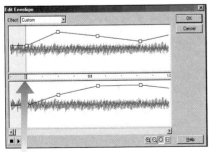

Click, Drag, & Release

How-To Hints

Using Fades to Fix Abrupt Beginnings and Endings

When you adjust the beginning or ending of a sound as described in step 6, use fades to make the abrupt beginning and ending more natural sounding.

Adjusting the Start and End of a Sound

You can use the Start and End adjustment sliders to cut out silence or unwanted sound at the beginning or ending of an audio file. This can help preserve synchronization, and is a great way to trim unnecessary file size from an exported file.

End

How to Add Sound to a Button

Adding sound to your buttons can make a button seem more real by providing audible clues to the current state of the button or the action being performed on the button. You associate sounds with the various states of a master button symbol. As a result, the sounds will follow the symbol and be present in every instance of the symbol that you place on the Stage.

Begin

1 Select the Button

First, select the Button symbol to which you are adding sound by clicking on its name in the **Library** window. If you don't have a button of your own, use one from the common library by choosing **Window, Common Libraries, Buttons**. Double-click on one of the folders in the list to expand it. Drag and drop a button to add it to the Stage. The button now also appears in your current movie library.

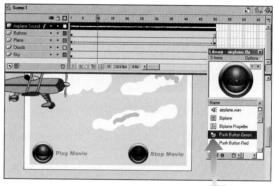

Click

2 Edit the Button Symbol

You add the sound to a Button symbol's Timeline. Right-click (**Ctrl**+click for Macintosh) on the desired button in your current movie library. Choose **Edit** from the pop-up to access the symbol's Timeline. Alternatively, double-click the Button symbol in your current movie library to enter edit mode.

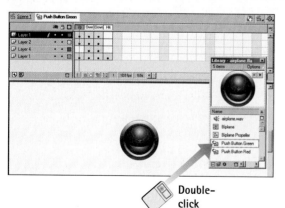

Double-click

3 Add a Sound Layer

Just like the movie itself, the Button symbol's Timeline can contain multiple layers. The new sound layer will appear directly above the layer you select. To add the new layer, click on the **Insert Layer** button to create a new layer in the Timeline. Name the new layer Sound Layer.

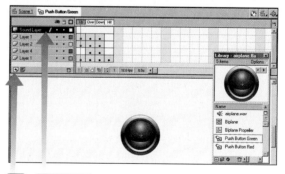

Click

4 Add a Sound to the Down State

As you learned in Part 10, "Buttons and Actions," a button has three main states: Up, Over, and Down. You can assign a sound to any or each of these states. To do so, click in the frame corresponding to the desired state. The Down state—when a user clicks on the button—is the most common place to add sounds. Press **F6** to add a keyframe to the Down state on the sound layer.

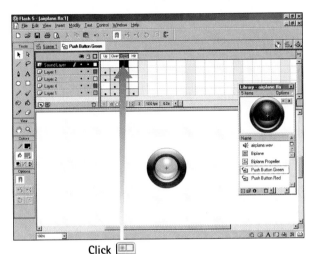

Click

5 Specify the Desired Sound

Use one of the methods you learned in Task 1 to add the desired sound to the Down state. In the example shown here, a button sound is selected from the common Sounds library (choose **Windows, Common Library, Sounds** to open it). After you add your sound, click on the **Scene** tab (Windows) or **Page** tab (Mac) to exit symbol-editing mode.

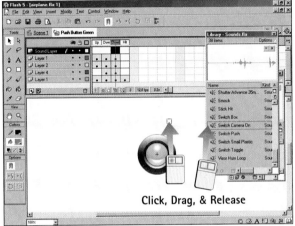

Click, Drag, & Release

End

How-To Hints

Test the Button Sound

There are two ways to test your button sounds. Drag your new button onto the Stage. You can press **Ctrl+Enter** to test the movie, and click on the button. To enable buttons so that you can test them from the Stage, choose **Control, Enable Simple Buttons.** Then press **Enter** to play the movie. Click on the button to hear the new button sound play.

Multiple Sound Layers

Remember that it is normally better to use more layers than fewer in your movies. The same is true with buttons. If you are adding a sound to each of a button's three states, it is best to add a new layer for each sound.

Synchronizing the Sound

For the button behavior to match the desired sounds, it is important to remember to choose **Event** from the **Sync** drop-down list in the **Sound** panel. This links the sound to the triggering event. We'll cover more **Sync** options in the next task.

How to Choose a Synchronization Option

After you've added the sound to your movie, you choose how the sound behaves in relation to the rest of the movie. You can specify the behavior of the sound symbol (which affects all instances of the sound) or individual instances. In either case, use the **Sync** drop-down list to set the desired option.

Begin

1 Open the Sound Panel

To edit the sound symbol, choose the desired sound from your current movie library, or click the sound in the Timeline. Open the **Sound** panel, and then click on the **Sync** drop-down list.

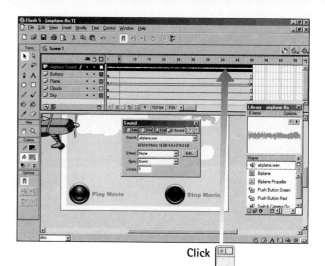

Click

2 Start with Event Sync

An event sound begins playing at the keyframe in which it's placed and plays in its entirety, even if the rest of the movie has stopped, or if another instance of the same sound starts before the first instance ends. In this example, an airplane appears on the screen in the third frame. The keyframe that starts the airplane sound also appears on the third frame. To synchronize the start of a sound to the occurrence of an event, choose the **Event** option from the **Sync** drop-down in the **Sound** panel.

Click

3 Use the Start Sync

The **Start** option works the same as the **Event** option with one difference: It ensures that a second instance of a sound will not begin playing until the first instance has ended. In this example, one plane exits the screen at frame 33, as does its sound. The sound for a second airplane is set to **Start** sync. So, even though its waveform begins at frame 21, the second plane sound begins playing at frame 34. This prevents "layering" of the sound that can occur if one or both of the instances are set to Event sync.

Click

4 Stop a Sound with Stop Sync

The **Stop** sync option ends an Event or Start sync sound at a specific keyframe. To stop a sound, press **F6** to add a keyframe where you want the sound to end. Choose the sound you want to stop from the **Sound** drop-down, and then choose **Stop** from the **Sync** dropdown. Here, the first airplane sound naturally stops at frame 33. But because there are two instances of the same sound, placing a Stop sync here will end both sounds. In this example, add a keyframe and Stop sync to the second airplane sound at frame 48. Without the Stop sync, the second airplane sound continues to play until the sound file ends.

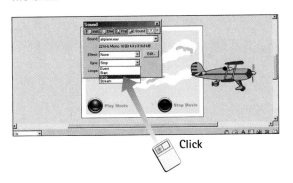

Click

5 Use the Stream Sync

To synchronize the sound for delivery over the Internet, choose the **Stream** sync. When you stream a sound, Flash forces the animation to keep pace with the sound, even if it has to drop frames to do it. Unlike Event and Start sounds, if the movie stops, the streamed sound stops. Further, a streamed sound plays only while the playback head is in one of the frames that the sound occupies.

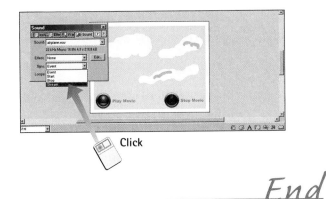

Click

End

How-To Hints

Keeping Up with Synchronized Sounds

When you include a streaming sound in your movie, the sound attempts to play normally. If your movie is complex, Flash may have trouble drawing the Stage fast enough. Flash reduces visual quality, and can even drop visual frames to keep pace with the streaming sound. This could cause undesirable visual results. Make sure to test your movie thoroughly to achieve the effects you want.

Think of the Possibilities

When you synchronize the beginning and end of a sound with an object or sequence in the movie, you create realistic animations with an extra dimension of aural input. Subtle sounds can shape the overall experience in ways that the audience cannot even consciously identify. Don't underestimate the importance of music, dialog, and sound effects. At the same time, use sound prudently. Because audio causes your final file size to increase rapidly, put careful thought into where and how to use audio in your movies.

How to Stop All Sounds

You can stop all the sounds that are currently playing in a movie at one time. You can assign the Stop All Sounds action to a specific keyframe in a movie (as shown in the following example), or to a button. For example, you can create a button that enables a user to turn off the audio portion of the movie while he or she continues to view the video portion. The following example illustrates how to stop all sounds in the middle of a movie.

Begin

1 Create the Keyframe

For this example, choose **Insert Layer** to create a new layer at the top of the timeline. Name the new layer Actions Layer. Now, click in the frame where you want all sounds to stop. Set a keyframe by pressing **F6** on the keyboard.

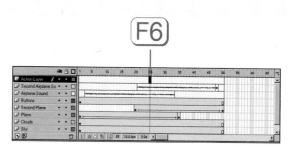

2 Open the Frame Actions Panel

Click on the keyframe you created in step 1 to select it. Choose **Window, Actions** to open the **Frame Actions** panel.

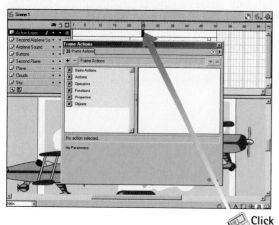

Click

3 Access Basic Actions

Click on the icon for **Basic Actions** to expand the list of available options.

 Click

4 Add the Stop All Sounds Action

Double-click on the **Stop All Sounds** action to add it to the Actions list.

Double-click

5 Test the Movie

Click on the **Close** button to dismiss the **Frame Actions** panel. To test the movie, choose **Control, Test Movie.** All sounds stop playing at the frame on which you entered the frame action.

Click

End

How-To Hints

A Simple, but Powerful Action

Notice that the Stop All Sounds action has no parameters. The action is either on if you've added it to your Actions list, or off if you haven't. But keep in mind that it is a powerful action, and disables all the sounds in your movie. In fact, it disables all the sounds in all the Flash movies currently playing. In other words, make sure that you really want silence before you decide to use this action!

Task

Saving and Publishing Files

*Y*ou're almost there! You've learned a lot about Flash throughout this book, but you're not quite done. All this knowledge of yours is great, but it doesn't mean much unless you deliver your project. That's what we discuss in this part.

When you save a Flash project (.fla), you merely protect your "work in progress." However, only people with Flash installed on their computers can view...and *edit*...your movie. Flash provides a number of ways that you can deliver your movie so that other people can see, but not edit it.

When you *export* your Flash movies, you choose a single file format into which to convert your movie. You can export a single frame as a GIF, JPG, or PNG. You can also export a series of frames as animated GIFs, or to QuickTime and AVI movie formats. The Flash Player format (.swf) is the main delivery method for the Internet. It supports *all* the functionality of a Flash movie and keeps file sizes manageable. To view a Flash Player movie in a browser, a special plug-in or add-on is required. You can also create a stand-alone Flash Player movie, called a *projector*.

To create all the files you need to deliver your Flash animation on the World Wide Web, use the **File, Publish** command to *publish* your Flash movie. This process creates the Flash Player file and writes the proper HTML code required to play your movie. You can also generate optional graphics files to display as an alternative when visitors to your Flash site do not have the Flash Player available to them.

You've put a lot of work into creating your Flash movie, so you want to get this final step right. It's very involved, but this part breaks it down into manageable steps. When you're done, it will hardly be a challenge at all for you to deliver your Flash content! ●

How to Optimize Movies

You've already learned throughout this book that one of the best ways to optimize file size is to use Flash symbols because they consume less space than individually drawn objects. During the publishing process, Flash automatically takes other steps toward optimizing a movie. For instance, it places duplicate shapes in the file only once. Flash converts nested groups (groups of groups) to a single group. Several manual techniques can help optimize your overall movie. This task gives tips to help you optimize elements and lines, text and fonts, and colors.

Begin

1 Sound

When you import a sound, it's usually best to use the MP3 file format. MP3 files maintain a high degree of sound quality. This format is highly compressed, so the file size is much smaller than a WAV or AIFF file.

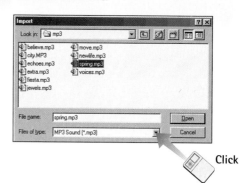

Click

2 Tweened Animation

It is always more efficient (from a file-size point of view) to use tweened animations rather than developing frame-by-frame animations. The series of keyframes required in the latter type of animation quickly increases file size. Try to limit the amount of change that takes place between keyframes, because it takes a lot of processor time. Again, focus on quality versus file size. Avoid animating bitmap images.

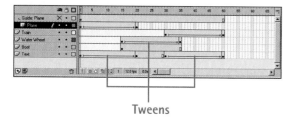

Tweens

3 Elements and Lines

Even though it doesn't directly affect file size, group elements and lines whenever you can. Also, keep animated elements on separate layers from static elements. Keep different line types to a minimum. Dashed, dotted, and ragged lines create larger files than solid lines. Because of the nature of these tools, lines that you create with the Pencil tool are more efficient than those you create with the Brush tool.

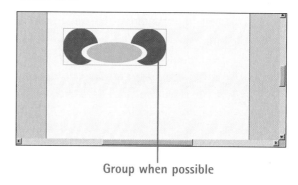

Group when possible

4 Text and Fonts

Make judicious use of fonts, font styles, and font colors. Too many different fonts and styles not only make for larger files sizes, they often also make for bad graphic design! Keep font colors to a minimum as well, for the sake of your design. Too many different fonts, sizes, and colors create a page that is far too distracting for the reader to view. When selecting font options, try to narrow the range of fonts you embed.

Limit font styles

5 Alter Instances

If you can, adjust the parameters of an instance of an existing symbol instead of creating a new symbol. For example, you could create two circles, one green, and one blue. But you gain efficiency when you add two instances of the blue circle, and change the tint of one of them to green.

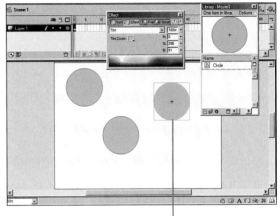

Reuse symbols where possible

6 Gradients

Gradient fills look great, but they also take up much more space than solid fills. Their use quickly increases your file size substantially. Be careful how often you use gradient fills.

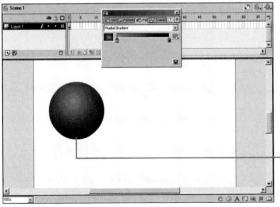

Limit gradients!

End

How-To Hints

Trade-offs and More Trade-offs

By now it's becoming clear that producing art for the Web is a series of one trade-off after another. To keep your Flash movies lean and mean, you constantly negotiate the struggle between complexity, artistic quality, and efficiency. That's just the way it is on the Web. Until it changes, you must become a master at striking the perfect compromise.

TASK 2

How to Optimize Curves

When you import line art from other programs, your objects can contain many unnecessary curves. A curved line or object stroke in Flash might look like one "curve," but it might actually contain multiple curve segments. Flash can optimize your curves for you by reducing the number of segments in a curve. Optimizing your curves can go a long way toward helping to keep your final file size down. This task shows you how to do this.

Begin

1 Select the Objects

Click to select the object or objects that you want to optimize. The object can be a curved line, or a shape with a curved stroke. To optimize the curves of a symbol, you must enter symbol-editing mode and apply optimization there. Of course, this affects all instances of that symbol.

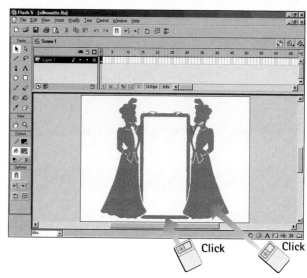

Click   Click

⬆Shift

2 Choose the Optimize Command

Choose **Modify, Optimize** to access the **Optimize Curves** dialog shown here. Alternatively, use the keyboard shortcut **Ctrl+Alt+Shift+C** (Windows) or **Cmmd+Opt+Shift+C** (Macintosh).

3 Set the Smoothing Amount

Click and drag the **Smoothing** slider to set a smoothing amount in the range from **None** to **Maximum**. The more you move the slider toward the **Maximum** setting, the smoother the curves will be. It also results in smaller file sizes.

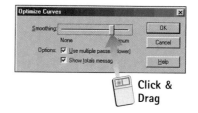

Click & Drag

4 Decide on Multiple Passes

Decide whether to use multiple passes during the smoothing process. If you leave this option unchecked, you might have to repeat the smoothing process several times to fully optimize a curve. If you check the **Use multiple passes (slower)** option the first time you run optimization, Flash automatically repeats the optimization function until it fully optimizes the curve.

 Click

5 Show a Summary

To see a summary of the optimization results, choose the **Show totals message** option. This causes an alert box containing summary information to appear at the end of the optimization process.

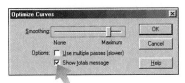

 Click

6 Complete the Optimization Process

Click on **OK** to activate the optimization command, and view the results on the stage. You might need to experiment with different settings until you achieve acceptable curve smoothing results.

End

How-To Hints

Optimization Versus Quality

Your results will vary depending on the curve with which you are working. Generally, the more you optimize (that is, the closer you move the slider to **Maximum**), the less the results look like the original curve. Once again, the trade-off exists here between optimization and quality.

Classic Lines

"Hey, good lookin', what's your sign?" No, we don't mean *that kind* of classic line! Instead, we mean the kind you see on a '53 Buick: smooth, yet strong; graceful, yet forceful; elegant, yet efficient. No wasted motion as the sweep of the curve draws you in. A line that is full of style and confidence. You want to create these kinds of lines in your Flash movies. Keep your curves simple and optimize them. You won't be sorry.

TASK 3

How to Test Movie Download Performance

As with any Web design project, you want to make sure you know a little something about the connection speeds at which your target audience views your content. Do your users connect with a 28.8 modem, a 56K modem, or a T1 connection? After you determine the worst-case connection speed, you can test your Flash movie from inside Flash to see where potential problems lie. This task walks you through a test of the download performance of your movie.

Begin

1 Test a Scene or the Entire Movie

Choose **Control, Test Scene** to test the current scene. Alternatively, use the keyboard shortcut **Ctrl+Alt+Enter**. To test the entire movie, choose **Control, Movie,** or use the keyboard shortcut **Ctrl+ Enter.** After a short download, the test environment opens, and the movie or scene begins to play.

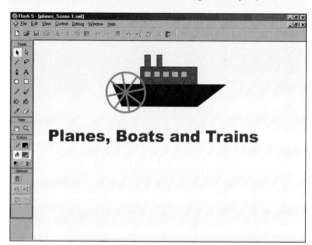

2 Choose a Download Speed to Test

Choose a download speed from the **Debug** menu. You'll need to know a little something about the connection speeds your target audience is likely to use when it views your Flash site. Choose a preset speed from the list, or choose **Customize** to define your own settings.

Click

3 View the Bandwidth Profiler

Choose **View, Bandwidth Profiler** to toggle this option on and off. Click on the bars of the graph to see the summary details for that frame appear on the left. The red line in the graph indicates the point at which the movie will be required to pause while information downloads from the Web server. If the bar for a frame extends above the red line, the movie will have to pause at that point.

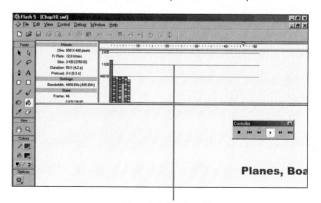

Bandwidth Profiler

4 Set View Options

You can view the Bandwidth Profiler graph in either Streaming view or Frame by Frame view. For Streaming view (the default), choose **View, Streaming Graph,** or the keyboard shortcut **Ctrl+G.** For Frame by Frame view, choose **View, Frame By Frame Graph,** or the keyboard shortcut **Ctrl+F.**

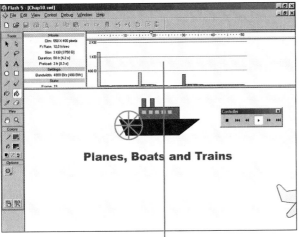

Frame by Frame view

5 Show Streaming

Choose **View, Show Streaming.** A green progress bar begins to grow from left to right across the Timeline indicating the amount of the file that is currently downloaded to the local machine. When enough information has been downloaded, playback begins. If the Playback Head catches up to the streaming bar, the movie pauses while more information downloads.

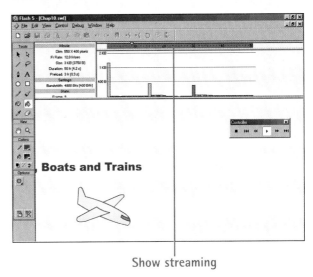

Show streaming

6 End the Performance Test

After running your tests and making notes about problem areas, choose **File, Close** or click on the **Close** box to end the performance test. This also exits the test window, and reopens the main Flash editing window.

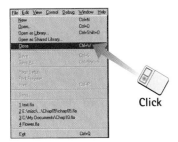

Click

End

How-To Hints

Opening Existing Shockwave Files

After the **Bandwidth Profiler** is open, you can evaluate any existing SWF file with it. Choose **File, Open** and navigate to the SWF file you want to test.

How to Choose Your Publishing Formats

The first step in the publishing process requires that you select the file formats to which you want to publish. The following task describes the many different ways that you can publish your Flash movies. You select these formats from the **Publish Settings** dialog.

Begin

1 Open the Publish Settings Dialog

Choose **File, Publish Settings** to open the **Publish Settings** dialog. Alternatively, type the keyboard shortcut **Ctrl+Shift+F12**.

Click

2 Publish a Flash Movie

Notice that the **Flash (.swf)** and **HTML (.html)** options are checked by default. With both of these options checked, when you publish a Flash movie, you also publish a Web page that displays your movie in a Web browser. Flash automatically generates the code based on the settings you select in the **Flash** and **HTML** tabs. You'll learn more about these in Tasks 5 and 7.

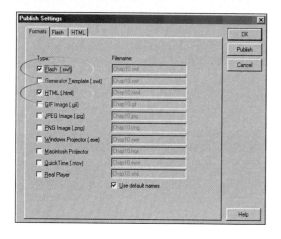

3 HTML Settings

Use the **HTML** tab to make choices that determine the HTML tags and attributes that Flash generates for the Web page that accompanies your Flash movie. The properties adjust position, alignment, image quality, playback options, page dimensions, and more. You'll learn more about these in Task 7.

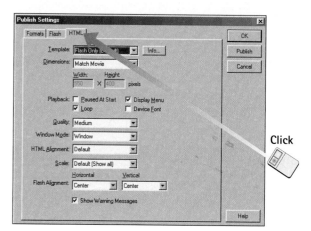
Click

4 Publish Bitmap Files

Flash also enables you to publish your Flash movies as GIF, JPG, or PNG bitmap images that can be viewed in any Web browser. If your Flash movie contains buttons, Flash generates the appropriate code to designate the buttons as clickable "hotspots" in an image map. These hotspots enable the user to navigate to other pages in your Web site. Bitmap images are perfect for creating static versions of Flash navigation bars. You'll learn more about these in Task 8.

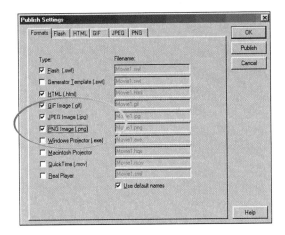

5 Publish Projector Files

Projector files are self-contained Flash movies that use an EXE (Windows) or HQX (Macintosh) extension. Projector files can be viewed outside a Web browser, and are excellent for presentations and other instances when a Web browser is not required for viewing. You'll learn more about how to choose projector settings in Task 9.

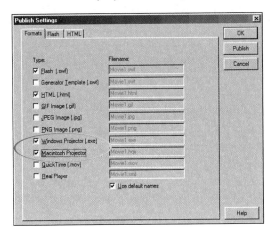

6 QuickTime and RealPlayer Movies

Flash also enables you to publish your Flash movies so that they are compatible with two other popular streaming media formats: QuickTime and RealPlayer. These streaming media options are discussed further in Tasks 11 and 12.

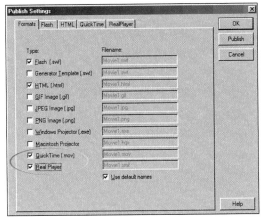

How-To Hints

How Many Formats Should You Publish?

It depends. Each project that you create has different needs, and Flash offers publishing options that should suit any of them. If your project is geared for the Internet, you'll most often use the default SWF and HTML method to publish your Web page. To accommodate as many different browser types as possible, select a bitmap format such as JPG to create image maps that users can use to navigate to other Web pages in your site. Use projector files for projects that users can view offline, without connecting to the Internet.

End

How to Select Flash Publishing Options

The **Flash** tab in the **Publish Settings** dialog enables you to configure the settings for Flash SWF movies that you publish. The options in this tab control the loading order of the layers in your movie, whether your file is protected from others debugging or editing your movie, how to compress sound, and which version of Flash will be the highest version supported.

Begin

1 Choose a Load Order

Use the **Load Order** drop-down to choose the order in which the Flash player loads the layers in your Flash movies. **Bottom up** loads the lowest layers first; **Top down** to load, the top layers first.

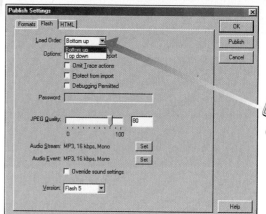

Click

2 Choose Options and Password

The **Generate size report** option creates a report that lists the amount of data in each frame. Check the **Protect from import** option to prevent other Flash users from importing your Flash movie into their own Flash projects. If you want others to help you remotely debug problems in your movies, check the **Debugging Permitted** option. Enter an optional password that applies to both these options.

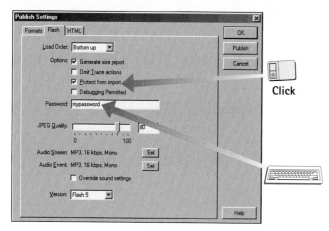

Click

3 Set JPEG Quality

Adjust the **JPEG Quality** slider to control the amount of compression that is used for bitmaps in your Flash movies. A setting of **100** provides the highest image quality, but also makes your Flash movies larger. Lower the setting to reduce the size of your Flash movies. You might need to experiment to achieve the right balance between file size and image quality.

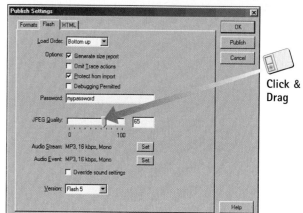

Click & Drag

4 Specify the Audio Properties

Two settings are provided for audio files. The **Audio Stream** settings control the quality of audio files with **Sync** set to **Stream.** Use the **Audio Event** settings to control the audio output quality sounds with **Sync** set to **Event** or **Start.** Click on the **Set** button next to each option to specify settings in the **Sound Settings** dialog. These settings are explained in more detail in the following task.

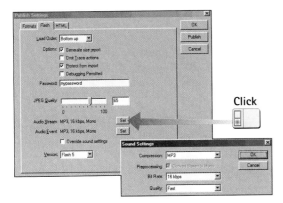

Click

5 Choose a Flash Version

Flash 5 includes many features and enhancements that are not available in previous versions of Flash, including many new ActionScript commands. However, you can also design your Flash 5 projects so that they are compatible with any version of Flash, and then choose the appropriate version from the **Version** drop-down.

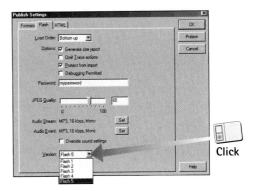

Click

6 Publish the File

To exit the **Publish Settings** dialog without publishing your project, click on **OK.** The settings you enter remain in the **Publish Settings** dialog. To publish the Flash movie with the settings you select, click on the **Publish** button. Flash publishes the movie to the same folder in which your original Flash project (.fla) is located. Then click on the **OK** button to exit the **Publish Settings** dialog.

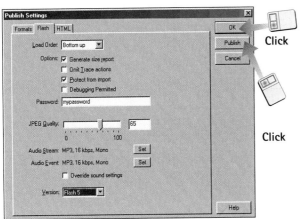

Click

Click

How-To Hints

Protect Your Work!

The **Protect from Import** setting, discussed in step 2, prevents other Flash users from opening your Flash movie and using it in their own work—but make sure that you don't place yourself in the same position! *Always* keep a backup copy of your original FLA projects on hand in the event of a hard drive crash. Although you can assign a password that unlocks a protected SWF file, you'll have to re-create symbols and tweens when you import an SWF file into Flash.

Provide Links for the Flash Player

With each new release of Flash, you have a host of visitors who are using earlier versions of the Flash Player. Provide notification on your Web site that you're using Flash 5, and place a link on your site for people to download the most current Flash Player from the Macromedia Web site. The URL is http://www.macromedia.com.

End

TASK **6**

How to Compress Sound Files

The Flash **Publish Settings** dialog, described in the previous task, enables you to choose compression settings for streamed audio and event audio files that you use in your Flash movies. The difference between these two types of files is subtle. You generally use streamed audio files for long pieces of audio such as background music or lengthy narration. Event sounds are used for button clicks and brief sound effects in your movies. The compression settings that you choose from are the same, regardless of its sync setting. The following task explains how to use some of the compression settings.

Begin

1 Choose a Compression Type

Click the **Set** button next to the **Audio Stream** or **Audio Event** options area in the **Flash Publish Settings** dialog. This opens the **Sound Settings** dialog. The first option that you choose is the **Compression** option. Choose **Disable** to publish your Flash movies using the sound settings as they are individually set in the Movie Library. The **ADPCM** file format is suitable for short sounds such as button clicks. Choose **MP3** compression for music and narration. Choose **Raw** to publish your Flash movies without compressing the sound.

2 Choose ADPCM Options

If you selected ADPCM options in step 1, configure the sound options as follows. Mono files are half as large as stereo files, and can sound equally as good. Check the **Convert Stereo to Mono** option to create mono files. Choose a sample rate from the **Sample Rate** drop-down. The options range from 5kHz sample rates—barely good enough for voice—to 44kHz—CD-quality audio. Higher values result in larger movie file sizes. When possible, choose either 11kHz or 22kHz. The **ADPCM Bits** setting also affects the amount of data that is streamed for your audio file. Decrease the bit rate to produce a smaller file, but note that this setting also reduces audio quality.

3 Choose MP3 Options

If you selected MP3 options in step 1, you can select a bit rate and audio quality from the **Sound Settings** dialog. Bit rates for MP3 files range from 8kbps (8,000 bits per second) to 160kbps. Larger bit rates produce better quality, but also produce larger file sizes. Values between 32kbps and 56kbps are generally good to start with, and then you can increase or decrease appropriately to find a balance between quality and file size. Choose **Fast, Medium,** or **Best** from the **Quality** drop-down to control the amount of compression used for the MP3 file.

4 Choose Raw Sound Options

If you choose **Raw** from the Sound Settings dialog, as discussed in step 1, Flash will not compress your audio files. Raw audio files consume the greatest number of bytes and, as a result, are difficult if not impossible to stream over the Internet. However, you might be able to use these settings in stand-alone projector files for hard-disk–based presentations. You can save raw files in stereo or mono, and can also choose bit rates from 5kHz (barely good enough for voice) to 11kHz (telephone quality), 22kHz (radio quality), and 44kHz (CD quality).

5 Choose OK

After you configure your sound options, click on OK to return to the Flash **Publish Settings** tab.

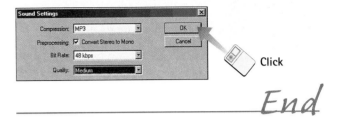

Click

End

How to Select HTML Publishing Options

There is a wide variety of HTML publishing options in Flash. The HTML settings control how Flash generates the HTML Web page that accompanies your Flash movie. When visitors navigate to your site, the Web page serves as a container for your Flash movie. Depending on the options you select here, the HTML code controls the placement, size, and quality of the Flash movie that displays on the page.

Begin

1 Choose a Template

Use the **Template** drop-down to select an HTML template from which to generate your Flash HTML page. Click on the **Info** button beside the **Template** drop-down to read a brief description of each template. Where appropriate, the **Info** description also includes other publishing options that you must choose. For example, if you select **Image Map**, the Info box tells you to select **GIF, JPEG,** or **PNG** on the **Formats** tab.

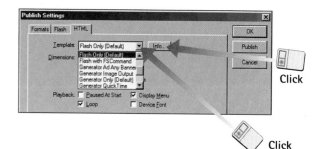

Click

Click

2 Specify Dimensions

The **Dimensions** drop-down enables you to select an option for movie size. Choose **Match Movie** to create a Flash movie that displays at the same size as your movie project. If you want to create a movie that is sized differently than your movie project, choose either **Pixels** or **Percent,** and enter the appropriate dimensions in the **Width** and **Height** fields.

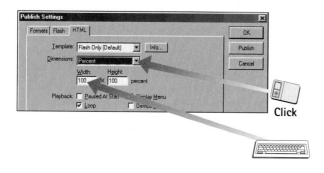

Click

3 Choose Playback Options

The **Playback** section provides four options that control how the user interacts with the movie. Choose **Paused At Start** to begin the movie only after the user clicks on a button or chooses **Play.** Deselect the **Loop** option to play the movie only once. Choose the **Display Menu** option to display a shortcut menu when the user right-clicks on the Flash movie on your Web page. Check **Device Font** (in Windows only) to substitute fonts that do not reside on the user's system with anti-aliased system fonts. This option can result in Flash movies that do not appear exactly as you designed them.

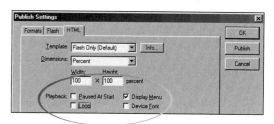

4 Select Movie Quality

The **Quality** drop-down enables you to choose a movie quality at which to publish your movie. To publish a movie that focuses more on playback speed than image quality, choose **Low** or **Auto Low**. To publish a movie that attempts to balance speed and quality, choose **Auto High** or **Medium**. To publish a movie that displays at the best quality, but places less importance on speed, choose **High** or **Best**.

Click

5 Specify the Window Mode

The **Window Mode** drop-down, provided only in the Windows version of Flash, enables you to choose a window mode for your Flash movie. The default is **Window,** which displays the Flash movie in its own rectangular window on a Web page. You can also place your movie in an **Opaque Windowless** HTML page. This enables you to use dynamic HTML to hide Web page elements behind the Flash movie. Choose **Transparent Windowless** to show the Web page background through any transparent areas in your Flash movie. Note, however, that this last option can reduce the playback speed of your movie.

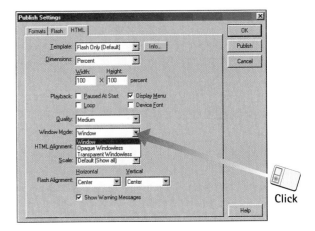

Click

6 Set Alignment and Scale

The **HTML Alignment** drop-down controls how the movie is aligned to your Web page. The **Default** option centers the movie horizontally and vertically. You can also align the movie to the **Left, Right, Top,** or **Bottom** of the Web page. Choose **Default** from the **Scale** drop-down fit the movie into the browser window both horizontally and vertically, without distorting it. Borders may appear on the top and bottom, or sides, with this option. The **No border** option displays the movie so that it completely fills the screen without distortion, but it crops the larger of the two dimensions. **Exact fit** fits your movie in your browser window and distorts the image as necessary.

Click

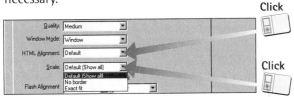

Click

End

How-To Hints

Creating a Movie That Fills the Browser Window

You've often seen Flash movies that fill an entire browser window, regardless of the display resolution setting. To publish a movie such as this, choose **Percent** from the **Dimensions** drop-down, and enter **100** in the Height and Width fields. Choose **Default (show all)** from the **Scale** drop-down to display your movie without distortion, using borders along the top and bottom or sides as necessary.

8

How to Publish Your Movie as Image Maps

You can publish bitmap versions of your Flash navigation bars. The static bitmaps become GIF, JPG, or PNG image maps that people can use to navigate to the appropriate pages in your site. You can also publish small, short Flash movies as animated GIF files. Although the file size of an animated GIF will be much larger than the equivalent Flash movie, you can place it on any Web page and view it with any Web browser.

Begin

1 Choose Image Map and Bitmap Format

First, click on the **HTML** tab in the **Publish Properties** dialog and choose **Image Map** from the **Template** drop-down. Then, choose the bitmap format (GIF, JPEG, or PNG) from the **Formats** tab. Finally, click on the **GIF, JPEG,** or **PNG** tab to configure bitmap options as described in the following steps.

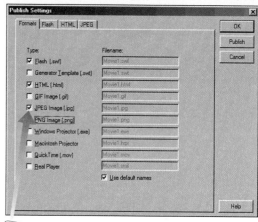

 Click

2 Configure GIF Settings

The **GIF** tab appears if you select the GIF format for your image map. You'll probably want to use a static image for your image map, so choose **Static** from the **Playback** section. File sizes will be smaller if you choose **None** from the **Dither** drop-down. If your Flash movie uses colors from the Web 216 (default) palette, without transparencies, choose **Web 216** from the **Palette Type** drop-down. The **Transparent** drop-down enables you to choose a color that appears invisible on your Web page. Use the **Options** section to select other optimization and dithering options.

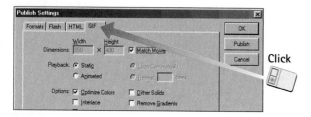 Click

3 Configure JPG Settings

JPG image maps generally result in the smallest file size while enabling you to use true-color images. Use the **JPEG** tab to configure properties for Flash movies that are saved as JPG image maps. Adjust the **Quality** slider toward the left to create a smaller (but lower quality) JPG image. Move the slider toward the right to increase quality, but note that this also increases file size. Check the **Progressive** option to gradually display the JPG image in increasing clarity while it downloads to the user's browser.

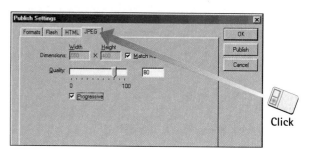 Click

4 Configure PNG Settings

The PNG format combines many of the features of GIF and JPG in one. The PNG format is supported by fewer browsers, and file sizes are generally not as compact as JPG. However, PNG images support transparency and alpha, which allow for some interesting effects in your Web pages. To take advantage of transparency and alpha, choose **24-bit with Alpha** from the **Bit Depth** drop-down. Additional options are similar to those you see in the **GIF** and **JPEG** tabs, already discussed in steps 2 and 3.

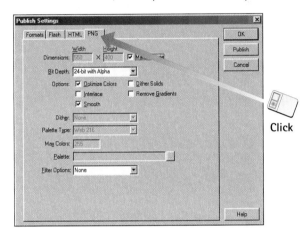

Click

5 Publish the Files

After you configure your image map and bitmap options, choose **Publish** to publish the image maps to the same folder in which your Flash project file appears. Then, click on **OK** to exit the **Publish Settings** dialog.

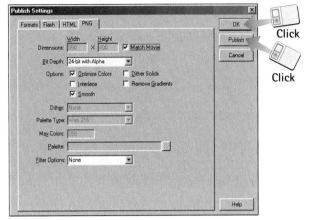

Click

Click

End

How-To Hints

Publishing Image Maps and Flash Movies at the Same Time

You can publish your Flash project as an image map and as a Flash movie (.swf) at the same time. To do so, choose **User Choice** from the **Template** drop-down in the **HTML** tab. You must use GIF or JPG bitmap format with this option.

9

How to Publish Flash Projectors

Sometimes you want to deliver your Flash movie outside of an HTML page. In that case, you still need to provide a way for everyone to see your movie, even if they don't have Flash on their computers. Flash projectors come to the rescue. Projectors are stand-alone applications that can be played back on most computers. You can create Windows and Macintosh projectors. This task shows how to create a projector file.

Begin

1 Access the Publish Settings Window

As usual, before you publish, you must specify the publish settings. Creating a projector is no exception. Choose **File, Publish Settings** to access the publish settings.

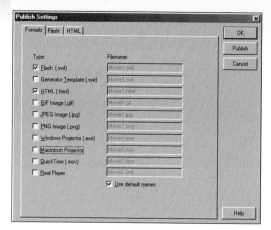

2 Choose the Projector Option

On the **Formats** tab, from the **Type** checklist, check the appropriate option for the projector you want to create. Choose either **Windows Projector (.exe)**, **Macintosh Projector,** or both options.

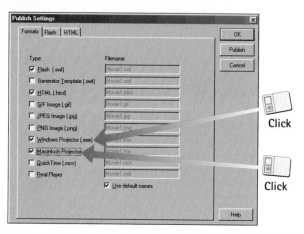

Click

Click

3 Name the Projector File

You can accept the default name for the projector, or give it a new name. To specify a name, click on the **Use default names** box to uncheck it. This makes the name fields editable. Double-click in the name field for the projector file to highlight the default name. Type in the new name. Make sure to include the proper file extension (.exe for Windows, .hqx for Macintosh). Press the **Tab** key to move out of that field.

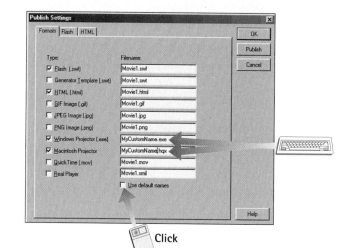

Click

4 Publish the Projector File

Click on the **Publish** button to create the projector file from the **Publish Settings** window. Flash publishes the file to the same location that holds the original Flash project file. You can skip this step if you would rather publish later using the **File, Publish** command discussed in Task 5.

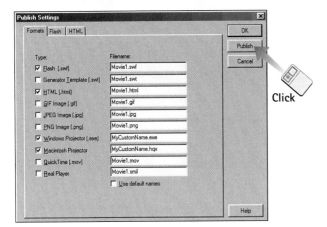

Click

5 Close the Publish Settings Window

Click on the **OK** button to close the **Publish Settings** window.

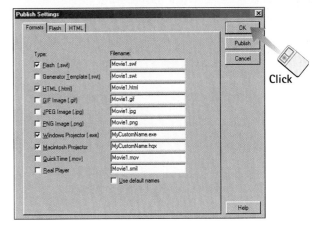

Click

6 Test the Projector File

Navigate to the new projector file on your computer, and test to make sure that it opens and plays properly. See Task 10 for details on playing a projector file.

Click

End

10

How to Use the Stand-Alone Player

A projector file uses the Flash Player for playback. You can use the Player's commands to control playback of the file. This task explores some of the possibilities.

Begin

1 Open the Projector File

Navigate to the location on you computer where you saved the projector file. Double-click on the icon to open the projector. The file opens, and begins playback immediately (by default) or when the user clicks on a button in the Flash movie if you designed it as such.

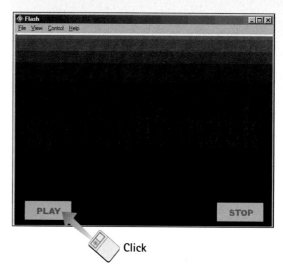

Click

2 Control Playback

Choose **Control, Play** to toggle between playing and stopping the projector.

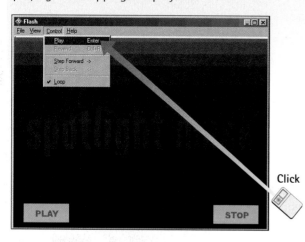

Click

3 Navigate Through the Projector

Choose **Control, Rewind** to reset the play position back to the beginning of the file. **Step Forward** and **Step Backward** enable you to step through the projector movie in small increments.

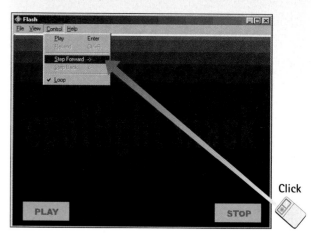

Click

4 Loop Playback

Choose **Control, Loop** to toggle looped playback mode on and off. When in looped playback mode, the projector plays continuously, starting over from the beginning every time it reaches the end. This continues until you choose **Control, Play** to toggle playback off, or exit the projector.

Click

5 Adjust the View

Choose **View, 100%** to show the artwork at regular size, or **Show All** to show the artwork at whatever size is necessary to fit it all in the projector window. Click and drag a corner or edge of the projector window to resize it. The **Zoom In** and **Zoom Out** options enable you to resize the artwork within the window. Choose **View, Full Screen** to resize the artwork and window so they occupy the entire computer screen. The **Quality** option enables you to lower or raise the image quality depending upon performance needs.

Click

6 Access the Context Menu

Right-click (Windows) or **Ctrl**+click (Macintosh) anywhere in the projector window to access the context menu. Here you will find most of the same menu options available in the regular menus.

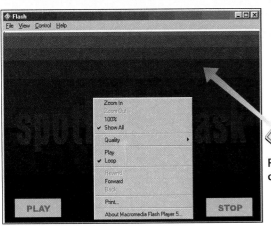

Right-click

7 Exit the Projector

Choose **File, Exit** to exit the projector. Alternatively, press the keyboard command **Ctrl+Q** (Windows) or **Cmmd+Q** (Macintosh), or click on the window's **Close** button.

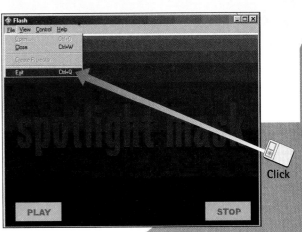

Click

End

How to Publish QuickTime Movies

When you publish your Flash movie in QuickTime format, you can view it in the QuickTime player. If your Flash movie contains any other QuickTime movies within it, Flash publishes them on separate layers and superimposes your Flash movie with the QuickTime movie in the same player. Flash movies that are published as QuickTime movies retain all the interactive features that you design in your projects, but offer the additional advantage of streaming QuickTime videos at the same time.

Begin

1 Publish with QuickTime

Choose File, Publish Settings to open the Publish Settings dialog. Check QuickTime (.mov) in the Formats tab to display the QuickTime tab.

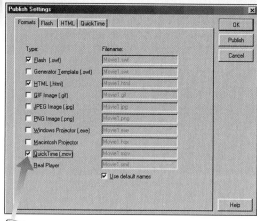

Click

2 Select Movie Dimensions

To publish a QuickTime movie that is the same dimensions as your Flash file, check the **Match Movie** check box. Uncheck this option to publish a movie that is sized to dimensions you enter in the **Width** and **Height** fields.

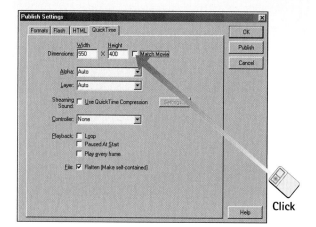

Click

3 Choose Alpha and Layering Options

The **Alpha** setting determines how other layers display in conjunction with your Flash movie. Choose **Transparent** to display underlying areas through the transparent areas in your Flash movie. Choose **Copy** to make your Flash movie opaque, so that all contents behind the Flash movie are masked. Choose **Auto** to use both of the previous options as necessary. The **Layer** options control which layer your Flash movie appears on (**Top, Bottom,** or **Auto**).

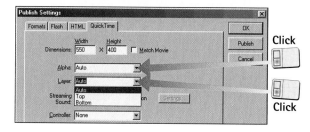

Click

Click

4 Configure Sound Options

If you want to use QuickTime compression for the audio that is included in your Flash movie, check the **Streaming Sound** option, and then click on the **Settings** button to open the **Sound Settings** dialog. More information about these options is included in your QuickTime documentation.

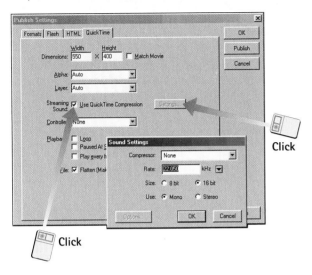

Click

Click

5 Select the Controller

Use the **Controller** drop-down to choose the type of QuickTime controller within which you want to display your movie. The options are **None**, **Standard**, and **QuickTime VR**.

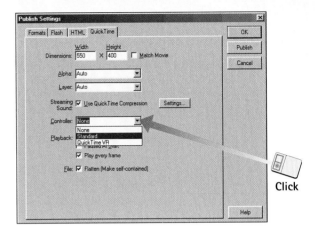

Click

6 Choose Other Playback Options

To loop your QuickTime movie, check the **Loop** option in the **Playback** section. To prevent the movie from playing until the user interacts with the QuickTime player, check the **Paused At Start** option. Check the **Play every frame** option to display every frame in your QuickTime movie. This option might cause skipping in the audio.

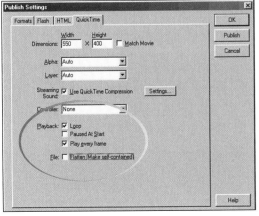

How-To Hints

Flattening Your QuickTime Movies

By default, your Flash movie is published as a separate Flash movie that links to any external movies that you imported into your Flash project. Movies don't work correctly if files are missing, and you might forget to include the external files on your site. However, you can flatten the QuickTime file so that your Flash movie and its associated QuickTime movies appear in the same file. To do so, choose **Flatten (Make self-contained)** from the **File** section of the **QuickTime** tab. This results in a bigger movie file, but it also makes your movie work correctly!

End

12

How to Publish RealPlayer Movies

The RealPlayer format enables you to publish streaming media files that are targeted for one or more connection speeds. Your Flash movies play within the RealPlayer, which you can download from **http://www.realplayer.com**.

Begin

1 Choose RealPlayer Format

Choose **File, Publish Settings** to open the **Publish Settings** dialog. Check **Real Player** in the **Formats** tab to display the **RealPlayer** tab.

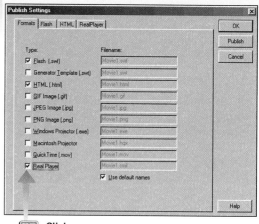

Click

2 Select Tuning Options

Check the **Export Tuned Flash** option to control the bitrate at which your Flash movie is published. Enter a new bitrate in the **Bitrate** field, or click on the arrow to raise or lower the bitrate with a slider. Higher bit rates result in higher quality, but are more difficult to stream on slower connections.

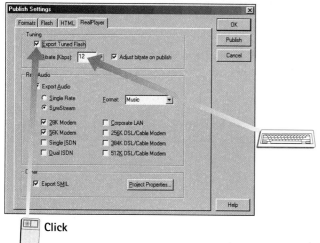

Click

3 Configure RealAudio Options

Use the **Real Audio** section to specify connection speed and streaming options for the audio in your RealPlayer movie. To publish the RealPlayer file in a single speed, choose **Single Rate**, and select the connection speed from the list of available options. Finally, choose the **Format** that most closely represents the audio content in your Flash project (**Music, Music in Stereo, Voice Only,** or **Voice with Background**).

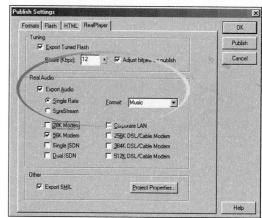

4 Select a Streaming Speed

People connect to the Internet using various connection speeds, and you can use the **SureStream** format to accommodate them all. Connection speeds range from 28.8 modems to 512K DSL or cable modems. If you're publishing your file to the Internet, try to keep all connection speeds in mind. If your movies are targeted for an intranet, choose **Corporate LAN** for the best results.

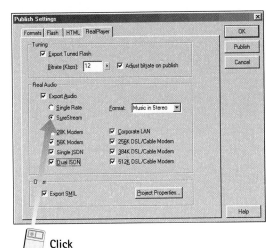

Click

5 Add Project Properties

Click on the **Project Properties** button to open the **Project Properties** dialog. This enables you to enter data that displays in the RealPlayer. Enter **Media Title, Author** information, **Copyright** information, **Keywords** for searching, and a **Description** of the media file. Click on **OK** to return to the **Publish Settings** dialog.

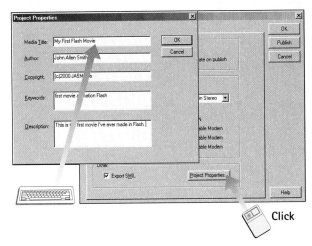

Click

6 Publish the Movie

To publish your RealPlayer movie with the settings you specified, click on the **Publish** button. The file is published to the same folder in which your Flash project resides. Click on **OK** to exit the **Publish Settings** dialog.

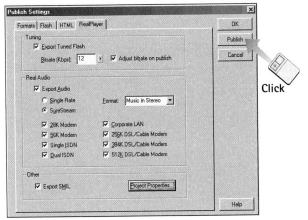

Click

How-To Hints

Multiple Connection Speeds

RealPlayer files are very popular because you can publish one file to accommodate several different connection speeds. Don't assume that everyone connects to the Internet at the same speed that you do. Try to accommodate as many different types of users as you can. Check as many different speed options as you think you'll need to support. Then, find some friends to help you test how your Flash movies look at all those connection speeds.

End

TASK *13*

How to Export Static Images

You can export an image of the stage at the current frame for use in other projects. Flash's image export supports a number of different formats. This task explains the process of exporting an image.

Begin

1 Select the Image

Click on a frame in the Timeline to select everything on that frame and layer, or directly select an image on the Stage.

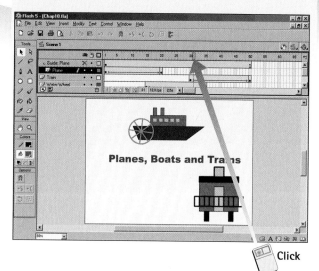

Click

2 Choose the Export Image Command

Choose **File, Export Image**. This opens the **Export Image** dialog.

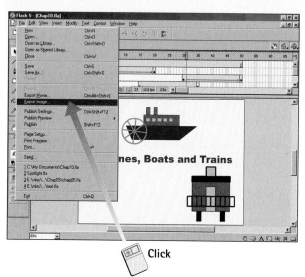

Click

3 Choose a File Format

From the **Save as type** drop-down list (Windows) or the **Format** drop-down list (Macintosh), choose the file format in which to save the file. You can save the image as an editable vector graphic with the **Adobe Illustrator (.ai)** format, or choose one of the many bitmap formats including GIF, JPEG, and PNG.

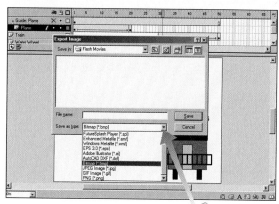

Click

4 Name the File

Navigate to the folder into which you want to save the file. Then, enter a name for your image file in the **File name** text field (**Save as** on the Macintosh). Click on the **Save** button. The **Export** options box opens.

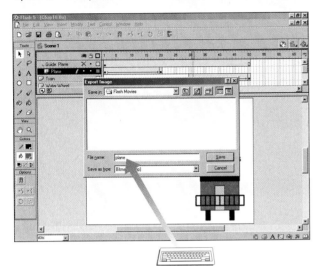

5 Set the Export Options

The options in the **Export** options box vary depending on the file format to which you are saving. Typically these choices involve the inevitable trade-off between file size and image quality so, once again, a good deal of experimentation is in order.

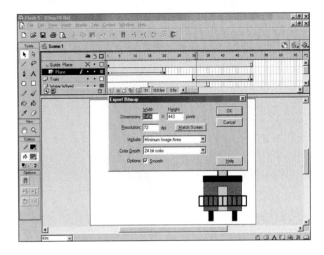

6 Click on OK

Click on **OK** to complete the export of the image.

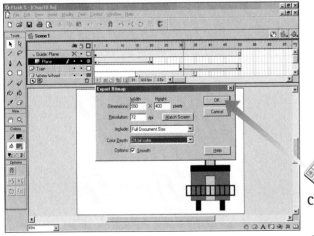

Click

End

How-To Hints

More About Formats

When you export an image as a vector-graphic file, you can edit it in another vector-graphic editing program such as FreeHand or Illustrator. When you save the image as a bitmap file, you can edit in bitmap image editors such as Photoshop, but you cannot edit the image in Flash or other vector-based image editing programs. You could, of course, import the graphic into Flash as a bitmap as discussed in Part 4, "Importing Artwork."

TASK *14*

How to Export Movies

You can also export your entire movie as a file that can be used in another project. For instance, you might export your movie as an .AVI movie file (in Windows) or QuickTime .MOV file (Macintosh) for use in a video production project. Several other options exist as well. This task shows how to export your Flash movies.

Begin

1 Choose the Export Movie Command

Choose **File, Export Movie**. This opens the Export Movie dialog.

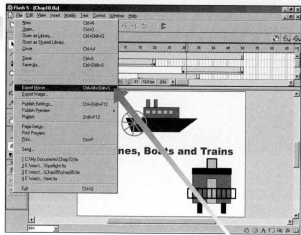

Click

2 Choose a File Format

From the **Save as type** drop-down list (Windows) or the **Format** drop-down list (Macintosh), choose a file format in which to save the file. Choose from among several movie formats and still image formats. Of special note: In Windows, you can choose **.wav** to save the audio only as a WAV file.

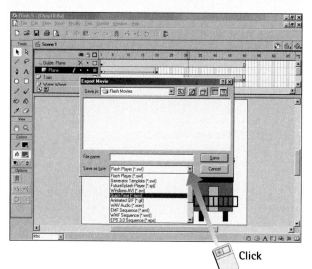

Click

3 Name the File

Navigate to the folder into which you want to save the file. Then, enter a name for your image file in the **File name** text field (**Save as** on the Macintosh).

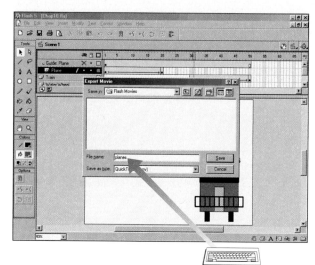

4 Set the Export Options

Click on **Save** to enter values and make choices for the various export options. See previous tasks for a further discussion of many of these options.

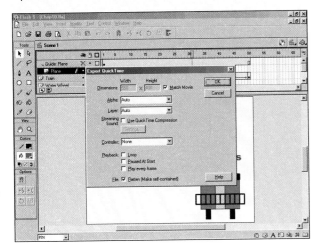

5 Click on OK

Click on **OK** to complete the export of the movie.

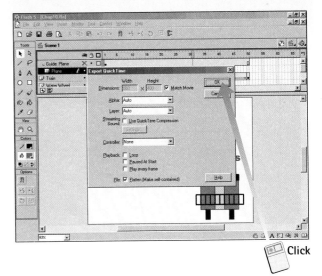

Click

End

How-To Hints

Using Exported Movies in Video

Flash can also be an excellent tool to help you develop animations, text, and titling for videotape as well. Develop your Flash movies as you normally would, but make sure that the height and width of the movie are the same as the media files you are using in your video project. Save your movies to AVI or MOV format, using little to no compression in the exported movie. Use the final AVI or MOV file in your favorite video-editing software!

Flash Resources

*L*earning Flash is an ongoing process. In this appendix, you will find a listing of Flash resources on the Web. There are several online Flash communities that offer online tutorials, source .fla files, bulletin boards, news, and links to other sites. You can also find resources for audio, images, and fonts. Additionally, we've included a couple of inspirational sites that you may want to visit.

Tutorials and Communities

Macromedia

http://macromedia.com/support/flash/

You can't beat going straight to the source.

Moock.Org

http://www.moock.org

General resource not only for Flash but for all things Web.

Colin Moock's site is a great resource because it not only makes information on Flash easy to understand, but he puts it in the context of the whole Web. This is the site to check out if you need to find the process to make Flash talk to JavaScript or to find out why your Flash movie isn't showing up even though you've used the embed tag.

The Flash Academy

http://www.enetserve.com/tutorials/

This site offers intermediate-to-advanced tutorials in the form of Shockwave files. They're easy to click through and follow along with.

Flash Kit

http://www.flashkit.com

This site offers downloadable tutorials so that you can see the .fla source files as well as click through the tutorials. It offers sounds as well.

Virtual-FX

http://www.virtual-fx.net/

Tutorials on all levels, from beginner to advanced action scripting, are offered at this site. There also is a library of open source .fla files, articles, and links to other Flash sites.

Flashlite

http://www.flashlite.net/

Good source for tutorials and Flash news.

Flazoom.com

http://www.flazoom.com/

Good source for links to Flash sites and Flash news.

Content Sites

Audio/Sound Sites

Music 4 Flash

http://www.music4flash.com/

This is a good resource. It offers free sounds but also has some high-end options if you want to pay for them. It's a thorough site so those who are unfamiliar with the use of sound can get a lot of info. It also has a lot of links to other resources.

ACIDplanet.com™

http://www.acidplanet.com/

ACID™ is a loop-based music creation tool made by Sonic Foundry (http://www.sonicfoundry.com). At ACIDplanet.com, you can download a free version of the software, ACID™ XPress, download free music loops that change frequently, and buy loop collections on CD.

Winamp

http://www.winamp.com/

This one can be tricky, but it offers MP3 files that can be converted to AIFF or WAV files. Good selection.

Wavcentral

http://www.wavcentral.com/

This offers wave files and so much more. It's a good place to find sound (WAV only) as well as miscellaneous effects.

Images/Photos

Clip Art

http://www.clip-art.com/

This site offers a variety of bitmap clip art in cartoon style. It also offers tutorials on image optimization as well as free downloads.

Clip Art Connection

http://www.clipartconnection.com/

Site for free clip art.

GettyOne

http://www.gettyone.com/

GettyOne is an umbrella site that offers a host of sites from high-end (expensive) to low-end (cheap) image options. It's a powerful resource, but you can't legally get free images. Images are divided into royalty-free and licensed images. Keep in mind that royalty-free is not actually free; it means you pay only once, as opposed to a licensed image, which you have to pay for every time you use it. Artville and Photodisc are good low-cost options.

Artville

http://www.artville.com/

Artville, as mentioned before, can be accessed from GettyOne. It has both illustrations and photos.

Photodisc

http://photodisc.com

Another site accessible from GettyOne, Photodisc is a searchable site that offers low-cost, low-resolution files.

Fonts and Miscellaneous

T-26

http://www.t26font.com/

This site is a digital type foundry started by Carlos Segura, an internationally known designer who lives in Chicago. It's not free, but the fonts are beyond compare.

GS Homepage

http://nebula.spaceports.com/~huge//

This Web site offers a selection of free fonts.

Émigré

http://www.emigre.com/

Émigré is a great source for fonts. Keep in mind that they're not free.

Inspirational Sites

Pray Station

http://www.praystation.com

This is a site from a group working out of the MIT Media Lab. Joshua Davis is the mastermind behind this site and many others, such as barneys.com. The site is created with Flash and features a calendar in which to access daily projects. You can also download .fla source files.

Communication Arts

http://www.commarts.com/interactive/index.html

Communication Arts is a magazine that covers the graphic/ad and design community. The interactive section of their Web site always has a site of the week, and often it's a Flash site.

Glossary

.fla file   An editable Flash file.

.swf file   A Flash file meant only for distribution—it can be watched, but not edited.

A

ActionScript   The computer language that Flash uses for actions.

Animated graphics   Moving images of any type. Often, Flash graphics and animated GIFs are image types seen on the Web.

Aspect ratio   The ratio of height to width. Like a television or movie screen, the shape of a Flash animation remains the same—no matter its size.

B

Bitmapped graphic   *See* Raster graphic.

Blank keyframe   A keyframe that causes nothing to appear on Stage. *See also* Keyframe.

Button   An item that a user can click that causes an action.

Button state   A visual version of a button. For example, during clicking, the button is in its "down" state; when dormant, it is in its "up" state. When the mouse is hovered over the button, the button is in its "over" state.

Button symbol   A symbol used to create interactive buttons that respond to mouse events. *See also* Symbol.

C

Coordinates   Numbers signifying a place in a Cartesian plane, represented by (x,y). The top-left pixel in Flash, for instance, is written (0,0) or (0x,0y).

D

Down state   A button state that occurs when the user clicks the button with his mouse.

E

Export   To move a file or object from a Flash file. Often, the term *export* is used to discuss the creation of distributable Flash files.

F

Focus   The state of being active. In Flash, a dark line indicates which option has focus in a Timeline. *See also* Timeline.

Frame rate   The rate, stated in frames per second (fps), at which each frame in an animation is played back for the user.

Frame-by-frame animation   Animation using a series of keyframes with no tweening that creates a flipbook-like animation Flash file.

G

Graphic symbol   Used for static images and to create reusable segments of animation. The animation that appears in a graphic symbol is locked into the same Timeline as the main movie.

Grid   Like grid paper, a grid is used for precise placement of objects in a Flash file. *See also* Ruler.

Guide layer   A special layer that does not export when you export a Flash file. This layer can be used to help registration of various elements of a Flash file.

H

Hit state   The clickable area of a button.

Hyperlink   Text or an object (such as an image) that can be clicked to take a user to related information, as used on the World Wide Web.

Hypertext Markup Language (HTML)   The language read by Web browsers to present information on the Internet.

I

Import   To bring a file or object into a Flash file.

Instance   An occurrence of a symbol used from the library—especially helpful because although more than one instance can exist, only the master symbol must be saved; thus, file sizes are kept small. *See also* Library and Symbol.

Interface   The design with which users interact.

J–K

Keyframe   A frame in which you establish exactly what should appear on Stage at that particular moment in time.

L

Layer   Aptly named, one of a "stack" of media in a Flash file Timeline. This is especially useful in animation because only one object can be tweened per layer.

Library   A storage facility for all media elements used in a Flash file.

M

Masking   A kind of layer property with at least two layers: one for the Mask and one that is Masked (like Motion Guide and Guided). The graphical contents of the Mask layer will determine which parts of the Masked layer will show through.

Morph   A kind of animation that naturally transitions one shape to another. *See also* Shape Tween.

Motion Guide   A Guide layer that has an adjacent layer (below it) that is set to "Guided." Tweened objects in the "Guided" layer will follow a path in the "Guide" layer.

Movie Clip symbol   Symbols that contain interactive controls, sounds, and even other Movie Clips. Movie Clips can be placed in the Timeline of Button symbols to create animated buttons. Movie Clips follow their own internal Timeline, independent of the main Timeline. *See also* Symbol.

N–O

Onion Skin tools   Tools that enable you to edit one keyframe while viewing (dimly) as many frames before or after the current frame.

Over state   A button state that occurs when the user passes his mouse over a button.

P

Panning   An effect that makes a sound seem to move from left to right (or right to left).

Parameter   A specifier used in ActionScript.

Q

QuickTime   A video format created by Apple. A common file format found on the Internet.

R

Raster graphic   An image file format that contains the color information for each pixel. Raster graphics' file sizes are relatively large.

RealPlayer   A streaming video player created by Real Networks. RealMedia (RealPlayer files) is a common format to find on the Internet.

Registration   The process of making sure things are properly aligned (often from one frame to another). *See also* Guide layer.

Rollover sound   A sound effect that plays any time a user places his cursor over a button.

Ruler   Like a physical ruler for Flash, a ruler is used for precise measurement of objects in a Flash file. *See also* Grid.

Runtime   The point at which the user is watching your movie (as well as when you're testing the movie).

S

Scale   To resize as necessary.

Scene   A component part of a Timeline in a Flash file.

Scrub   A technique to preview your animation by dragging the red current frame marker back and forth in the Timeline.

Shape Tween   A utility to create a fluid motion between two objects. *See also* Tween.

Smart Clip   A movie clip with unique parameters in it that performs certain actions.

Stage   The large, white rectangle in the middle of the Flash workspace where a file is created. What is on Stage is what the users will see when they play your Flash file.

Statement   A single line of code in a script. *See also* ActionScript.

Static graphics   Graphics with no animation or interactivity. The computer-image equivalent of a photograph or a painting.

Symbol   Although any object in a library is technically a symbol, symbols mainly refer to either a Graphic, Movie Clip, or a Button that is stored in the library. This is especially useful because no matter how many instances of a symbol are used, it only has to download once, and changes made to the master symbol are immediately reflected in all instances already used. *See also* Button symbol, Graphic symbol, Library, and Movie Clip symbol.

Sync   The timing between an animation and a corresponding sound. You choose sync settings in the Sound panel.

T

Tile effect   A raster graphic used as the "fill" color used in any shape you draw.

Timeline   Object on the Flash workspace that contains the sequence of frames, layers, and scenes comprising an animation.

Tween   Used as a verb, "to tween" is to have something be done between two things. For example, you can use a Shape Tween to morph a solid circle into a doughnut.

U

Up state   Normally a button's default state, this occurs when the user has not clicked or passed over the button with his mouse.

V–Z

Vector graphic   A vector graphic file contains all the "math" to redraw the image on screen. A vector graphic's file size remains small, and the image can be scaled to any size without any degradation to image quality. Flash .swf files are saved as vector graphics.

Index

windows
Narrow State, 20
Wide State, 20

Library command (Window menu), 20

line segments, creating (Pen tool), 45

Line style
Ink Bottle tool, 58
Pencil tool, 41

linear gradients, 36

lines
endpoint connections, 24
gradients, filling, 39
optimization, dotted versus solid, 228
straight, tolerance settings (Preferences dialog box), 25
straightening, 25
text, space adjustments (Text tool), 92
width adjustments (Ink Bottle tool), 59

linking layers to mask layer, 111

loading
movies into one another, 180-181
.swf movies, layer order, 236
Web-safe color palette, 35

locating registration points, troubleshooting, 139

Lock Fill modifier, 62-63

locking
gradient fills, 62-63
grouped objects, 125
guide layers, 109
layers, 104
range of, 105

looping sounds, 217

lossless (GIF) compression, bitmap files, 83

M

Macintosh
bitmap files, importing, 67
Flash
exiting, 7
launching, 6

Macromedia Web site, tutorial resources, 258

Magic Wand modifier
bitmap fills, modifying, 78-79
properties, setting, 79

Main toolbar, 8-9

margins, text, adjusting (Text tool), 92

mask layers
creating, 110-111
layers
linking, 111
unlinking, 111

master symbols, instances, breaking apart, 166-167

Menu bar, 8

menus
Control, 11
Edit, 10
File, 10
Insert, 10
Modify, 11
Text, 11
View, 10
Window, 10

Modify menu commands
Break Apart, 74-75, 166-167
floating panels, 11
Group, 95, 124
Movie, 14
Optimize, 230-231
Smooth, 25
Straighten, 25
Trace Bitmap, 72
Ungroup, 95

modifying
background colors on Stage, 57
gradients
radius, 39
shapes, 38
text field width (Text tool), 89

Moock.org Web site, tutorial resources, 258

morphing objects (Shape Tweens), 206-207

Motion Guide command (Insert menu), 204

motion paths, changing (Motion Tweens), 204-205

motion tweens
movement options, 196-197
objects
color changing options, 202-203
fade options options, 203
motion path options, 204-205
scaling options, 200-201
rotation options, 198-199

mouse
Click Accuracy setting (Preferences dialog box), 25
right-click action, layer insertion, 98

Movie Clips
adding to main movie, 154
animated buttons, 155
creating, 154
symbol type, creating, 154

Movie command (Modify menu), 14

Movie Properties dialog box, 14

movies
animated GIF files, 242-243
backgrounds, custom palettes, 15
bitmap files, 235
container, 180-181
creating, 14-15
default settings, saving, 15
download performance, testing, 232-233
exporting, 254-255
Flash SWF format
audio properties, 237
JPEG quality, 236
load order, 236
passwords, 236
framerates, setting, 14
guide layers, creating, 108
HTML format
alignment settings, 241
dimensions, 240
movie quality, 241
playback options, 240
templates, 240
window modes, 241
layers
copying, 102
creating, 98
cutting, 103
deleting, 102
hiding, 106
locking, 104-105
naming, 99
pasting, 103
properties, 99
reordering, 99
selecting, 100-101
unlocking, 104
viewing, 106-107
Movie Clips, adding to, 154
objects, zooming in/out, 16
optimization
curves, 230-231
fonts, 229
gradients, 229
instances, 229
line types, 228
sounds, 228
text, 229
tweened animation, 228
panning (Hand tool), 17
pixel sizes, 14